WiMAX CRASH COURSE

WiMAX
Crash
Course

Steven Shepard

McGraw-Hill
New York   Chicago   San Francisco   Lisbon
London   Madrid   Mexico City   Milan
New Delhi   San Juan   Seoul   Singapore
Sydney   Toronto

The McGraw-Hill Companies

Library of Congress Cataloging-in-Publication Data is on file.

1 2 3 4 5 6 7 8 9 0   DOC/DOC   0 1 9 8 7 6

ISBN 0-07-226307-5

The sponsoring editor for this book was Jane Brownlow and the production supervisor was Jean Bodeaux. It was set in New Century Schoolbook by Patricia Wallenburg.

Printed and bound by RR Donnelley

This book is for my good friend and colleague,
Phil Cashia. Thanks for your friendship,
your kindness, and the many hours of engaging
conversation. As always, LOFOG.

CONTENTS

Contents

X

Contents

ACKNOWLEDGMENTS

First, a very special thanks to Roger Deeringer for his insights into WiMAX and its evolving role in the world. This book would be far thinner—and far less content-rich—were it not for him. Also, thanks to Kenn Sato for his usual high degree of editing skill and literary pushback.

I also thank the following people for their generous contributions and counsel: Phil Asmundson, Kim Barker, Paul Bedell, Jane Brownlow, Phil Cashia, Steve Chapman, Anthony Contino, Jonathan Dunne, Andy Harrs, Dave Heckman, Issac-Aaron Jayaraj, Tony Kern, Charles Krempa, Dee Marcus, Roy Marcus, Gary Martin, Paul McDonagh-Smith, Tom McNulty, Jim Nason, Alan Nurick, Chris O'Gorman, Dick Pecor, Karen Schopp, Mary Slaughter, Steve Tadeo, Fernando Toledo, Calvin Tong, and Craig Wigginton.

Sabine, Steve, and Cristina, thank you for being my family. I am so proud of all of you.

FOREWORD

Once more, and this time with feeling.

I write this book as a complement to the small collection of good technology-focused WiMAX books that are already in circulation. This title, like my other books, contains plenty of technology, but its primary focus is on markets, applications, revenue impacts, and integration. In reality, it's a business book more than a technology book. Embryonic though the technology is at the time of this writing (the current standard is still in draft form, and the next one isn't due for months), it has a growing base of supporters that includes component manufacturers, systems manufacturers, and a significant number of service providers. Prestandard hardware is on the market, numerous global trials are under way, and an industry standards group, the WiMAX Forum (www.wimaxforum.org), has been constituted by key influencers, including Intel, Proxim, BT, Alvarion, AT&T, and Samsung.

I have monitored the evolution of WiMAX for the last two years with great interest not because of how it works or what it does but because of what it catalyzes. WiMAX is an accelerator, and it wields its influence on the areas where businesses focus *their* attentions: revenue enhancement, cost containment, competitive advantage, and risk mitigation. Properly deployed, it will have far-reaching, global impacts—and that's where I focus *my* attention.

With 50 clients operating in more than 90 countries, I am blessed with the opportunity to see firsthand the impact that new technologies have on the developed, developing, and undeveloped worlds. I have watched as problems of conduit congestion, infrastructure disruption, and onerous permitting processes in major cities have been resolved through the judicious selection of broadband wireless as an alternative to optical infrastructure. I have watched the frenzy in the developing world that occurs when liberalization and privatization take effect, bringing on a spate of competitive positioning by emergent players and the attendant deployment of innovative technologies. I also have watched magic happen: the arrival of a small town's first phone in Africa and the buzz of potential that it creates among vendors and shopkeepers who crave connections to the global market and everything that access to the Internet promises.

We are a big industry, so big that it's easy to get lost in the mundane daily grind of "doing telecom." There are chips to be manufactured, systems to be assembled, code to be debugged, standards to be written, networks to be managed, and customers to be billed. Working in the middle of that operational maelstrom, it's easy to forget why we do what we do.

For a long time I unwittingly operated under the belief that the telecom industry exists for the telecom industry, that it is an end unto itself. That assumption came to a jarring and abrupt halt when I began working in the third world and had an opportunity to see firsthand what we *really* do. Yes, we satisfy shareholders and employ large numbers of people because of the products we make and sell, the services we offer, and the targeted solutions we craft. However, beyond that, at the critical customer touchpoint where magic happens and sparks fly, we empower commerce, create markets, build businesses, and motivate thought leadership. Our networks make it possible to consider what could be, and our services and applications make it happen. In many ways we are the ultimate change agent, and in the years to come our influence will be felt most strongly in the realm of globalization.

In *The Lexus and the Olive Tree*, Tom Friedman describes a phenomenon that he calls "the Golden Arches Theory." That theory eerily and accurately observes that no two countries with a McDonald's have ever waged war against each other. As silly as that observation sounds, its implications are quite serious: When a country reaches a stage of economic development at which its citizens have enough disposable income to spend some of it at McDonald's, that country becomes a paid member of the global economic team. When that happens, when national economies become interlinked into a single global economy, the Golden Arches Theory is lived out: If I attack *you*, I attack *me*. As the checker-playing, Armageddon-bent supercomputer said to Matthew Broderick's character in the movie *War Games*, "An interesting game, Professor Falken. The only winning move is not to play."

This book is about WiMAX, but more than that, it is about the *promise* of WiMAX. Numbers as large as $500 billion[1] have been tossed about as being indicative of the upward economic impact of broadband; imagine what happens when broadband mixes with global roaming. That, among other things, is the value that WiMAX brings to the table.

We begin with the vision: What will be possible when WiMAX arrives? We then discuss application scenarios before walking through the technology's brief history (it hasn't been around long enough to have a *real* history). Next, we dive into the inner workings of WiMAX and explain how it interworks with other technologies. Then we introduce the evolving application set that WiMAX enables before discussing the increasingly chaotic but very interesting world of regulation as it relates to broadband wireless. We conclude with a brief discussion about the players in the WiMAX game, followed by a peek into the future. WiMAX has the potential to be highly disruptive, but like all capable technologies, it can be enormously facilitative. We wrap up the book with a discussion of strategies for integrating and deploying WiMAX.

All my books include a comprehensive acronym list and a glossary. Thanks to all the readers who have lobbied for its inclusion; this book has it as well.

Thank you, readers, for your continued support. This book is for you.

December 2005
Steven Shepard
Steve@ShepardComm.com
Johannesburg, Mexico City, Nedile Lodge, Paris, Williston

---

[1] Crandall, Robert W., and Charles L. Jackson, *The $500 Billion Dollar Opportunity: The Potential Economic Benefit of Widespread Diffusion of Broadband Internet Access.* Criterion Economics, LLC, July 2001.

ABOUT THE AUTHOR

Steven Shepard is the president of the Shepard
Communications Group in Williston, Vermont. A
professional author and educator with 24 years of
varied experience in the telecommunications
industry, he has written books and magazine arti-
cles on a wide variety of topics. His books include:

- *Telecommunications Convergence: How to
  Profit from the Convergence of Technologies,
  Services and Companie*s (McGraw-Hill, New York, 2000)
- *A Spanish-English Telecommunications Dictionary* (Shepard
  Communications Group, Williston, Vermont, 2001)
- *Managing Cross-Cultural Transition: A Handbook for Corporations,
  Employees and Their Families* (Aletheia Publications, New York,
  1997)
- *An Optical Networking Crash Course* (McGraw-Hill, New York,
  February 2001)
- *SONET and SDH Demystified* (McGraw-Hill, New York, 2001)
- *Telecom Crash Course* (McGraw-Hill, New York, October 2001)
- *Telecommunications Convergence, Second Edition* (McGraw-Hill,
  New York, February 2002)
- *Videoconferencing Demystified* (McGraw-Hill, April 2002)
- *Metro Networking Demystified* (McGraw-Hill, New York, October
  2002)
- *RFID Demystified* (McGraw-Hill, New York, July 2004)

- *Managing Supply Chain Technology* (with Jack Garrett; in progress)
- *Telecom Crash Course, Second Edition* (McGraw-Hill, New York, June 2005); and
- *VoIP Crash Course* (McGraw-Hill, New York, July 2005)

How to Do Everything with VoIP will be published by McGraw-Hill in early 2006.

Steve is also the Series Advisor of the McGraw-Hill *Portable Consultant* book series.

Mr. Shepard received his undergraduate degree in Spanish and Romance Philology from the University of California at Berkeley and his master's degree in International Business from St. Mary's College. He spent eleven years with Pacific Bell in San Francisco in a variety of capacities including network analysis, computer operations, systems standards development, and advanced technical training, followed by nine years with Hill Associates, a world-renowned telecommunications education company, before forming the Shepard Communications Group. He is a fellow of the Da Vinci Institute for Technology Management of South Africa, a member of the Board of Directors of Champlain Community Television, a Founding Director of the African Telecoms Institute, and a member of the Board of Trustees of Champlain College in Burlington, Vermont. He is also the Resident Director of the University of Southern California's Executive Leadership and Advanced Management Programs in Telecommunications, and adjunct faculty member at the University of Southern California, The Garvin School of International Management (Thunderbird University), the University of Vermont, Champlain College and St. Michael's College. He and his wife Sabine have two children.

Mr. Shepard specializes in international issues in telecommunications with an emphasis on strategic technical sales; services convergence; the social implications of technological change; the development of multilingual educational materials; and the effective use of multiple delivery media. He has written and directed more than 40 videos and films and written technical presentations on a broad range of topics for more than 70 companies and organizations worldwide. He is fluent in Spanish and routinely publishes and delivers presentations in that language. Global clients include major telecommunications manufacturers, service providers, software development firms, multinational corporations, universities, professional services firms, advertising firms, venture capital firms, and regulatory bodies.

CHAPTER 1

Introduction to Wireless and WiMAX

I am in a car in Raleigh-Durham, traveling at 70 miles per hour. On my lap is a rather heavy laptop with a strange little pigtail antenna sticking out of the side. I'm wearing a headset that is plugged into the laptop.

I suppose it's a good idea to tell you that I am not driving. My friend William, who owns the car and works in Research Triangle Park, has that responsibility. My job is to be impressed with what is going on with the laptop. At this moment, as we round the curve on the highway, heading for the airport, I am chatting with four people online, downloading my e-mail, surfing the Web for information about a nearby camera store, talking on the headset over a Skype connection, and occasionally going to a Web window that is showing a scene from the webcam in William's laboratory: "If you see Walter come in, let me know so that I can call him and tell him not to get Rick at the airport since we're doing it already." All these applications are working well, all of them are working simultaneously, and all of them are sharing access to a trial Worldwide Interoperability for Microwave Access (WiMAX) radio cell that William's company has built and installed on top of a building near his office. I am impressed.

Now the scene shifts: I am standing beside a dusty African crossroads in Limpopo province in the northernmost reaches of South Africa. Vendors beside me are selling melons, cell phone chargers, mousetraps, and ironwood animal carvings. Just across the street a family of baboons sits on the guardrail, closely watching the small pile of melons, waiting for an opportunity to dash across the street and steal one. The owner watches the baboons equally closely (during the three hours I was there, I saw five melons snatched).

I am not here to buy melons or watch thieving baboons. I am here to visit the telephone company central office, which is just behind me (Figure 1-1). Housed in a shipping container, it is one of several hundred exchanges that have been deployed rapidly throughout the region as a way to bring connectivity services to rural Africa. Along the back wall of the container are arrayed several standard racks of switching equipment that provide service to mobile callers in the area; along one side wall hang telephones for the use of anyone with a prepaid calling card but no mobile phone. Facing the phones is a small administrative desk. The shipping container is at once a central office exchange, a public phone office, and a business office where bills can be paid and assistance can e requested for setting up small businesses.

On the roof of the shipping container, hidden from view by the leftmost ventilation globe, a high-gain antenna points off into the bush to an invisible receiver across the plains. The signal that runs between the two

Figure 1-1
A central office in northern South Africa made from a shipping container.

is a WiMAX backhaul connection, part of a trial being conducted by the incumbent carrier in that country.

The scene shifts again: The power industry in most countries has one of the most widely deployed distribution infrastructures in the world. Those long, looping catenaries, strung between pylons, carry power from generation facilities to substations where the power is stepped down, filtered, and distributed to subscribers.

One of the challenges power companies face is the fact that the cable strung between the towers is extraordinarily heavy in spite of the fact that it is made of aluminum. To reduce its dead weight, the cable is hollow, and to make the cable more useful without adding to the weight, it is filled with ribbons of optical fibers: terabits of bandwidth. For years the power industry has been its own best bandwidth customer, using its wholly owned optical capacity to move load-sharing and telemetry data.

Of course, commodity industries such as power and telecommunications providers are always looking for the next great thing they can offer to enhance their revenues. It didn't take long for the engineers in the industry to realize that their internal requirements used only a fraction of the available bandwidth. The second conclusion they quickly reached was that the leftover bandwidth could be sold to enterprise or residence customers as long as they had a way to connect (a local loop) to those customers. The local loop problem was solved in two ways. The first was through the creation of an out-of-band transport scheme called Broadband over Power Line (BPL), sometimes called Power Line Transport (PLT) (see Figure 1-2). The range of frequencies set aside for this technology lies between 3 and 30 MHz, which is far above the 50- or 60-Hz frequency band within which AC power is transported. Unfortunately,

Figure 1-2
Optical fiber
ribbons
wrapped
within
aluminum
power cable,
making BPL
possible

this range of frequencies creates interference for other services, most notably amateur radio. Amateur radio is the incumbent user within this space, and so it will win the battle if push comes to shove.

The second solution is to use WiMAX. If a power company installed a WiMAX node at the substation that provides power to a local area and connected the node to its optical transport network, it could deliver broadband wireless service to all customers within a 30-mile radius of the substation. That is a very powerful service.

The scene shifts one more time: In downtown Houston a hospital has outgrown its physical facilities and now occupies multiple buildings in the greater metro area. For reasons related to security, privacy, and operational effectiveness, the hospital has come to realize that it needs to upgrade its interoffice connectivity. Unfortunately, when the hospital's representatives meet with their service provider, they are chagrined to learn that the conduit within which they need to install additional fiber is completely exhausted and that the wait time from the city for permits to install additional conduit space is over a year. Does this mean that they cannot get the broadband transport they require to comply with patient and government safety and privacy mandates? The answer is yes if optical is the only answer. The good news is that there is another option: WiMAX. By installing WiMAX in the area, the hospital can operate its own broadband wireless network. The cost is lower than that of installing an optical network, the network can be installed almost immediately, and the bandwidth is extremely high.

These four examples—Raleigh-Durham, South Africa, the power infrastructure, and a metro broadband alternative—illustrate the opportunities that lie ahead for the Worldwide Interoperability [standard] for Microwave Access. Initially designed as a backhaul solution, WiMAX will soon evolve to offer point-to-multipoint broadband solutions and will become a force to be reckoned with in the broadband provisioning arena. The technology is being deployed in trials all over the world. The city of

Tokyo is being "wired" for WiMAX right now, and San Francisco is being eyed as the next broadband wireless city.

Casting a Jaundiced Eye

The Internet is rife with urban legends about strange and wonderful things that have occurred to people all over the world. Let's see if I can remember the best of them.

- Flash your headlights at night at an oncoming car that has its headlights turned off and you will be killed by the gang member in the lightless car who is driving around looking for a headlight-flashing do-gooder.

- Accept a drink from a stranger in a bar. Hours later you will wake up in a bathtub filled with ice, minus at least one kidney and with a note telling you to go to the nearest hospital.

- Forward this e-mail to your friends and Microsoft and AOL will send you checks for about $250 each.

Here's the best urban legend: WiMAX will kill off all wireline transport, destroy the need for third-generation (3G) infrastructure and wireless fidelity (WiFi), and provide 100 Mbps to as many customers as want it up to 30 miles from the WiMAX tower. Sorry, folks, but this just isn't the case. WiMAX is a very good technology that offers great promise in certain applications. It is not, however, the end-all and be-all solution to access and transport challenges any more than Synchronous Optical Network (SONET), E-1, and Code Division Multiple Access (CDMA) were the only solutions to the problems they went after.

Those of you who have heard me speak or have read my other books are familiar with my warnings about asking a lot of questions. The fact that a technology claims to be able to do certain things does not mean that those things will actually work, since many of the claimed capabilities deliver in a laboratory setting but not in the real world where atmospheric conditions and the vagaries of the user community hold sway. Therefore, my most important message to you is this: *Question everything*. If a technology claims to be able to do something and that claim seems a bit wrong, question it. The most important question you can ask as a successful person in your company is this: *Are you sure?*

I am not trying to undermine WiMAX or anything about it (I am writing a book about it, after all). I am, however, trying to overlay a patina of reality on the WiMAX scene because WiMAX is surrounded by a sea of hype in which it is easy to drown. There is no question that WiMAX holds great promise for the industry. It is a powerful broadband alternative, does not require line-of-site, is based on a set of internationally accepted standards and spectrum set-asides, will soon support mobility, operates in both point-to-point mode and point-to-multipoint mode, and has the broad support of major corporations in the manufacturing and service provider sectors. However, it remains immature. It has not been implemented in a large and meaningful way and therefore has not been thrashed by the rigors of a real implementation. The nonmobile version of the standard has been accepted and is undergoing trials in Spain at the time of this writing. 802.16e, the mobile version of WiMAX, is undergoing draft review (fourth quarter of 2005) and will be ratified fully by mid-2006.

Let's talk about this market for a moment. Many analysts (me included) believe that the success of broadband wireless lies largely in the realization of the mobile triple play. If a service provider had the ability to deliver voice, video, and data seamlessly and efficiently to a mobile device, the promise of true convergence would be realized and the customer would become sticky, in effect unable or unwilling to head off to a competitor's network. For the longest time third-generation systems have been held up as the facilitators of broadband wireless, but it has become increasingly clear that these networks are not up to the task. Service providers most likely will have to build parallel infrastructures if they want to play in the broadband wireless game, and for reasons associated primarily with capital cost, they are reluctant to do that. They have little choice, however, because of the availability of alternative solutions [cable, Digital Subscriber Line (DSL)].

The technology they probably will deploy is *Orthogonal Frequency Division Multiplexing* (OFDM). OFDM is central to the emerging fourth-generation wireless standards (can't we get the third generation working first?) and is an important component of WiMAX, as we'll see later in this book. Although mobile WiMAX is seen as being a major contender for the deployment of mobile broadband Internet and an ideal technology for the deployment of the mobile triple play, it remains in limbo, not yet completely standardized. Consequently, proprietary broadband wireless solutions have emerged in the interim.

Flarion came into the broadband wireless game several years ago with its FLASH-OFDM air interface technology, which was designed for the delivery of high-speed Internet access to mobile devices. FLASH is an acronym for Fast Low-Latency Access with Seamless Handoff, and OFDM is an acronym for Orthogonal Frequency Division Multiplexing. Flarion's product is based on the OFDM airlink, a wireless access technique that combines the best aspects of time division multiple access (TDMA) and code division multiple access (CDMA) to address the demands of mobile broadband data and Voice over Internet Protocol (VoIP) users. Flarion's Flash-OFDM has been upgraded with "Flexband," which claims data rates two to three times faster than those of current systems and the ability to support hundreds of users per base station at a cost to the service provider of no more than $10 per month. According to Flarion, one 1.25-MHz Flexband carrier channel will deliver peak data rates of 5.3 Mbps downstream and 1.8 Mbps upstream, with 2.5 Mbps of throughput up to 6 Mbps at 5 GHz. A 5-MHz Flexband multicarrier system, fully implemented, results in the transport of 186 voice calls per sector and data rates as high as 15.9 Mbps in "burst mode" and 6 Mbps sustainable over a long period. Each base station supports three signals per sector and three sectors per unit.

The increased throughput claimed by Flarion is a direct result of a frequency-monitoring capability known as BeaconTone. BeaconTone monitors the levels of interference between the various subsignals into which OFDM splits the radio signal and then, in real time, chooses the best possible transmission path to maximize throughput.

It should come as no surprise, then, that Flarion announced in August 2005 that it was to be acquired by Qualcomm for approximately $600 million. The companies' products are highly complementary, and will result in the ability to serve numerous underserved areas around the world. Watch this dance closely.

Other players are in contention for the space WiMAX would have. Navini Networks, an active member of the WiMAX Forum, offers portable plug-and-play WiMAX products. Its Ripwave portable non-line-of-sight (NLOS) product line includes customer modems, base stations, and element management systems (EMSs) that operate throughout the WiMAX spectrum.

WiBro (wireless broadband) is a wireless broadband access technology that is being developed by the Korean telecom industry. In early February 2002 the Korean government allocated 100 MHz of spectrum in the 2.3-GHz band for broadband wireless applications, and in late 2004 WiBro Phase 1 was standardized by the Telecommunications Technology Association (TTA) of Korea.

WiBro base stations offer an aggregate data rate of 30 to 50 Mbps and cover a service radius of as much as three miles. WiBro supports differentiable quality of service, and as a result, devices based on the standard will support streaming video and other loss- and delay-sensitive traffic types.

WiBro differs from WiMAX in one significant respect: It relies entirely on licensed spectrum. On the one hand, this represents a clear advantage for WiBro because the licensed nature of its operating range protects it from interference from unlicensed devices that use the same spectrum. On the other hand, its dependency on licensed spectrum could prove to be a hindrance to worldwide acceptance. Furthermore, whereas WiMAX leaves much of the design consideration up to the equipment providers, WiBro is very rigid in this regard, potentially adding to the barriers to its acceptance.

That being said, WiBro continues to advance in the market. SK Telecom and Hanaro Telecom are in a partnership to roll out WiBro throughout Korea, and in November 2004 Intel and LG Electronics agreed to promote interoperability between WiBro and WiMAX technologies. In September 2005 Samsung signed an agreement with Sprint Nextel Corporation to provide equipment for a WiBro trial.

Ultimately WiBro will merge with WiMAX, but in the meantime the technology is pushing the limits of broadband wireless.

Flarion has been the most successful player so far in the mobile market. It has conducted trials with Nextel, T-Mobile, and Vodafone in Japan, and the results have been quite good. However, Flarion faces the same challenge that all small companies face: the availability of major original equipment manufacturer (OEM) backing that will provide the quality of service (QoS) and commercial viability that large carriers expect. Even with the support of Qualcomm, major barriers remain. Flarion has always argued that OEM support will come as soon as the mobile carriers make a commitment to FLASH-OFDM technology, but this is a classic chicken-and-egg proposition. The mobile carriers are reluctant to take any steps toward a new technology that will cannibalize or cheapen the investment they have made in 3G infrastructure. Also, they are concerned that the deployment of an alternative access technology will siphon revenues from 3G. Finally, none of the wireless carriers is willing to be the first to take a risk on what is perceived to be a largely untested new technology.

This combination of challenges, combined with the fact that none of the trials Flarion has had under way have yet gone commercial, is a vexing problem for the company. In response, Flarion has turned its attention to markets in which short-term support may be easier to come by. A 450-MHz spectrum, for example, is currently available in many parts of the world, particularly in eastern and northern Europe. It works well for the delivery of broadband data services to rural environments. Recognizing this, Flarion went after that sector by forging an OEM deal with Siemens. Since WiMAX cannot currently operate in the 450-MHz band, the only option for mobile wireless data transport has been CDMA450. Consequently, Flarion offers a viable alternative in these regions and has the added advantage of the 450-MHz licenses held by T-Mobile, an investor in Flarion.

With FlexBand, Flarion also appeals to the service providers that are most eager to offer the elusive quadruple play (voice, video, data, and wireless): cable and satellite providers.

If it is to stay in this space, Flarion will have to act quickly because WiMAX vendors will be in hot pursuit of potential customers in that space as well. In fact, early entrants are establishing beachheads there with pre-WiMAX equipment, and they tend to be large, well-established companies that already have a name in the broadband space—compared with Flarion, which is in many ways still trying to prove itself. A case in point is Clearwire, which owns NextNet and is deploying a pre-WiMAX network across the United States that will be leased to cable companies and other would-be broadband wireless providers in the triple-play space. South Korea Telecom, which is deploying WiBro across Korea, is also entering the U.S. market through a venture with EarthLink. Thus, decisive, bold moves are required, and they're required *now*.

Alliances and strategic partnerships will be critical to Flarion's success and, by extension, to Qualcomm's, and all indications point to the fact that the combination of Flarion's actions in the 450-MHz arena and FlexBand's technological advantages could position the company well with major vendors. A functional and efficient OFDM implementation is important in the marketplace because the systems manufacturers are looking not only to offer a better solution and a cost-effective parallel to their in-place 3G networks but also to go after the Millennial Generation, for which mobility is a lifestyle choice, as well as cable providers and wireless companies that want to get into the quad play game or become Mobile Virtual Network Operators (MVNOs).

Qualcomm leads the pack in this arena, largely because of its Media-FLO network. Qualcomm's Forward Link Only (FLO) technology (Figure 1-3) is designed to deliver multimedia content effectively to mobile devices. FLO is an OFDM-based interface that is designed to multicast large volumes of rich multimedia content to wireless subscribers. It relies on multicasting technology in a single-frequency network to reduce the cost of delivering the same content to multiple simultaneous users.

Chapter 1

Figure 1-3
Qualcomm's FLO technology. Users access the network via the FLO-based antennae shown on either side of the diagram.

FLO primarily targets cell phones and personal digital assistants (PDAs), which are morphing rapidly into multipurpose devices that serve as telephones, address books, calendars, chat devices, game consoles, Internet access portals, cameras, MP3 players, and so on. Based on exhaustive studies conducted over the last year, the most compelling application among these devices is the ability to make and receive phone calls.

Because all mobile device applications share access to the battery, power can be exhausted rapidly through the inefficient use of the device or network connectivity. FLO optimizes power consumption and frequency usage. As a result, FLO-based devices will exhibit battery life that is similar to that of a standard cell phone.

MediaFLO will deliver as many as 100 content channels to a mobile device, 15 of which will be live streaming video. The best part is that it works with both CDMA and Universal Mobile Telephony System (UMTS) networks.

In December 2005, Verizon and Qualcomm released the following press release, a sign of things to come:

MediaFLO Service to Provide Video Content of Unprecedented Quality to Subscribers' Wireless Phones

BEDMINSTER, NJ—December 01, 2005—QUALCOMM Incorporated (Nasdaq: QCOM), a leading developer and innovator of Code Division Multiple Access (CDMA) and other advanced wireless technologies, and Verizon Wireless, which operates the nation's most reliable wireless networks, today announced that QUALCOMM and its subsidiary MediaFLO™ USA Inc. are working together with Verizon Wireless to bring its customers real-time mobile video over the MediaFLO multicasting network in the United States. QUALCOMM and Verizon Wireless expect to launch mobile TV services over the MediaFLO network in approximately half of the markets already covered by Verizon Wireless' CDMA2000 1xEV-DO-based broadband network, enabling Verizon Wireless to offer real-time mobile TV services of unprecedented quality to its subscribers. Verizon Wireless will be the first U.S. wireless service provider to offer MediaFLO when the network is commercially available.

Following the initial launch, QUALCOMM and MediaFLO USA Inc. will continue to expand the MediaFLO network throughout other markets that cover the Verizon Wireless V CAST and Broadband Access service areas. Verizon Wireless plans to offer mobile TV service to its subscribers through MediaFLO-enabled EV-DO handsets and use the MediaFLO network to deliver mobile TV services when the network begins commercial operation.

"MediaFLO USA's network will allow us to provide compelling real-time multimedia services to wireless customers, complementing our industry-leading wireless voice and data services—including our successful V CAST broadband multimedia service," said John Stratton, vice president and chief marketing officer for Verizon Wireless. "As we aggressively expand our mobile multimedia offerings, MediaFLO will help us continue providing the most innovative multimedia services in the nation."

"Using the MediaFLO technology and network, Verizon Wireless will be able to offer its customers a real-time TV-like experience on their wireless phones unlike anything available on the market today," said Dr. Paul E. Jacobs, CEO, QUALCOMM. "With the MediaFLO network, we have developed a wireless multicasting solution that will offer high-value, high-quality branded content at an affordable cost to service providers."

A number of other companies are working on WiMAX alternatives (note: alternative but interoperable) that are designed to satisfy the requirements of triple play providers. Both Motorola and Siemens have demonstrated impressive trials, and it is clear that the list will continue to grow. It is equally clear that all these companies understand that if they are to succeed with their plans, they must build them around the emergent but very real Internet Protocol Multimedia Subsystem (IMS) that is about to hit the market. We'll discuss IMS shortly, but suffice it to say here that no technological innovation in the last 50 years will have a greater impact on telecommunications services than IMS, and WiMAX and its closely related cousins will figure prominently in its evolution.

WiMAX, Convergence, and IMS

Now that we have cleared the debris from the last bubble, it's time to start a new one, and in fact that process already has begun. The sections that follow describe IMS, how it works, and how it will have the impact I believe it will have.

IMS Fundamentals

IMS is a standards-based networking and service delivery architecture that falls into the realm of the well-known concept of the Next-Generation Network (NGN). It is a multimedia architecture for both wireline and wireless Internet Protocol (IP)-based services. Using a version of Session Initiation Protocol (SIP) that has been accepted by the Third-Generation Partnership Project (3GPP), it gives traditional service providers the ability to offer a new range of multimedia services in a converged delivery model, using whatever access techniques they wish to employ.

The goal of IMS is to provide a set of services that combine the best of what is available from the legacy telephone network [public switched telephone network (PSTN)] and the best of what the Internet has to offer. Most important, it will facilitate the delivery of services to users regardless of their location, the devices they are using, and the access modality over which they are currently connected. Because IMS is modular and is designed to adapt to environmental changes (market demand, technology shifts, etc.), service providers can rest assured that it will adapt to their changing requirements as the need arises.

IMS depends on open IP standard protocols, and this guarantees its universal applicability within the realm of global data networks. Because it was created by and for the mobile services world, it seamlessly combines the best of the Internet with the best of cellular telephony to bring the two domains together.

IMS was created by an organization called the Third-Generation Partnership Project. Its primary responsibility traditionally has been the creation of standards for third-generation mobile telephony systems, with a focus on W-CDMA (wideband CDMA).

IMS first appeared on the scene in the 3GPP's Release 5 standard, which established the rules for the migration from second-generation to third-generation wireless systems. At the time Universal Mobile Telephony System (UMTS) was emerging as a major force for the harmonization of GSM and CDMA networks, multimedia applications were creating interest in SIP-based systems, particularly as NGNs were beginning to appear. Release 6 added interoperability with wireless local area networks (LANs); both releases were backward-compatible with legacy GSM and Generalized Packet Radio System (GPRS) networks.

Meanwhile, a different organization came into the picture. 3GPP2 arrived on the scene with its CDMA2000 Multimedia Domain (MMD) based on 3GPP IMS, which added CDMA2000 to the global mix of supported standards. Release 7 incorporated the requirements of wireline networks, completing the convergence between fixed and wireless. Shortly thereafter, a migration plan appeared for the evolution from Internet Protocol Version 4 (Ipv4) to Ipv6, and although it has not been adhered to, the strategy is in place.

Critical Elements

Perhaps the most important and relevant characteristic of IMS is that it is designed to work with literally any network: UMTS, GPRS, WLAN, WiMAX, WiFi, DSL, CDMA2000, and cable. In fact, it works quite well with legacy (nonpacket) circuit-switched telephone networks through a gateway device. Because the system is designed around IP, access networks with different characteristics can interoperate seamlessly. Because of the interworking between wireless and wireline networks, users can roam freely among member networks, using the applications they subscribe to regardless of the network to which they are connected.

Service delivery in IMS is remarkably straightforward, and the modular design of the architecture (see Figure 1-4) supports Push-to-Talk over Cellular (POC), videoconferencing, multiplayer gaming, screen sharing, VoIP, and any other IP-based services that can be controlled by SIP.

What is IMS, really? It is a foundation on which a service delivery environment can be built for the creation and delivery of voice, video, data, and other multimedia services. With IMS, these services can be converged and delivered to subscribers on demand, however and whenever they like, serving as lifestyle enablers. Imagine a technology innovation designed from day 1 to enhance a desirable lifestyle rather than be accommodated by it. Through the combination of the database and management capabilities of IMS with traditional services that include

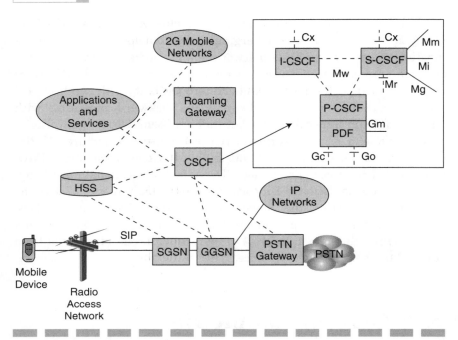

Figure 1-4
Proposed IMS reference architecture.

Signaling System Seven (SS7) and SIP data, Short Message Service (SMS) and Instant Messenger (IM) buddy lists, location data, presence information, purchase histories, and subscriber preferences and profiles, new combinations of services can be created on demand that adapt instantaneously to user behaviors and profiles. SMS could be interlaced with voice and video services, all IP-based, to deliver multiparty video-conferencing for individuals or for use in schools.

Again I ask, Exactly what is IMS? The answer continues to evolve and change as more players and other technologies are added to the overall IMS vision. Functionally designed to converge voice and data services with end-to-end QoS over a packet-based infrastructure and to combine wireline and wireless infrastructures logically under a shared set of end-to-end signaling and billing capabilities, IMS will play a relatively clear role in the evolving network definition. That role continues to grow more complex, however, as time passes. A collection of mobile providers that are interested in expanding their purview to include alternative data technologies have begun to petition for inclusion of both WiFi and WiMAX in the IMS vision. To round out the table banging, cable television providers are beginning to clamor for inclusion alongside traditional wireline providers so that they will not be left out of the game.

The Next-Generation Network

The Next-Generation (in some countries the New-Generation) Network is a concept that has been banging around the service provider domain for years and is just now coming to fruition. It is driven by a set of enterprise, consumer, government, and investor requirements and purports to reframe network service delivery relative to the IMS vision of a user-centric network.

Not surprisingly, enterprise and residence customers exhibit an ongoing demand for integrated data, voice, and video; support for any service, anywhere, with high speeds and media flexibility; support for on-demand circuit, bandwidth, and service provisioning; support for highly flexible virtual private networks; a need for security, storage, and application layer routing; and the ability to integrate network (telecom) and information (IT) systems easily and seamlessly.

Consumer and government groups have a related but different set of requirements. Those requirements include broadband access to every home; business-capable telecommuting services; reasonable prices for bundled data, voice, and video services; access to firewall and intrusion protection services; availability of on-demand video; and, finally, access to and support for high-speed peer-to-peer networking and applications.

Finally, there is the investment community that must fund IMS. Not surprisingly, it wants increased revenue, enhanced profitability, larger served areas, and enhanced productivity.

Service providers have their own set of challenges. They currently must deliver data, voice, and video services over expensive, service-specific, largely stand-alone networks that are incapable of delivering the flexible integrated services that the market demands. They realize that they must offer a wide range of access methods and protocols that better fit the needs of differentiated profitable services and must build IP and Multiprotocol Label Switching (MPLS) networks that rely on fairly complex redundant architectures.

In essence, then, the IMS network can satisfy all these groups if it offers the following:

- The mobility of wireless
- The reliability of the PSTN

- The universality of the Internet
- The security and service isolation capability of private line
- The flexibility of IP and MPLS to support integrated data, voice, and video services
- The high bandwidth of optical networks
- The operational efficiency of a common, consistent infrastructure

In essence, IMS is a philosophy, a model, an architecture for service delivery.

As the NGN concept continues to develop, three overarching characteristics are emerging. They are *infrastructure convergence*, which is simply the convergence of multiple service-specific networks onto a common MPLS core through Multiservice Edge (MSE) routers that deliver layer 2 and layer 3 virtual private network (VPN) services; *service convergence*, the convergence of data, voice, and video services onto flexible and ubiquitous IP and MPLS networks; and *network simplification*, the elimination of complex tiered architectures and redundancy to create more scalable, reliable, and manageable networks that rely on point-of-presence (POP) architectures.

Numerous organizations have contributed to the definition of NGN, including the International Telecommunication Union (ITU). They have a remarkably simple view of it that aligns nicely with the IMS vision, as illustrated in the following quotes:

"Nothing should be done in the network that can be efficiently done in an end system."

"An NGN is a packet-based network able to provide telecommunications services and able to make use of multiple broadband, QoS-enabled transport technologies in which service-related functions are independent from underlying transport-related technologies."

We have spent quite a few pages talking about the role of IMS in the evolving network. In essence, IMS is the ultimate incarnation of convergence. It represents the seamless and highly functional coming together of technologies (wireless, wireline, and IP), services (voice, video, data), applications (gaming, television, content on demand, location-based services), companies (strategic alliances and partnerships), and philosophies (access to *my stuff* versus access to the network).

If service providers can really do what IMS makes feasible—deliver anywhere, anytime content to any device—service suddenly takes on a whole new meaning and the network inverts its reason for being. Instead of customers being forced to adapt their demands to the limited capabilities of the network, the massively more capable network simply will adapt to the whims of the customer.

I hope you are beginning to see why I believe that IMS represents the single most powerful communications innovation to come along in a very long time. What is the role of WiMAX in this? If broadband wireless become universally available and if roaming becomes a reality with WiMAX as it is anticipated to do, the two technologies will become mutually supportive and will serve as critical underpinnings in the evolving converged multiservice network.

First Things First: Radio Basics

Before we launch into a discussion of WiMAX, we should set the stage with an overview of wireless technology in general. Those of you who are familiar with radio frequency (RF) basics can skip this section or read it quickly for review.

What if I were to tell you the following? "I have a new service that I want to sell you, similar to the one you use today. But I should warn you that it isn't quite as good as the one you use today. However, it does *cost* more." Interested? Ready to sign up? No? Sounds insane? You say you'd never do such a silly thing?

So… You don't own a cell phone?

The fact is that wireless deployment always involves some kind of trade-off between QoS and added convenience. Before we go too deeply into the inner workings of the WiMAX anatomy, let's cover radio basics. I realize that this may be old hat for more experienced readers; if you fall into that category, feel free to skip ahead.

The path employed between a user's device and the network to which that user wants to connect, whether wireless or wireline, is defined by characteristics such as distance, quality (signal level, noise, and distortion factors), and bandwidth. Distance is important because it places design limitations on the network, making it more expensive as circuit length increases. Over distance signals tend to weaken and become noisy, and specialized devices such as amplifiers, repeaters, and regenerators are required to strengthen and clean up the signal periodically to

Figure 1-5
*Signal
degradation
over distance.*

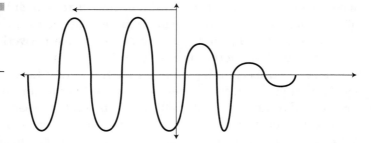

ensure intelligibility and recognizability at the receiving end. This is illustrated in Figure 1-5.

Quality Issues

Quality is related to distance in the sense that the two share many affecting factors. Those factors include distance, noise, and distortion.

Distance

Those who remember their elementary physics will recall that the power of a radiated signal decreases as a function of the square of the distance from the source; in other words, it does not decline in a linear fashion (Figure 1-6). The farther a device is from the antenna that is generating the signal, the faster the signal decreases in strength. This is why cellular systems are designed the way they are. First, they rely on a cellular

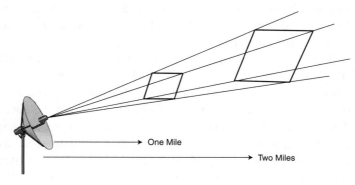

Figure 1-6
*The strength of
a transmitted
signal
decreases
according to
the square of
the distance
between the
transmitter and
the receiver.*

One Mile

Two Miles

system (Figure 1-7) in which multiple towers (antennas) are used to blanket a large area. Second, they depend on low-frequency transmission power, which allows them to achieve the third characteristic: frequency reuse. As shown in Figure 1-8, all the cells with the same patterns use the same transmit and receive frequencies. Because they are low-power emitters and are sufficiently distant from one another, they do not interfere with one another. Finally, cellular systems rely on a technique called

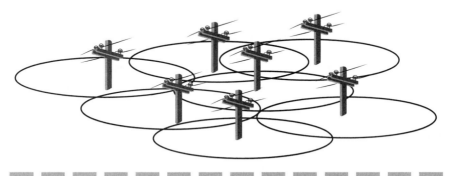

Figure 1-7

An array of low-power cells in a cellular network. Notice how the coverage areas overlap, allowing handoff of a call to occur from one cell to another. Also, because of low power and distance, frequencies can be reused.

Figure 1-8

Central switch "authority" commands endpoints to "hop" as instructed.

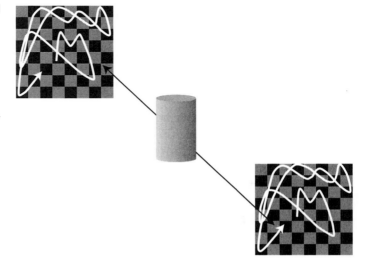

handoff; this simply means that as the signal from one cell gets weak, a stronger signal in an adjacent cell picks up the call before it is dropped.

With the use of a cellular architecture, there is no need for a single high-power transmitter whose signal will fade rapidly as users drive away from it. Instead, signal strength remains relatively uniform because of handoff.

Physical Impairments

A series of factors can diminish the signal radiated by an antenna. In the South, for example, it is well known that because of their waxy or resin-rich leaves, magnolia and pine trees adversely affect transmitted signals far more than do the leaves of deciduous trees. In the Northeast, where I live, we know when the snow is starting to fall because the cable signal, which is collected at the head end by a large satellite downlink, starts to hiccup.

Physical structures can pose problems as well. How many times have you had to tell the person you're talking to that you'll call him or her back because you're about to drive into a tunnel or into an area where the signal strength drops to zero? There's a reason Verizon Wireless uses its "Can you hear me now?" advertising slogan.

Signal level is clearly important, as is noise. Noise is a function of extraneous signal components "stomping" on what otherwise would be a clear signal. It is a random event caused by factors such as lightning, flickering fluorescent lights, whirling electric motors, sunspot activity, and squirrels chewing on wires, to name a few. It is also unpredictable and largely random. Noise therefore cannot be anticipated with any degree of accuracy; its effects can only be recovered from. This is why layer 2 error detection and correction protocols were created: to provide a mechanism for detecting errors related to noise events and correct them where possible.

Distortion, in contrast, is a measurable, predictable characteristic of a transmission channel and is usually frequency-dependent. For example, certain frequencies transmitted over a particular channel will be weakened, or attenuated, more than will other frequencies. Think about the last time you listened to music on hold over your mobile phone. Pretty lousy, wasn't it? This is the case because the rich frequencies that make up a music signal are affected differently by the bandwidth-limited channel of the cellular network. Remember the last time you attended a parade? What was your first clue that the band was approaching? You heard the low-frequency beat of the bass drums and tubas long before you saw the band or heard the higher frequencies of the trumpets and trombones. Higher-frequency signals weaken faster than do signals at lower frequencies and therefore do not travel as far without amplification and regeneration.

If we can measure this, we can condition the channel to equalize the treatment that all frequencies receive as they are transmitted down that channel. This process is known as *conditioning* and is part of the higher cost of buying a dedicated circuit for data transmission. It works well in a physical facility, but how do you condition an air interface? Answer: *You can't.* Therein lies the greatest challenge faced by engineers and service providers: finding a way to guarantee quality of service that is consistent in all circumstances when the characteristics of the "circuit" are constantly changing.

Bandwidth

Bandwidth is the last characteristic we will discuss here, largely because of the ongoing demand for wireless data services. Whether the application is television broadcast to a mobile device, location-based services, Web access, e-mail downloads, mobile gaming, or videoconferencing, the continued expansion of rich media (i.e., multimedia content) demands greater levels of available bandwidth. Bandwidth, which typically is measured in bits per second (or megabits or gigabits per second), is a measure of the number of bits that can be transmitted across a facility in a one-second period. In most cases it is a fixed characteristic of the facility and is the characteristic that most customers pay for. WiMAX, with its remarkably high bandwidth and service radius, is a serious contender for the broadband wireless data space.

Facilities often are called *channels* because physical facilities frequently are used to carry multiple streams of user data through a process called *multiplexing*. Multiplexing allows multiple users to share access to a transport facility either by taking turns or by using separate frequencies within the channel. If the users take turns, as shown in Figure 1-9, the multiplexing process is known as *time division multiplexing* because time is the variable that determines when each user gets to transmit through the channel. If the users share the channel by occupying different frequencies, as shown in Figure 1-10, the process is called *frequency division multiplexing* because frequency is the variable that determines who can use the channel.

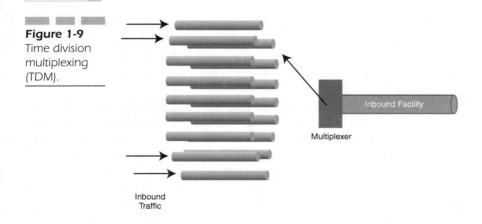

Figure 1-9
Time division multiplexing (TDM).

Figure 1-10
Frequency division multiplexing (FDM).

It often is said that in time division multiplexing, users of the facility are given *all* the frequency *some* of the time because each user is the only one using the channel during his or her timeslot. In frequency division multiplexing, users are given *some* of the frequency *all* the time because each user is the only one using his or her particular frequency "band" at any point. Multiplexing is as much a part of the wireless world as it is of the world of physically connected facilities; for example, a person with a mobile device can simultaneously talk on the phone and surf the Web as long as the wireless facility over which that person is connected offers ample bandwidth to support the demands of both applications.

Analog versus Digital Signaling: Dispensing with Myths

Frequency division multiplexing normally is considered an *analog technology*, whereas time division multiplexing is thought of as a *digital technology*. The word *analog* means "something that bears a similarity to something else," whereas *digital* means "discrete." Analog data, for example, which typically are illustrated as some form of sine wave such as the one shown in Figure 1-11, are an exact representation of the values of the data being transmitted. The process of using the manipulable characteristics of a signal to represent data is called *signaling*.

We should introduce a few terms here. When one is speaking of signaling, the proper term for digital is *baseband*, whereas the term for analog signaling is *broadband*. When talking about data (not signaling), the term *broadband* means "big channel."

The sine wave, undulating along in real time in response to changes in one or more of the parameters that control its shape, represents the exact value of each of those parameters at any point in time. The parameters are amplitude, frequency, and phase. We will discuss each one in turn. Before we do, though, let's relate analog waves to the geometry of a circle. This is one of the best ways to demonstrate the relationship between the various characteristics of a transmitted signal.

Consider the diagram shown in Figure 1-12. As the circle rolls along the flat surface, the dot will trace the shape shown by the dotted line. This shape is called a sine wave. If we examine this waveform carefully, we notice some interesting things. First, every time the circle completes a full revolution (360 degrees), it draws the shape shown in Figure 1-13. Thus, halfway through its path, indicated by the zero point on the graph, the circle has passed through 180 degrees of travel. This makes sense, since a circle circumscribes 360 degrees.

Figure 1-11
Sine wave.

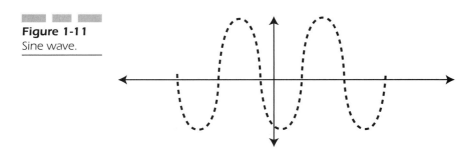

Figure 1-12
Creating a sine
wave.

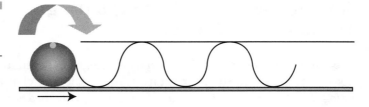

Figure 1-13
Sine wave.

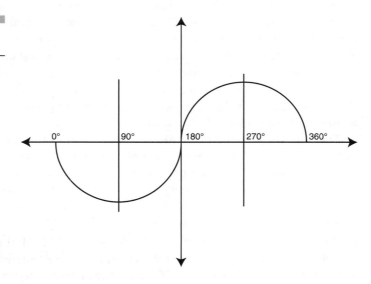

The reason this is important is that we can manipulate the characteristics of the wave created in this fashion to cause it to carry varying
amounts of information. Those characteristics—amplitude, frequency,
and phase—can be manipulated as follows.

Amplitude Modulation

Amplitude is a measure of the loudness of a signal. A loud signal, such as
the one currently thumping through the window of my office from the
subwoofer in the back window of the car that belongs to the kid across
the street, has high-amplitude components (but also has very-low-fre-
quency components, as evidenced by the fact that I can hear him coming
when he's still in southern Vermont), whereas lower-volume signals are
lower in amplitude. Examples are shown in Figure 1-14. The dashed line
represents a high-amplitude signal, and the solid line represents a

Figure 1-14
Amplitude
modulation.

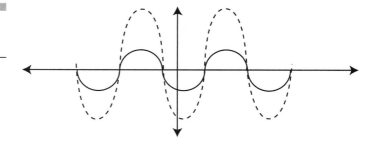

lower-amplitude signal. How could this be used in the data communications realm? Let's let a high-amplitude signal represent a digital 0 and a low amplitude signal represent a digital 1. If I then send four high-amplitude waves followed by four low-amplitude waves, I have transmitted the series 00001111. This technique is called *amplitude modulation* (AM); *modulation* simply means "vary." This is how AM radio works; that is why it's called AM.

Frequency Modulation

Frequency modulation (FM) is similar to amplitude modulation except that instead of changing the loudness of the signal, we change the number of signals that pass a point in a given second, as illustrated in Figure 1-15. The left side of the graph contains a lower-frequency signal component, and a higher-frequency component appears to its right. We can use this technique the same way we used AM: If we let a high-frequency component represent a 0 and a low-frequency component represent a 1, I can transmit the 00001111 series by transmitting four high-frequency signals followed by four low-frequency signals.

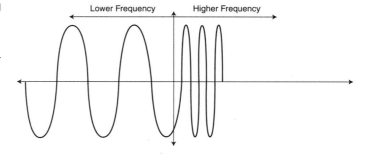
Figure 1-15
Frequency
modulation.

Lower Frequency   Higher Frequency

An interesting historical point about FM is that the technique was invented by the radio pioneer Edwin Armstrong in 1933. Armstrong created FM as a way to overcome the problem of noisy radio transmission. Before the arrival of FM, AM was the only technique available, and it relied on modulation of the loudness of the signal *and* the inherent noise to make it stronger. FM did not rely on amplitude but instead on frequency modulation, and it therefore was much cleaner and offered significantly higher fidelity than did AM radio. Keep in mind that signals pick up noise over distance; when an amplifier amplifies a signal, it also amplifies the noise.

Many technical historians of World War II believe that Armstrong's invention of FM transmission played a pivotal role in the outcome of the war. When the war was in full swing, FM technology was available only to the Allied forces. AM radio, the basis for most military communications at that time, could be jammed by transmitting a more powerful signal that overloaded the transmissions of military radios. FM, however, was not available to the Axis powers and therefore could not be jammed as easily.

Phase Modulation

Phase modulation (PM) is a little more difficult to understand than the other two modulation techniques. *Phase* is defined mathematically as "the fraction of a complete cycle elapsed as measured from a particular reference point." Any questions? Let's make that definition make sense. Consider the drawing shown in Figure 1-16. The two waves in the diagram are exactly 90 degrees "out of phase" with each other because they do not have a common start point: Wave B begins 90 degrees later than wave A. In the same way we used amplitude and frequency to represent 0s and 1s, we can manipulate the phase of the wave to represent digital data.

A few years ago I saw a real-world example of how phase modulation can be used in a practical way. I was in Arizona with a film crew, shooting a video for one of my corporate clients. The theme of the video was based on the statement that if "we don't deploy technology intelligently, the competition will leave us in the dust." Building on that phrase, we rented a ghost town in Arizona and created a video metaphor around it. In the last scene of the show a horse-drawn wagon loaded with boxes of technology products is heading off into a bloody Arizona sunset, but just before the wagon disappears over the hill, it skyrockets into the sky on a digital effect that looks like a rocket trail.

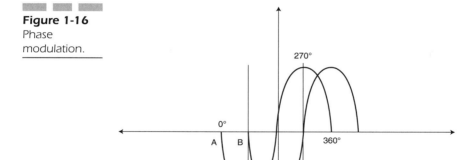

Figure 1-16
Phase
modulation.

We loved it. The only problem was that when we got back into the post-production studio and began to assemble the final show, we discovered to our horror that the sound of an airplane could be heard behind our narrator. Since airplanes didn't exist in the Old West, we had a big problem. Our audio engineer asked us to pipe the sound into the audio booth. Listening to the recording, he went to his wall of audio CDs and selected a collection of airplane sounds. He listened to several of them until he found one that was correct. Setting the levels correctly so that they matched those of the video sound track, he inverted the CD signal (180 degrees out of phase with the sound track signal) and electronically added it to the sound track.

The airplane noise disappeared from the narration.

Digital Signaling

Data can be transmitted in a digital fashion as well. Instead of a smoothly undulating wave crashing on the computer beach, we can use an approximation of the wave to represent the data. This technique is called *digital signaling*. In digital signaling, a mathematical phenomenon called the Fourier series is called into play to create what most people call a square wave (see Figure 1-17). In the case of digital signaling, the *Fourier series* is used to approximate the "square" nature of the waveform. The details of how the series works are beyond the scope of

Figure 1-17
Square wave.

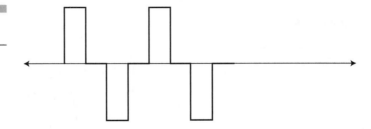

this book, but suffice it to say that when the infinite series of odd harmonics of a fundamental wave are combined mathematically, the ultimate result is a squared-off shape that approximates the square wave that commonly is used to depict digital data transmission. This technique is called digital signaling, as opposed to the amplitude, frequency, and phase-dependent signaling techniques used in analog systems.

In digital signaling, 0s and 1s are represented as either the absence or the presence of voltage on the line and in some cases are represented by either positive or negative voltage or both. Figure 1-18 shows a technique in which a 0 is represented by the presence of positive voltage and a 1 is represented as zero voltage. This is called a *unipolar signaling scheme*. Figure 1-19 shows a different technique in which a 0 is represented as positive voltage and a 1 is represented as negative voltage. This is called a *nonreturn to zero signaling scheme* because zero voltage has no meaning in this technique. Finally, Figure 1-20 demonstrates a *bipolar signaling system*. In this technique, the presence of voltage represents a 1, but note that

Figure 1-18
Unipolar
signaling
scheme.

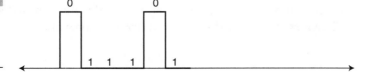

Figure 1-19
Nonreturn to
zero (NRZI)
signaling
scheme.

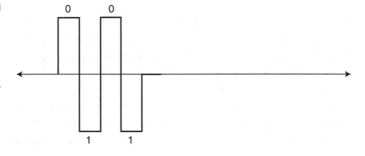

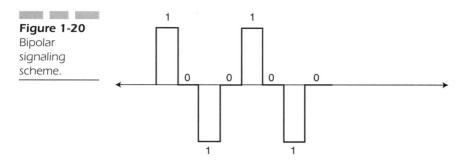

Figure 1-20
Bipolar
signaling
scheme.

every other 1 is opposite in polarity to the one that precedes it *and* the one that follows it. Zeros, meanwhile, are represented as zero voltage. This technique, which is called *alternate mark inversion* (AMI), is used commonly in T- and E-Carrier systems for reasons that will be discussed later.

There are other techniques in use, but these are the most common.

Clearly, both analog and digital signaling schemes can be used to represent digital data, depending on the nature of the underlying transmission system. It is important to be clear about the difference between *data* and *signaling*. Data is the information that is being transported, and it can be either analog or digital in nature. For example, music is a purely analog signal because its values vary constantly over time. It can be represented, however, by both analog and digital signaling techniques. The 0s and 1s that spew forth from a computer are clearly digital information, but they too can be represented either analogically or digitally. For example, the broadband access technology known as *Digital Subscriber Line* is not digital at all: There are analog modems at each end of the line; that means that *analog signaling techniques* are used to represent the *digital data* that are being transmitted over the local loop.

Does this help? It should, but before we return to the details of WiMAX, let's add one more piece: ways to take advantage of waveform characteristics to transmit high-bit-rate signals.

Combining Signaling Techniques for Higher Bit Rates

Let's assume that we are operating in an analog network. Under the standard rules of the analog road, one signaling event represents one bit. For example, a high-amplitude signal represents a 1 and a low-amplitude signal represents a 0. But what happens if we want to increase the bit rate? One way to do that is to signal faster. Unfortunately, the rules of physics limit the degree to which we can do that. In the 1920s a senior researcher at Bell Laboratories who has become something of a legend in the field of communications came to the realization that the bandwidth of the channel over which information is transmitted has a direct bearing on the speed at which signaling can be done across that channel. According to Harry Nyquist, the broader the channel is, the faster the signaling rate can be. In fact, the signaling rate can never be faster than two times the highest frequency a channel can accommodate.

Unfortunately, the telephone local loop historically was engineered to support the limited bandwidth requirements of voice transmission. The traditional voice network was engineered to deliver 4 KHz of bandwidth to each local loop,[1] and that means that the fastest signaling rate achievable over a telephony local loop is 8000 baud. However, during the late 1980s and early 1990s it was common to see advertisements for "9600-baud modems." This is where the confusion of terms becomes obvious: As it turns out, these were *9600-bit-per-second modems*, and that is a big difference. A 9600-baud modem was patently impossible. This introduces a whole new problem: How do we create higher bit rates over signaling rate–limited (and therefore bandwidth-limited) channels?

To achieve higher signaling rates, one of two things must be done: broaden the channel, which is not always feasible, or figure out a way to have a single signaling event convey more than a single bit.

Consider the following example. We know from our earlier discussion that we can represent two bits by sending a high-amplitude signal followed by a low-amplitude signal (the high-amplitude signal represents a 0, and the low-amplitude signal represents a 1). What would happen, though, if we combined amplitude modulation with frequency modulation? Consider the four waveforms shown in Figure 1-21. By combining the two possible values of each characteristic (high and low frequency or amplitude), we create four possible states, each of which can represent two bits, as shown in Figure 1-22. We can have a high-bandwidth, high-frequency signal; a high-bandwidth, low-frequency signal; a low-bandwidth, low-frequency signal; and a low-bandwidth,

---

[1] One way in which this was done was through the use of load coils. Load coils are electrical traps that tune the local loop to a particular frequency range, allowing only certain frequencies to be carried. This created a problem for digital technologies, as we will discuss later.

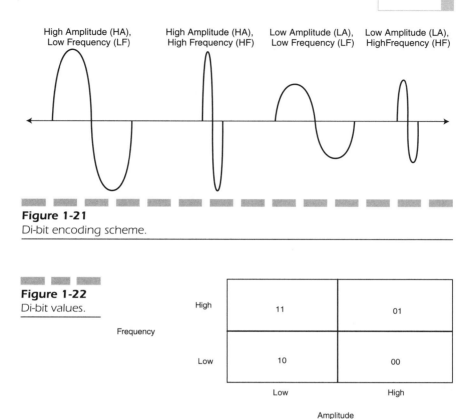

Figure 1-21
Di-bit encoding scheme.

Figure 1-22
Di-bit values.

high-frequency signal. Consider what we have just done: We have created a system in which each signaling event represents two bits; this means that our bit rate is twice our signaling rate.

It's time to introduce a new word: *baud*.

Baud is the signaling rate. It may or may not be the same as the bit rate, depending on the scheme being used.

Let's take this concept a step farther. Figure 1-23 shows a system in which we are encoding four bits for each signal, a technique known as quad-bit encoding. This scheme, which sometimes is called *Quadrature Amplitude Modulation* (QAM, pronounced kwam), permits a single signal to represent four bits; that means that there is a 4:1 ratio between the bit rate and the signaling rate. Thus, it is possible to achieve higher bit rates in the bandwidth-limited telephony local loop by using multibit encoding techniques such as QAM. The first "high-bit-rate modems" (9600 bits per second) used this technique or a variation of it to overcome the design limitations of the network. In fact, these multibit schemes are

Figure 1-23
Quadrature
amplitude
modulation
(QAM).

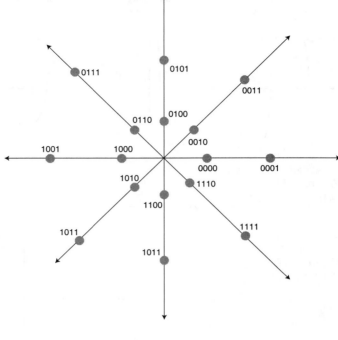

Figure 1-24
Quadrature
amplitude
modulation
(QAM), this
time with noise
added to the
constellation.

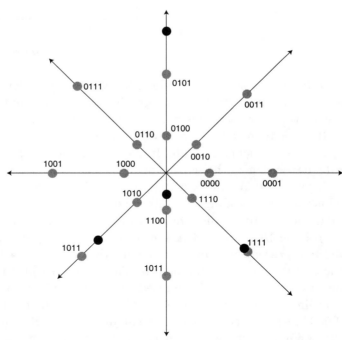

used by the cable industry to achieve the high bit rates those companies need to operate their multimedia broadband networks.

There is one other limitation that must be mentioned here: noise. Figure 1-24 shows a typical QAM graph, but we have added noise in the form of additional points on the graph that have no implied value. When a receiver sees them, how does it know which points are noise and which are data? Similarly, the oscilloscope trace of a high-speed transmission shown in Figure 1-25 would be difficult to interpret if there were noise spikes intermingled with the data. There is a well-known relationship between the noise level in a circuit and the maximum bit rate that is achievable over that circuit, a relationship that was first described by Bell Labs researcher Claude Shannon, widely known as the father of information theory. In 1948 Shannon published *A Mathematical Theory of Communication*, which is universally accepted as the framework for modern communications.

We won't delve into the complex but fascinating mathematics that underlie Shannon's theorem; suffice it to say that his conclusions are seminal: The higher the noise level in a circuit, the lower the achievable bandwidth. The bottom line is that *noise matters*. It matters so much, in fact, that network designers and engineers make its elimination the first order of business in their overall strategies for creating high-bandwidth networks. This is one of the reasons optical fiber-based networks have become critically important in modern transport systems: They are far less subject (though not immune) to noise and absolutely immune to the

Figure 1-25
Oscilloscope trace.

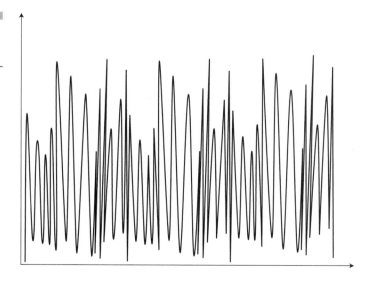

electromagnetic interference that plagues copper-based networks. This is also the reason wireless networks are so sensitive to noise: They do not operate within a bounded channel, and the signal can be affected by so many environmental factors that engineers go to great lengths to overcome the limitations of the wireless world. To a great extent they succeed, although not entirely.

Let's dive a bit deeper into the workings of WiMAX. Earlier we talked about the characteristics of radio waves and how they can be modified (and therefore persuaded to carry information) by changing their frequency, amplitude, and phase. Let's discuss those characteristics in a bit more detail.

The term *megahertz* (MHz) refers to a radio wave that is cycling a million times per second (1 MHz). By extension, a *1-gigahertz signal* (GHz) cycles a billion times a second. This is true in all wireless environments. For example, consider the radio in your car (okay, your older car). The FM band spans the range of frequencies from 88 MHz to 108 MHz. In other words, FM radio signals cycle between 88 and 108 million times per second, depending on the channel to which you're listening. By definition, then, the wavelength of the signal at the top of the FM band is much shorter than the wavelength of the signal at the bottom because instead of packing 88 million of them into a 1-second interval, it has to pack 108 million into the same space.

I've discussed only FM here, but there are other frequency ranges that are worth considering. For example, amplitude modulated (AM) radio operates in the range of frequencies that lie between 535 kHz and 1605 kHz. Maritime communications, which are used for ship-to-shore and some nautical navigation applications, are found in the range of 30 to 535 kHz. Shortwave radio, which sometimes is called amateur radio, is found between the top end of the AM band and the bottom of the VHF television band.

Similarly, the range of frequencies between 1605 kHz and 54 MHz hosts multiple applications. The range of 1605 kHz to 30 MHz provides a home for amateur radio, government radio, international shortwave broadcast, and fixed and mobile communications. The range of 30 to 50 MHz hosts government and nongovernment applications and fixed and mobile communications applications, including police, fire, forestry, highway, and railroad services. The band from 50 to 54 MHz is the site for amateur radio, and the frequency range from 40 to 50 MHz is used in nuclear magnetic resonance (NMR) and magnetic resonance imaging (MRI) applications, both of which are critical for medical radiological diagnostics systems.

Television and FM radio, as mentioned earlier, are scattered across this region of the spectrum. The frequencies for VHF television channels 2 to 4 span the range from 54 to 72 MHz; 72 to 76 MHz is reserved for government and nongovernment services, including a standard aeronautical beacon at 75 MHz. VHF television channels 5 and 6 lie between 76 and 88 MHz, and FM radio ranges from 88 to 108 MHz, sandwiched between VHF television channels 6 and 7.

Above FM one finds aeronautical navigation applications in the range of 108 to 122 MHz. These applications include localizers, radio ranging, and airport control systems. From 122 to 174 MHz there is a general services band for both government and nongovernment signals, including fixed and mobile devices and amateur broadcasts.

Television channels 7 through 13 span the range between 174 and 216 MHz, and the spectrum from 216 to 470 MHz is assigned to fixed and mobile communication applications, including some aeronautical navigation and citizens-band (CB) radio. The band from 470 to 890 MHz includes a broad range of UHF television channels, from 14 to 83.

The list continues. The band from 890 to 3000 MHz supports aeronautical and amateur radio applications, television studio-transmitter relays, and a variety of other applications. In the middle of the range there are radar bands between 1300 and 1600 MHz.

The spectrum from 390 to 1550 MHz is used for satellite communications in the range known as L-Band. The Global Positioning System (GPS) relies on two carrier frequencies in this band for transmitting navigation data.

Finally, at the top of the heap there is radar. Although some radar bands are found between 1300 and 1600 MHz, most of these so-called microwave applications fall between 3000 and 30,000 MHz (3 to 30 GHz). Microwave ovens operate at or around 2450 MHz, and some amateur and radio navigation systems use the range of 3 to 30 GHz.

Some of the more common defined bands are shown on the next page.

The Issue of Licensed Spectrum

Although much of the available spectrum is *unlicensed*, meaning that it is freely available to all users, the rest of it is licensed, meaning that a formal government license is required for permission to operate within the range of frequencies covered by the license. In the United States, the

Frequency	Application
450 MHz	Public-service radios, rural cellular services
700 MHz	UHF bands for television and future wireless services
850 MHz	Cell phone services, including advanced 3G wireless wide area network services
900 MHz	Cellular service
1700 MHz	Cellular service
1800 MHz	Cellular service
1900 MHz	Cellular service
2100 MHz	Cellular service
2300 MHz	Amateur radio, satellite (U.S.)
2400 MHz	WiFi, home cordless, baby monitors, microwave ovens, "unlicensed" or, technically, the ISM (industrial, scientific, and medical) band
2.5–2.6 GHz	Proposed for WiMAX and other services, also IMT-2000 extension band
3.4–3.6 GHz	Proposed for WiMAX and other services in Europe and China; used by the U.S. government for radio location and amateur radio
5.7 GHz	WiFi, cordless phones, commercial use, proposed for WiMAX (European fixed broadband wireless access)

Federal Communications Commission (FCC) is responsible for the assignment of operating licenses.

As with any licensing activity, this one is fraught with challenges. For example, years ago, when consumer wireless applications were limited to radio and television, the television industry applied for and was granted the exclusive right to operate within a vast swath of spectrum. Over the years, however, much of its operation has gone to cable, meaning that a huge percentage of the spectrum assigned to that industry is unused. The same thing is true of much of the analog frequency that was granted to early cellular operators.

This is important because of a single, simple observation. I often hear professionals in this industry say that "we are running out of spectrum because we don't have enough of it." In fact, that is not true: We have all the spectrum there is. The problem is that we don't manage it particularly well, as has been the case with many limited technological resources, such as IP addresses. One way to deal with the problem of responsible spectrum management is to give specific government agencies the responsibility for protecting the various ranges of spectrum over which they have administrative control. If they did not exercise this responsibility, any operator would be free to operate in any range of frequency he or she wished, and the result would be at best poor service quality and at worst interference with critical services such as airport beacons.

We've spent quite a bit of time talking about the environment in which WiMAX will operate, but we haven't discussed WiMAX itself. We'll do that now with a brief introduction to WiMAX technology.

WiMAX Technology: An Introduction

WiMax falls into the general category of wireless transmission known as *broadband wireless access* (BWA). WiFi also falls into this category and is widely deployed, popular, and highly functional. The only problem with WiFi, along with most BWA solutions, is that they tend to be expensive; they also tend to offer spotty coverage, and where they *do* offer coverage, it is usually over a small geographic area. So we have expensive, small, and spotty. Any questions?

What the market would like to have is a solution that offers the freedom of wireless, the high speed of broadband, and a coverage footprint that is similar to that provided by the cellular network. Although it is not yet commercially viable at the level at which we would like it to be, WiMAX does provide all these characteristics. Defined by the Institute of Electrical and Electronic Engineers (IEEE) under standard 802.16, WiMAX is the best solution on the table today for broadband wireless access. WiMAX will offer broadband access the same way the mobile network today offers voice and limited data connectivity, and based on the rigorous work being done by both standards bodies and manufacturers (at both the component level and the system level), WiMAX could pose a serious competitive threat to DSL and cable as a viable alternative to the broadband service they currently provide. Since it is designed to be easy to use, WiMAX could be as seamless a part of the "connectivity experience" as WiFi is today. Turn on your PDA, computer, or laptop and you are connected; it's as simple as that.

Let's look briefly at WiMAX from the perspective of functionality. Practically speaking, WiMAX operates analogously to WiFi, but because it does not necessarily require line-of-site transmission, it could provide service in areas where WiFi cannot penetrate or where DSL and cable facilities have not been installed. In practice, WiMAX includes two key components: a tower-mounted antenna similar to the cell towers one sees sprouting all over the landscape and some form of receiver. A WiMAX tower can provide service coverage over an area as large as 2500 square miles because of the way the system is designed (more on that later); the antenna can be as large as a roof-mounted dish (Figure 1-26) or as small as a card inserted in the personal computer (PC) card slot on a laptop.

The WiMAX tower can be mounted on a stand-alone pedestal or can be placed on a rooftop (Figure 1-27). From there it can connect directly to the greater network (e.g., the Internet) via a fixed facility such as an optical connection or a high-speed copper circuit or via a microwave back-

Figure 1-26
A roof-mounted WiMAX dish antenna. Courtesy Skylink Corp.

Figure 1-27
Rooftop-mounted WiMAX antenna.

haul connection using a point-to-point microwave hop, such as a focused WiMAX link that connects to another WiMAX tower. Because it combines the broad wireless coverage of WiMAX with the ability to connect to the wireline network and use WiMAX itself for backhaul, the technology is being watched as the ideal solution for providing BWA service in rural areas with sparse coverage, hence the scenario I described earlier in Africa.

WiMAX Service Options

This also demonstrates that WiMAX offers two different implementation options. The first is a line-of-sight option. In this scenario a fixed antenna, typically a small dish, is oriented so that it can "see" the antenna mounted on a remote WiMAX tower. This is far and away the more reliable of the two service options because it relies on an uninterrupted microwave connection between two antennas. These line-of-sight (LOS) systems operate at the higher end of the frequency band allocated for WiMAX, as high as 66 GHz. In radio terms, the higher the frequency, the greater the available bandwidth but the shorter the operating distance. Of course, with the shorter LOS distances comes reduced interference. LOS systems typically can operate at distances up to about 5 miles, and this provides a very rough service footprint of about 75 square miles. With high-end antennas, a WiMAX node could transmit as far as 30 miles to a router such as the one shown in Figure 1-28, thus allowing the technology to realize its full potential.

Non-line-of-sight WiMAX systems rely on a signal-encoding scheme called *Orthogonal Frequency Division Multiplexing*, which we will describe in detail later in this book. These NLOS systems are designed primarily for computer or laptop applications and rely on a much smaller antenna device. These systems operate at a much lower frequency range (2 to 11 GHz) and are therefore less susceptible to physical obstacles. Because OFDM is used, this capability is greatly enhanced.

Figure 1-28
Backhaul router.
Courtesy
Tasman Corp.

Ultimately, WiMAX will facilitate the deployment of what has come to be known as the Global Area Network (GAN). GAN, which is documented in IEEE standard 802.20, defines an environment in which a subscriber can roam the country—indeed, the world—and stay connected regardless of his or her location. This ties into the IMS concept as well, since one of the key tenets of IMS is anywhere, anytime, always-on connectivity and access to content on the user's terms, not those of the network. Clearly, WiMAX will play a key role in the deployment of this capability.

How WiMAX Works

WiMAX operates in a manner similar to that of WiFi. A computer equipped with a WiMAX radio card connects to the WiMAX-enabled network via a remote tower and then exchanges data (most likely encrypted) with that remote device at very high data rates. Whereas current WiFi devices operate at SONET Optical Carrier 1 (OC-1) speeds (54 Mbps), WiMAX can support bandwidth in excess of 70 Mbps. Although that 70 Mbps is shared among a collection of users, early trials have demonstrated that the allocated bandwidth competes favorably with that provided by DSL and cable modems.

However, the real advantage of WiMAX over WiFi is not bandwidth; it's the operating radius of the technology. Whereas WiFi operates at service radii of about 300 feet, WiMAX can deliver high-bandwidth connectivity to devices as far as 30 miles away because of the microwave frequencies that are used and the increased power of the transmitting device. Although physical obstructions will have a deleterious effect on transmission quality and distance, the use of OFDM helps overcome their effects. Since rural coverage is one of the most important applications for WiMAX, obstructions from buildings most likely will not pose a serious threat.

Let's summarize the requirements of the 802.16 WiMAX standard. It specifies an operating range of 30 miles between the remote device and the base station antenna at bandwidth levels that hover around 70 Mbps. Although line-of-sight is not required, it does enhance the capabilities of the technology if it is available. 802.16 operates in the frequency ranges that lie between 2 and 11 GHz and between 10 and 66 GHz and clearly defines a media access control (MAC) layer and multiple physical (PHY) layers.

WiMAX Deployment and Cost Considerations

WiMAX can be deployed in two distinct ways. The first is the WiFi analog: an NLOS implementation for roaming users (not in the cellular sense but in the sense that individual users can "wander" into the WiMAX "cell" and take advantage of the delivered bandwidth). The second technique is to place WiMAX in the center of an area of desired influence (Figure 1-29) and use it to provide LOS high-bandwidth connectivity to a community of relatively fixed users.

The first technique, which sometimes is referred to as "WiFi-MAX," most likely would be implemented by a city government. Multiple WiMAX base stations would be installed across the greater metro area, providing connectivity to financial centers and other major business centers. The service could be offered as a paid service for ad hoc use or as a "magnetic" free service to attract businesses to the area. As I write this, Tokyo is being "wired" with citywide WiMAX service. The Yozan Metro-Zone will support high-bandwidth IP connectivity for voice, video, and broadband data services. The $12 million implementation is expected to be complete by mid-2006.

The second technique is more complex but offers greater promise. By placing a WiMAX tower in the center of an area to serve as a high-speed

Figure 1-29
Arrows show possible locations for WiMAX antennas.

wireless hub, it could offer Internet access and content delivery over a broad area. Today subscribers pay a fee to cable companies and telephone service providers for network access. In the future, the same providers or, more interestingly, a collection of alternative providers might offer wireless broadband via WiMAX for a fixed monthly fee. For example, an Internet service provider (ISP) or another provider (e.g., the power company) could install a WiMAX base station in a suburban area. The customers then would buy a WiMAX card for their PCs, allowing them to receive the WiMAX signal. Access would be controlled through some form of encryption in much the same way a cable set-top box today cannot access the network without an authorization code. The subscriber would pay a monthly fee to the service provider (I use the term *service provider* loosely since that company could be a variety of types), a fee that could be significantly lower than that requested by the traditional players, because there is little to install physically, thus requiring far less initial expense.

Home users would continue to use their personal networks in much the same way. They might buy a WiMAX router (Figure 1-30) or even a dual-mode router that provides both WiMAX and WiFi, allowing the in-home network to remain unchanged. Because WiMAX supports VoIP, its use for voice service unquestionably will increase dramatically.

Let's summarize what we now know about WiMAX and where it sits in the pantheon of high-speed network services available today (see Figure 1-31). The range of wireless standards in place today supports a collection of networking capabilities defined by two key characteristics: bandwidth and distance. At the shortest operating distance we find the personal area network (PAN), which includes such standards as Bluetooth and the HiperPAN standard defined by the European Telecommunications Standards Institute (ETSI) for use in Europe. Next is the local area network, which includes 802.11 (WiFi), and the European Hiper-

Figure 1-30
A desktop
WiMAX router.
Courtesy
AirSpan Corp.

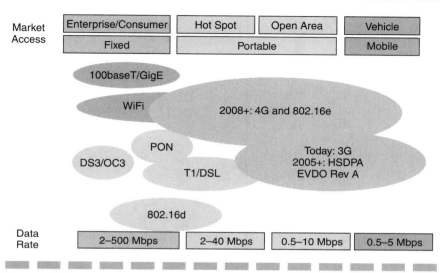

Figure 1-31
The broadband geography.

LAN standard, also published by ETSI. Third in the hierarchy is the metropolitan area network (MAN), which includes 802.16 (WiMAX) and the European HiperMAN and HiperAccess offerings. Finally, at the outer edge we find the proposed 802.20 IEEE standard and the European Third-Generation Partnership Project (3GPP) offerings such as Enhanced Data for GSM Evolution (EDGE) and other GSM capabilities that are yet to come.

Summary

In this chapter we have examined the driving forces behind WiMAX. They include the desire for more bandwidth, an increasing demand for mobility, the need for global roaming, the requirement on the part of the market to have anywhere, anytime access to content (hence the tight linkage between WiMAX and IMS), and the incessant demand on the part of service providers to extend their relevance and indeed their ability to survive. In Chapter 2 we look at the history of WiMAX and talk about its current status with an eye toward placing it in the collection of evolving network technologies.

WiMAX History and Support Organizations

There is a story I often use in describing the interplay between standards and the technologies they are designed to govern. We'll begin with the evolution and history of Worldwide Interoperability for Microwave Access (WiMAX) and a few related technologies and then introduce the companies that are most active in the design, deployment, and sale of WiMAX as a technology and a solution. The list probably will surprise you.

Consider this: If you visit any reasonable-sized university campus or business park and put on your architect's hat, you will notice a couple of things. First, in addition to the design of the buildings and the way they are sited relative to the land on which they stand, you will notice that the buildings are placed in such a way that the natural features of the land and the artificial features of the buildings complement each other. You also will notice that running between the buildings, nicely laid out in pleasing right angles, is a warren of concrete or redwood bark walkways that provide pedestrians with paths between the facilities.

If you look closely, you also will see a collection of what I like to call "goat trails" that are worn into the grass and run directly from building to building (Figure 2-1); those trails demonstrate that although the angular sidewalks are aesthetically pleasing, they violate the rule that the shortest distance between two points is a straight line. (I maintain that architects should dispense with the sidewalks altogether, wait six months, and then pave the goat trails. It makes a lot more sense and saves on concrete.) I call this a goat trail methodology; in much the same way that goats create ad hoc trail systems across the rocky hillsides in the wild, people create the technological equivalent whenever something new is introduced and there is revenue at stake.

Figure 2-1
Goat trails on
a college
campus.

If we look back at the evolution of wireless fidelity (WiFi) (not WiMAX), we note that what I just described is precisely what happened in that case. WiFi was introduced in 1992 when wireless local area network (LAN) companies began to make use of the 2.4-GHz spectrum component where WiFi operates today. It is important to note that the technology was released before the standards were complete, and manufacturers, seeing the promise of a new technological innovation and the opportunity to garner maximum market share in what they perceived would be a very large market, jumped on the bandwagon and began building WiFi devices. Standards development efforts followed, and the result was what one might expect: a collection of incompatible standards that created problems in the industry that were reminiscent of the "modem wars" of the early 1990s, when two competing and incompatible 56-Kbps modem standards were released, creating implementation paralysis throughout the industry.

Hence the goat trail comparison: WiFi was created as a result of a "path of least resistance" progression model in which developers rushed to create products. Although this resulted in the rapid introduction of WiFi products and services, it created a variety of problems, including the release of dysfunctional standards. For example, some of the spectrum that is available today for WiFi in the United States is not available in other parts of the world; in places where it is available, it cannot be used legally because it is reserved for military purposes or for some other proprietary application.

This is all reminiscent of the well-known "Apocalypse of the Two Elephants" that was described a couple of decades or so ago by Andy Tanenbaum, the author of *Computer Networks*. This colorfully named phenomenon (see Figure 2-2) describes the tragedy that results when the research and development (R&D) activity and the manufacturing activity collide, crushing the standards-creation process in the middle. It's a very sad thing.

Enter WiMAX

The concept behind broadband wireless in general and WiMAX in particular follows roughly the same developmental path as that of Digital Subscriber Line (DSL), as shown in Figure 2-3. Even though broadband wireless accounts for the smallest percentage of the overall growth of broadband access, its growth curve is steady and unwavering and is in

Figure 2-2
The
Apocalypse of
the Two
Elephants.

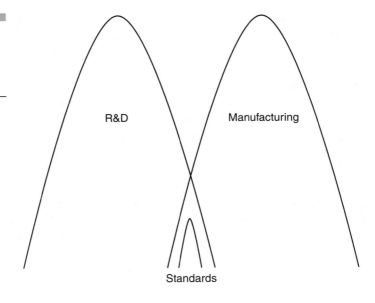

Figure 2-2
The
Apocalypse of
the Two
Elephants.

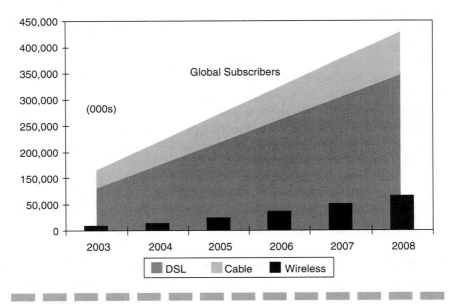

Figure 2-3
Growth in global subscribers by technology type. Source: Yankee Group.

fact accelerating at a rate faster than that of the other two. By 2010 analysts expect that there will be more than 450 million broadband users worldwide. That's not all: Analysts anticipate that by 2010 processors will have an eightfold increase in power and that there will be more than a billion Voice over Internet Protocol (VoIP) users worldwide. Storage is growing at a rate 12 times faster than increases in processor density; that means that the average personal computer (PC) will have a terabyte of onboard storage by 2010. There's no doubt about it: This evolution is serious, and it hasn't begun to slow down. In fact, it's accelerating.

Broadband Data by Sector

If we examine the sectors that make up the broadband data domain (see Figure 2-4), we see that it can be characterized by a collection of data points. Across the bottom of the diagram is the bandwidth range, and the top part depicts the market that is served by each technology and the type of access that is used in each case. At the highest bandwidth range we find both enterprise and consumer market fixed access applications, including 100BaseT (Fast Ethernet), Gigabit Ethernet, and WiFi in the LAN environment and Passive Optical Network (PON), DS3, Optical

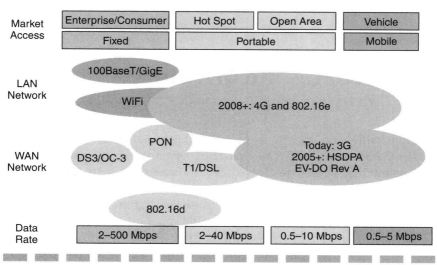

Figure 2-4
The broadband geography.

Carrier 3 (OC-3), and 802.16d in the wide area network (WAN) environment. Here we find data rates ranging from 2 Mbps to 500 Mbps.

In the middle of the range there are the so-called portable access solutions, which include both hotspot deployments and open area applications. These include the higher ranges of WiFi, fourth-generation (4G) systems, T1, and DSL. Bandwidth in this domain ranges from 2 Mbps to 40 Mbps. The other side of this midrange domain is the open area application, which currently includes third-geneation (3G) systems but also will include High-Speed Downline Packet Access (HSDPA) and later versions of Evolution–Data Only (EV-DO). Also included in this sector is the next generation of WiMAX, 802.16e, which adds mobility to the capabilities of the standard. Here one finds data rates in the range of 500 Kbps to 10 Mbps. Note that with each step outward on the scale there is a decline in available bandwidth but a marked increase in the flexibility of the technology.

Finally, on the far end of the scale there is vehicle-based mobility with access speeds ranging from 500 Kbps to as much as 5 Mbps and including HSDPA, EV-DO, and 802.16e.

This evolution demonstrates that the market is willing to exchange a high bit rate for flexibility. In fact, the combination of the two—a high bit rate and flexible service capabilities—is one of the great differentiators associated with WiMAX. Although it has its limitations, the various versions of it cover the technological services waterfront in an elegant and relatively seamless way.

Broadband Wireless Evolution

A remarkable evolution took place in the broadband wireless world between 2000 and 2005. The first transformative step was associated with capability: Data rates increased, the standards settled down, and chipset availability went from highly proprietary to high-volume availability. The second major change was the evolution from proprietary solutions to standards-based WiMAX solutions.

Consider Figure 2-5. In the period 2000–2001, broadband wireless was virtually 100 percent proprietary in nature, as is often the case with a new technological innovation. Data rates evolved from 2 Mbps to 11 Mbps, and the WiFi RF chipsets were based on 802.11b or were entirely

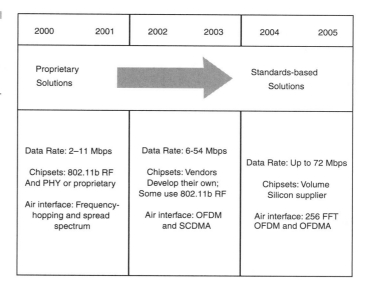

Figure 2-5
Standards and capability evolution in WiMAX.

2000	2001	2002	2003	2004	2005

Proprietary Solutions → Standards-based Solutions

Data Rate: 2–11 Mbps

Chipsets: 802.11b RF
And PHY or proprietary

Air interface: Frequency-hopping and spread spectrum

Data Rate: 6-54 Mbps

Chipsets: Vendors Develop their own; Some use 802.11b RF

Air interface: OFDM and SCDMA

Data Rate: Up to 72 Mbps

Chipsets: Volume Silicon supplier

Air interface: 256 FFT OFDM and OFDMA

proprietary. The air interface for these systems was based on spread-spectrum transmission schemes. Let's take a moment to define these important techniques.

Spread Spectrum

Spread-spectrum transmission is a simple concept that entails disguising a narrowband transmission within a broadband transmission by "spreading" or "smearing" the narrowband signal across the broadband carrier. This is done by using one of two basic techniques: *frequency hopping*, in which a control signal directs the two communicating devices to "hop" randomly from frequency to frequency to avoid eavesdropping, and *direct sequence*, in which the signal is combined with a random "noise" signal to disguise its contents under the command of a control signal that knows how to separate the signal "wheat" from the noise "chaff."

Frequency Hopping Spread Spectrum

The development of the frequency hopping spread spectrum (FHSS) is a story that is worth knowing because it is so much fun to tell and so remarkable in the telling. During World War II there was considerable concern among the Allied forces about the Axis powers' ability to defeat the target-following capabilities of radio-controlled torpedoes by jamming the radio signals that guided them to their targets. With that in mind, a pair of industrious entrepreneurs filed patent number 2,292,387, "Secret Communications System." The inventors were the orchestra composer George Antheil and the electrical engineer Hedy K. Markey (Figure 2-6), better known as the early film star Hedy Lamarr.

The technique described in their patent application is straightforward: A central base station, which is shown schematically in Figure 2-7, communicates with the two communicating endpoint devices, instructing them to "hop" randomly from frequency to frequency at ran-

Figure 2-6
Actress Hedy Lamarr, also the co-inventor of spread-spectrum technology.

Figure 2-7
Central switch "authority" commands endpoints to "hop" as instructed.

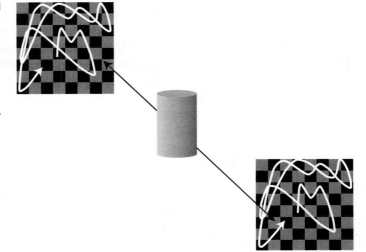

domly selected times and for random intervals, typically on the order of 5 ms or less. Only the base station and the two devices know when and where to jump and for how long. To any device wishing to eavesdrop on the conversation, the hopping process appears completely random. It isn't, however: The base station knows precisely what it is doing and when it is doing it, and so the hopping behavior is actually "pseudo-random"; this technique often is referred to as a "pseudorandom hopping code." It is used most commonly in Code Division Multiple Access (CDMA) cellular systems and is, as one might expect, used extensively in secure military communications systems.

Direct Sequence Spread Spectrum

Direct Sequence Spread Spectrum (DSSS), sometimes called Noise-Modulated Spread Spectrum, is different from its FHSS cousin. In frequency hopping, the "conversation" jumps from frequency to frequency on a seemingly random basis. In noise modulation, the actual signal is combined with a carefully crafted "noise" signal that disguises it. The otherwise narrowband signal, which is shown in Figure 2-8, is spread across a much wider channel, typically on the order of 1.25 MHz. The bits in the data stream are combined with "noise bits" to create a much broader signal, and as before, only the base station and the communicating devices

Figure 2-8
Spread
spectrum
graph.

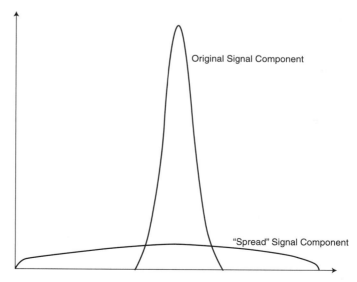

Original Signal Component

"Spread" Signal Component

know the code that must be used to extract the original signal from the noise. The code sometimes is called a chipping code, and the technique is referred to as producing a chipped signal.

These two techniques, FHSS and DSSS, formed the functional basis of the original wireless LAN standards that ultimately coalesced into the solution known as WiFi.

Between 2002 and 2003 things progressed rapidly. Supported data rates climbed to 54 Mbps, a speed previously attainable from solutions such as Synchronous Optical Network (SONET). At the component (chipset) level, vendors began to introduce their own silicon solutions, some of them based on the newly released Institute of Electrical and Electronic Engineers (IEEE) 802.11a standard. Vendors also evolved the air interface to include access solutions based on Orthogonal Frequency Division Multiplexing (OFDM) and Synchronous Code Division Multiple Access (SCDMA). SCDMA, which was developed in China and is based on intelligent antenna arrays, software-defined radio, and highly intelligent signal-processing software, remains somewhat proprietary and, though intriguing, is not yet ready for prime time. OFDM, in contrast, deserves some serious attention.

Orthogonal Frequency Division Multiplexing

Orthogonal Frequency Division Multiplexing is a multicarrier transmission scheme that works well for high-speed, full-duplex wireless transport. It was developed in the 1960s but has gotten a great deal of attention recently because the new generation of processors can perform the high-speed operations it relies on, making OFDM available to more applications.

OFDM works in an intriguing way, squeezing together a collection of adjacent modulated carriers, reducing bandwidth requirements but maintaining orthogonality among them to ensure that they do not interfere with one another (Figure 2-9). Put simply, signals are orthogonal relative to one another when they are maintained in separate space relative to one another—in effect, they are independent and noninterfering. Mathematically speaking, they occur at right angles to one another. DSL, WiFi, and WiMAX all use orthogonal multiplexing.

OFDM relies on frequency division multiplexing (FDM), which uses multiple frequencies to transmit multiple simultaneous signals in parallel across a facility even if the facility is wireless. Each signal compo-

Figure 2-9
Non-interfering
signals.

nent has its own frequency range, which is then modulated by the data it transports and then demodulated by the receiver, using filters to separate the individual carriers.

OFDM is similar to FDM but is significantly more efficient in spacing the subchannels (in fact, they actually overlap slightly). What OFDM does is locate frequencies that are orthogonal, and that allows the individual channels to overlap without interfering with each other. This is illustrated in Figure 2-10, where 10 subcarriers overlap each other by removing the guard bands. To demodulate the signal, a discrete Fourier transform (DFT) is required. Since fast Fourier transform (FFT) semiconductors are now widely available, this requirement has become trivial.

Figure 2-11 shows an example of OFDM in which there are 256 subcarriers, of which 192 carry data, 56 are nulls, and 8 are pilot frequencies. Fundamentally, in any given situation, any of the subcarriers could be used to indicate a 1 or 0 value. However, because of multibit encoding schemes such as Phase Shift Keying (PSK) and Quadrature Amplitude Modulation (QAM), the data throughput can be increased dramatically. The pilot subcarriers provide a point of reference that is used to minimize frequency and phase shifts during data transmission, and the null bands are used to center the DC carrier and provide guard bands between transmission streams.

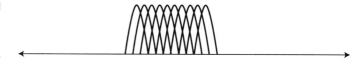
Figure 2-10
Overlapping
subcarriers.

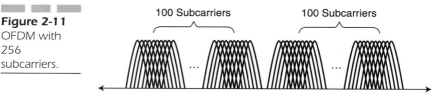
Figure 2-11
OFDM with
256
subcarriers.

100 Subcarriers   100 Subcarriers

Expanding on the Promise of OFDM

OFDM Access (OFDMA) permits reassignment of some of the subcarriers; in effect, some of them can be assigned to different users. Subcarriers 3, 9, and 11 could be assigned to user 1, and subcarriers 2, 10, and 12 could be assigned to user 2. By grouping subcarriers in this fashion, we create what are commonly known as subchannels. You see where this is going: With this capability, multiple users can be supported over a single multiplexed path. Advances in OFDMA silicon have dramatically improved the efficiency of the fast Fourier transforms that drive the overall scheme, reducing the FFT size from 2048 to 128, supporting channel bandwidth between 1.25 MHz and 20 MHz. As a result, the performance of lower-bandwidth channels is improved, as is that of higher-bandwidth carriers.

OFDM is highly resistant to multipath interference, a problem that occurs when multiple reflected signals arrive at the receiver with near simultaneity. OFDM deals with this well, overcoming many of the challenges of the unpredictable wireless environment in which many of the systems that use it operate. Consequently, it lends itself well to WiFi and WiMAX and is in fact a major component of both technologies.

WiFi Today

Today several 802.11 standards exist; 802.11b and 802.11g devices transmit in the unlicensed 2.4-GHz range, and 802.11a devices transmit at 5 GHz. Needless to say, this presents a radio compatibility problem that had to be overcome. As far as implementation history is concerned, 802.11b was the first version of the WiFi standard to reach the market. It is the least costly and offers the lowest bandwidth of the three, transmitting in the 2.4-GHz spectral band at speeds up to 11 Mbps.

Next in the developmental lineup was 802.11a. Operating at 5 GHz, it can handle transmission speeds up to 54 Mbps. Its biggest challenge, however, was its incompatibility with the widely accepted 802.11b. To remedy this, 802.11g was introduced; it operates in the same 2.4-GHz band as 802.11b but offers transmission rates at speeds equivalent to 802.11a: upward of 54 Mbps. As a result, not only is it compatible with 802.11b, it also benefits from the lower-cost unlicensed spectrum at 2.4 GHz.

802.11a and 802.11g rely on OFDM. 802.11b, in contrast, uses a different encoding technique called *complementary code keying* (CCK). As one knowledge base defines it, complementary codes are "binary complementary sequences with the mathematical property that their periodic auto-correlative vector sum is zero except at the zero shift." Although that definition may set the engineers in the audience all aquiver, it makes me feel like I'm reading the bridge column in the newspaper. In English, CCK is a technique that creates a set of 64 eight-bit "code words" that encode data for 11-Mbps data transmission in the 2.4-GHz band (802.11b). These code words are mathematically unique so that they can be distinguished from one another by the receiver even when there is substantial noise and multipath interference. As a result, CCK-based systems can achieve substantially higher data rates by eliminating the impact of effects that otherwise would limit their ability to achieve those rates.

It should be noted that CCK works only with the DSSS systems specified in the original 802.11 standard. It does not work with FHSS.

802.11 Physical Layer

All 802 standards address themselves to both the physical (PHY) and the media access control (MAC) layers. At the PHY layer, IEEE 802.11 identifies three options for wireless local area networks: diffused infrared, DSSS, and FHSS.

Whereas the infrared PHY operates at a baseband level, the other two operate at 2.4 GHz, part of the Industrial, Scientific, and Medical (ISM) band. It can be used for operating wireless LAN devices and does not require an end-user license. All three PHYs specify support for 1-Mbps and 2-Mbps data rates.

802.11 Media Access Control Layer

The 802.11 MAC layer, like Carrier Sense Multiple Access with Collision Detection (CSMA/CD) and token passing, presents the rules used to access the wireless medium. The primary services provided by the MAC layer are as follows:

- **Data transfer:** Based on a Carrier Sense Multiple Access with Collision Avoidance (CSMA/CA) algorithm as the media access scheme.

- **Association:** The establishment of wireless links between wireless clients and access points (APs).

- **Authentication:** Because any wireless device can associate itself with an access point, privacy and confidentiality are critical components in WiFi. True authentication is possible with the use of the Wired Equivalent Privacy Protocol (WEP), which uses a shared key validation protocol similar to that used in Public Key Infrastructures (PKIs). Only devices with a valid shared key can be associated with an AP.

- **Privacy:** By default, data are transferred "in the clear"; any 802.11-compliant device can potentially eavesdrop on PHY 802.11 traffic that is within range. WEP encrypts the data before the data are transmitted by using a 40-bit encryption algorithm known as RC4. The shared key used in authentication is used to encrypt or decrypt the data; only clients with the correct shared key can decipher the data.

- **Power management:** 802.11 defines an *active mode* in which a wireless client is powered at a level adequate to transmit and receive and a *power save mode* in which a client is not able to transmit or receive but consumes less power while in a "standby mode" of sorts.

In 2004 and 2005, WiMAX standards were nearly complete. Bandwidth increased to 72 Mbps, and components became available in large volumes at a reasonable price. The air interface, which finally was mature, incorporated 256 FFT OFDM and OFDMA. WiFi was mature, WiMAX had arrived, and the standards wars were just beginning.

IEEE 802.16 Wireless Point-to-Multipoint MAN

Since early July 1999 the *IEEE 802.16 Working Group on Broadband Wireless Access* has worked to develop standards for wireless metropolitan area networks (WANs) that have global relevance. IEEE 802.16 provides solutions that may be more economical than wireline options. The standards it has developed so far address demands for reliable high-bandwidth access over the famous first mile.

The 802.16 committee has developed a small collection of relevant standards.

The IEEE 802.16 WirelessMAN Standard, also known by its harder-to-remember name "Air Interface for Fixed Broadband Wireless Access Systems," addresses the requirements for wireless MANs. The initial standard, which took two years to develop, covers systems that operate between 10 and 66 GHz. It was approved for publication in December 2001 and was published in April 2002.

Next on the IEEE's list of publications is Amendment 802.16a, which expands the range of available spectrum to both licensed and unlicensed bands that range from 2 to 11 GHz.

Amendment 802.16c offers 10- to 66-GHz system profiles to help with the development of interoperability specifications. 802.16.2, another addition, is a recommended practice that discusses the "Coexistence of Fixed Broadband Wireless Access Systems" between 10 and 66 GHz. It was published in September 2001 and was followed in July 2004 by 802.16d, which added non-line-of-sight capability. 802.16e will add the capability for mobility and an improved air interface. Finally, 802.16f provides a management information base (MIB) for 802.16d, and 802.16g, to be released some time in 2007, will provide the capability for mobility management.

Let us summarize. In 2001, the IEEE released the original IEEE 802.16 standard, the first in a series of related broadband wireless MAN standards. Since that time the organization has added to that original standard through a series of amendments, each targeting a different capability.

In early 2002, the Wi-LAN organization joined Nokia, Ensemble, Harris, and CrossSpan and became a founding member of the 2- to 11-GHz group within the WiMAX Forum. Consequently, the charter of the WiMAX Forum was modified to promote a single global standard for broadband wireless access based on Wi-LAN's original and highly functional W-OFDM technology and the IEEE 802.16 and European Telecommunications Standards Institute (ETSI) HiperMAN standards operating in the 2- to 11-Ghz bands.

In September 2003, during the twenty-seventh session of the IEEE 802.16 Working Group, a new project, 802.16-REVd, was approved. Until its arrival, the 802.16 standard consisted of three documents within the 802.16 group: IEEE Standard 802.16-2001, IEEE Standard 802.16c-2002, and IEEE Standard 802.16a-2003. The standard commonly known as 802.16a is actually an amendment to IEEE 802.16-2001 and is not a stand-alone document. IEEE 802.16-REVd, which was in fact a combination of the prior three documents, was ratified and published in September 2004.

Finally, IEEE 802.16-e is an amendment to IEEE 802.16-2004 that, when ratified and published, will address the addition of true mobility to the 802.16 standard.

Of course, the IEEE is not the only WiMAX game in town, not by a long shot. Equally important is the WiMAX Forum.

The WiMAX Forum

The WiMAX Forum (www.wiMAXForum.org) was created with a single focus: to facilitate the deployment of broadband wireless networks based on the IEEE 802.16 standard by helping to ensure the compatibility and interoperability of broadband wireless access equipment. The organization is nonprofit and was formed in June 2001 by a collection of equipment and component manufacturers. It is the only organization that specifically brings compliance and interoperability to the wireless broadband industry with its testing and certification program, *WiMAX Forum Certified*. The goal of the organization is international standardization and interoperability: Every WiMAX Forum–certified device will be interoperable with all other WiMAX Forum–certified devices. Ultimately, this will lead to a more competitive industry, lower costs, greater levels of innovation, and stronger, healthier competition.

In essence, the WiMAX Forum strives for interoperability among all vendors and lobbies for regulatory changes that will enhance the value of WiMAX as a global standard. WiMAX products are not certified automatically; they must pass a rigorous testing procedure to be certified officially. To that end, hundreds of companies and organizations have joined the WiMAX Forum, demonstrating that they believe it to be a long-range strategy for broadband service delivery. These companies, which are listed and described below, are all over the map. They include component manufacturers, systems manufacturers, service providers, professional services firms, and end-user organizations. Thanks to the WiMAX Forum for their assistance in providing this list and to the many companies, many of them listed below, that gave permission to use descriptive data from their Web sites.

Alphabetical Listing of Member Companies

Consult the company Web sites that follow for additional information.

WiMAX Forum Companies

ADAPTIX
Adesta
Advance Data Technology Corporation
Aeroflex
Agilent
airBand
Air Broadband Communications
Air Communications
Air Network Solutions
AirNet Communications
Airpath Wireless
Airspan Networks
Airzed
Alcatel
Aloha Partners
ALPHA Networks
Alpha Technologies
Alps Electric
Altera Corporation
Altitude Telecom
Alvarion
American Tower
Amphenol
Analog Devices
Andrew Corporation
Anritsu Corporation
AOL
Aperto Networks
Aphelion Communications
Arab Telecommunication
Arasor Corporation

Arcadia Design Systems

Areva T&D

ARL Home Communications S.B.

ArrayComm

ARRIS

ATDI

AT&T

Atmel

AudioCodes

AUSTAR Entertainment

Award Solutions

Axtel

Axxcelera

Azaire Networks

Azimuth Systems

Azonic Systems, Inc.

Aztech Systems Ltd

Bandwidth.com

Barik

Beceem

Bechtel Telecommunications

BelAir Networks

Bell Canada

BellSouth Corporation

BII Group

Booz Allen Hamilton

bracNet

Bridgewater Systems

British Telecom

Broadcom

butlerNetworks

C-DOT

Cambridge Broadband

Cameo Communications

CATR

Celestica

Cellcom

Cellular South

CelPlan Technologies

Ceragon

CETECOM

China Motion Telecom

Chung-Shan Institute of Science & Technology

Cisco Systems

Clear Channel Broadcasting

Clearwire

Colubris Networks

COM DEV

Comba Telecom Systems

Comcast

Compliance Certification Services

CompUSA

Comsys Communication & Signal Processing

Covad Communications

Cushcraft Corporation

CWC

Dell

Deutsche Telekom

Digiweb

DiNi Communications

Dishnet Wireless Limited

Distributel

Dyaptive Systems

eAccess Ltd.

EDX Wireless

Eircom

Elcoteq

Elektrobit

Enertel

Enforta

Entel

Ericsson

Ertach

ETRI

European Antennas

Euskaltel S.A.

Filtronic

Finnet

Firetide

First Avenue Networks

Firstserver

Flextronics Software Systems

Fortress Technologies

France Telecom

Fujitsu

Funk Software

Fusion Communications Corporation

General DataComm

Genius Institute of Technology

Globalcom

GloBul

Golden Telecom

Hanaro Telecom

HCL Infinet

HCL Technologies

Hopling Technologies

Huawei Technologies

Huber+Suhner

Hughes Network Systems

Hypres

IDEA Cellular Limited

IDT Telecom

IIT (Institut International des Telecommunications)

InfiNet Wireless Ltd.

Info Quest S.A.

Innowireless

Inovaware Corporation

Integrated Devices

Intel

Intarlach Wireless

Interpeak

INTRACOM

Invenova

Iqara Telecom

Irish Broadband Internet Services

Iskra Transmission

Ixia

Jacket Micro Devices

Juniper Networks

Kapsch CarrierCom

Kathrein Werke KG

KDDI

KenCast

KT Corp.

Kyocera

Larsen & Toubro Infotech Limited

Lattice Semiconductor

LCC

LG Electronics

LitePoint

Lucent Technologies

MWeb

M/A-Com, Inc.

Marconi

Mascon Global Limited

Maxim Integrated Products

MediaRing

Merrimac Industries

MetroBridge Networks

MiCOM Labs

Microelectronics Technology Inc.

Microsoft Corporation

Midwest Wireless

MITAC Technology Corporation

Mitsubishi Electric

mmWave Technologies

Mobile Mark

MobilePro

Motorola

Mpower Communications

MSV

MTI Wireless Edge

MTN Group

Murandi Communications Ltd.

Navini Networks

NEC

Neotec

Nera Networks ASA

Netgear

Netopia

NextGenTel

NextNet Wireless

NextPhase Wireless

NextWave Telecom

NextWeb

Nippon Telegraph and Telephone

Nokia

Nortel

North Rock Communications

Orbitel S.A. E.S.P

Orthogon

P-Com

PA Consulting Group

Pacific Internet Corporation

Panasonic Electronic Devices Europe

Parks

PCCW

PCTEL

Pegasus Communications

PicoChip

Piepenbrock Schuster Consulting AG

PMC-Sierra

Portugal Telecom Inovao

POSData

PowerNet Global

PricewaterhouseCoopers

Prisma Engineering

Pronto Networks

Proxim

PT Indosat Mega Media

PT Telekomunikasi Indonesia, Tbk

Qwest

Radionet

Redline Communications

Redpine Signals

ReignCom

Reliance Infocomm Limited

RemotePipes

Resolute Networks

RF Integration

Rogers

Rohde & Schwarz

Runcom Technologies Ltd.

Samora Digital

Samsung

Sanjole

Sanyo Electric Co., Ltd.

Saudi Aramco

SBC

SC Lithuanian Radio & TV Center

Securitas Direct

Selex Communications

Semino Communications

SES Americom

SGS Taiwan Ltd.

Shorecliff Communications

Siemens Mobile

Sierra Monolithics

Sierra Wireless

Sify Limited

SiGe Semiconductor, Inc.

SingTel

SK Telecom

SkyPilot Networks

SkyTel

SkyWorks Solutions

SmartBridges

Softbank

SOMA Networks

Speakeasy

Spirent Communications

Sprint Nextel

SR Telecom

Starent Networks

Start Telecom

Stealth Microwave

Stratex Networks

Stretch

Strix Systems

Symmetricom

Syntronic AB

TDC Solutions

Tektronix

Telabria

TelASIC Communications

Telcordia Technologies

TeleCIS Wireless

Telecom Italia

Telecom Technology Center

Telediffusion de France

TeleLink AD

Telenor

TeliaSonera

Telkom SA

Tellabs

Telsima

Telus

The Cloud Networks

TietoEnator

Time Warner Telecom

TNO Information and Communication Technology

Tollgrade

TowerStream

Trackwise

TRDA

Trillion

TriQuint Semiconductor

Tropos

Tulip IT Services

UNITLINE

Unwired Australia

Urmet Telecomunicazioni Spa

UTStarcom

VCom Inc.

Vectron International

Venturi Wireless

VeriSign

Vivato

Warpera

WaveSat Wireless Inc.

WFI

Wi-LAN

Wi-MAN

WiMAX Telecom AG

WiNetworks

Wintegra

WirelessLogix

Wong's International (USA)

Xilinx

Z-Com

ZTE Corporation

Company Details

ADAPTIX

http://www.adaptix.com

ADAPTIX WiMAX-compatible technologies enable feature-rich service deployments to address the increasing flexibility and mobility demands of enterprise and residential broadband subscribers. ADAPTIX delivers unprecedented spectral efficiency through its patented FastSwitching-OFDMA, which provides highly granular control over all radio domains, including frequency, time, modulation, power, coding, and space. The result is a deployment and user experience agile enough for the rapidly changing broadband landscape and connectivity powerful and intelligent enough to support high-value services.

Adesta

http://www.adestagroup.com

Adesta is a nationwide systems integrator for communication networks, security systems, and intelligent transportation systems. We provide customers with a single point of contact to design, engineer, integrate, construct, manage, and operate and maintain networks and systems.

Advance Data Technology Corporation

http://www.adt.com.tw

Since 1988, ADT Corporation has established itself as one of Taiwan's leading EMC, RF, Safety, Telecom and Wi-Fi laboratories by providing clients with reliable compliance testing and certification services. By taking advantage of the extensive facilities and design consultations we offered, many electronic manufacturers and trading companies, both in Taiwan and overseas, have been able to quickly obtain global certification from various approval agencies in ADT one-stop shop integrated service.

Aeroflex

http://www.aeroflex.com

As well as being a global provider of high-technology solutions to the aerospace and defense industries, Aeroflex offers a full range of protocol and parametric test solutions for the cellular communications industry. Its products address infrastructure and mobile handset testing and support all stages of mobile phone development and deployment. Applications include R&D, conformance, production, installation and commissioning, field service, and network optimization for all key 2G, 2.5G and 3G wireless technologies.

Agilent

http://www.agilent.com

Agilent Technologies is a global, diversified technology company focusing on high-growth markets such as wireless communications. For engineers responsible for design, development or manufacturing of wireless systems or components (such as WiMAX, Bluetooth, WLAN, UWB and cellular), Agilent provides an array of test and measurement solutions and services.

airBand

http://www.airband.com

airBand Communications, Inc., strives to be the market leader in delivering cost-effective, reliable business class broadband communications services through a relentless focus on our customers, employees, and shareholders. airBand is ideal for growing companies that need flexibility to add bandwidth quickly or more mature companies that are looking to reduce IT costs or add business continuity and disaster recovery services.

Air Broadband Communications

http://www.airbb.com

Air Broadband Communications is an innovative company in the wireless networking sector offering a comprehensive line of wireless switches for enterprise and public WLAN (802.11) and WiMAX (802.16) networks. Air Broadband's wireless solution resides on the wired portion of the network between the various antenna elements and the protected side of network, providing IP Mobility, multi-vendor antenna Compatibility, wide Scalability, per user QoS and management capabilities for Wi-Fi, WiMAX and hybrid wireless markets.

Air Communications

http://www.aircomms.co.za

Air Communications is a Broadband Wireless Access and Telecom's Company offering a variety of integrated solutions in conjunction with its local and international partners. With over 18 years' experience in the Information and Telecommunication Industry, our in-house expertise is focused on customer service and service delivery. Air Communications is ideally positioned to capitalize on the projected, explosive growth of telecommunications in Africa. The key convergence of telephony and IP in conjunction with the evolution of fixed wireless and mobile wireless technologies has provided further opportunities to connect people on the continent.

Air Network Solutions
http://www.airnetsol.net
Air Network Solutions is a dynamic service provider specializing in wireless ISP provisioning in areas not served by DSL or cable broadband. In addition, with more than 50 years of combined telecommunications systems engineering expertise, Air Network Solutions provides high-end systems engineering consultancy services.

AirNet Communications
http://www.airnetcom.com
AirNet Communications Corporation is a leader in wireless base stations that allow service operators to cost-effectively and simultaneously offer high-speed wireless data and voice services to mobile subscribers. AirNet's patented OFDM, broadband, software-defined radio architecture supports: i) high-capacity wireless applications, utilizing its AdaptaCell SuperCapacity adaptive array technology, ii) wide area coverage solutions with its award-winning AirSite Backhaul Free technology, and iii) government communications users with its compact, rapidly deployable RapidCell technology.

Airpath Wireless
http://www.airpath.com
Airpath Wireless is the "enabling source" for providers to perform and manage their Wi-Fi networks and roaming activities. We provide the engines (billing and rating), management systems (authentication, provisioning and reporting), and services (clearing and call center) that enable Service Providers to offer seamless, global access to wireless broadband services across disparate networks. The Airpath Provider Alliance (APA) is the global standard for ubiquitous Wi-Fi roaming, with over 600 providers operating over 3,300 hotspots (and counting) around the world.

Airspan Networks
http://www.airspan.com
Airspan Networks provides broadband wireless systems and solutions to licensed and unlicensed operators around the world in frequency bands

between 900 MHz and 6 GHz. Airspan has deployments with more than 120 operators in 60 countries. Airspan's systems are based on efficient radio technology that delivers broadband services over wide area coverage. Airspan's systems can be deployed rapidly and cost-effectively, providing an attractive alternative to traditional wired communications networks.

Airzed

http://www.airzed.com
Airzed is the leading wireless broadband (Wi-Fi) service provider in Malaysia. Airzed brings you affordable high-speed wireless Internet access in many hotspot locations throughout Asia.

Alcatel

http://www.alcatel.com
Alcatel provides communications solutions to telecommunication carriers, Internet service providers and enterprises for delivery of voice, data and video applications to their customers or to their employees. Alcatel leverages its leading position in fixed and mobile broadband networks, applications and services to bring value to its customers in the framework of a broadband world. Alcatel operates in more than 130 countries.

Aloha Partners

http://www.alohapartners.net/
Aloha Partners is the largest owner of 700-MHz spectrum in the United States. Aloha has 166 licenses covering over 120 million people throughout the country. Aloha covers nearly two-thirds of the top 40 markets; the entire states of California, Nevada, Hawaii, and most of Arizona, Arkansas, Ohio, Oklahoma and Tennessee. Aloha plans to use the 700-MHz spectrum for wireless broadband services.

ALPHA Networks

http://www.alphanetworks.com
ALPHA Networks, Inc., is a distinctive leader in the Networking OEM/ODM industry, offering innovative and professional engineering, manufacturing, and service to worldwide brand-name networking customers. Our design and manufacturing engineers have exclusively been focused on developing high-quality, cost-effective networking products. Our strength is in utilizing the combining potential of Ethernet LAN/WAN, Wireless, and Broadband networking technologies to produce the perfect product strategy and solution.

Alpha Technologies

http://www.alpha.com

The Alpha Group represents an alliance of independent companies that share a common philosophy to create world-class powering solutions. Collectively, Alpha Group members develop and manufacture AC and DC power conversion, protection, and standby products. Applications for these products include broadband, telecom, AC/UPS, wireless, commercial, industrial, and distributed generation for a worldwide customer base. In addition, our companies provide a range of installation and maintenance services.

Alps Electric

http://www.alpsusa.com

ALPS ELECTRIC CO., LTD., is a global electrical component company established in 1948. ALPS is the leading provider of communication devices, peripheral products, magnetic devices, mechatronic devices and automotive products. In the communication field, ALPS has WLAN and Bluetooth module, GPS antenna, AM/FM tuner, VCO and many kinds of RF modules. ALPS's global network contains 22 production bases in 9 nations, including North America, Europe, China, Japan and other ASEAN member countries. ALPS also has 57 sales bases in 14 nations.

Altera Corporation

http://www.altera.com

Altera Corporation (NASDAQ: ALTR) is the world's pioneer in system-on-a-programmable-chip (SOPC) solutions, featuring the industry's most advanced programmable logic devices, associated software tools, intellectual property (IP) software blocks, and state-of-the-art design services. Altera's products offer the performance and cost required to address the PHY and MAC layers for next generation wireless standards.

Altitude Telecom

http://www.altitudetelecom.fr

Altitude Telecom is a French multitechnologies Telco operator for businesses and regional governments. Altitude Telecom is the only WLL operator in France (more than 500 customers currently connected) and offers lots of services such as VPN IP, LAN to LAN, ISP services, broadband Internet connections and web hosting.

Alvarion

http://www.alvarion.com

Alvarion is a premier provider of solutions based on Point-to-Multipoint (PMP) Broadband Wireless Access (BWA), a technology essential to the growth of broadband markets. Created through the merger of Breeze-COM and Floware, the Company supplies integrated BWA solutions to telecom carriers, service providers and enterprises all over the world.

American Tower

http://www.americantower.com

American Tower is the leading independent owner, operator and developer of broadcast and wireless communications sites in North America. American Tower owns and operates over 22,000 sites in the United States, Mexico, and Brazil. Additionally, American Tower manages approximately 2,000 revenue-producing rooftop and tower sites.

Amphenol

http://www.amphenol.com

Amphenol RF is the world leader in the design, manufacture and supply of RF interconnect systems for the Automotive, Broadband, Telecommunication, Military/Aerospace, WLAN/RFID, and Wireless Infrastructure markets. With the combination of our global footprint and experience extending over a half century, Amphenol is your RF Global Solutions Provider for the 21st Century.

Analog Devices

http://www.analog.com

Analog Devices, Inc. (NYSE: ADI), is a world-leading semiconductor company specializing in high-performance analog, mixed-signal and digital signal processing (DSP) integrated circuits (ICs). Since ADI was founded in 1965, its focus has been to solve the engineering challenges associated with signal processing in electronic equipment. ADI's products play a fundamental role in converting real-world phenomena such as temperature, motion, pressure, light and sound into electrical signals to be used in a wide array of applications ranging from industrial process control, factory automation, radar systems and CAT scanners to cellular base stations, broadband modems, wireless telephones, computers, cars and digital cameras.

Andrew Corporation

http://www.andrew.com

Andrew Corporation is the world's premier provider of complete RF subsystem solutions for evolving global communications. We are a global leader in the design, manufacture, and supply of communications equipment systems and services. Our products and services provide proven solutions for wireless, fixed-line, broadband service providers and broadcasters throughout the world.

Anritsu Corporation

http://www.eu.anritsu.com

The Anritsu Corporation is a multinational company producing high-quality test and measurement equipment for the communications industry. The company has three primary focus areas: wireless communication, wired/optical fiber IP communications and general purpose electronic instrumentation. Anritsu manufactures products in Japan, the United States, and the United Kingdom and has a sales and support network covering all major territories and already supplies T&M products for GSM, 3G, CDMA2000, Bluetooth and WLAN.

AOL

http://www.aol.com

America Online, Inc., is a wholly owned subsidiary of Time Warner, Inc. Based in Dulles, Virginia, America Online is the world's leader in interactive services, Web brands, Internet technologies and e-commerce services.

Aperto Networks

http://www.apertonet.com

Aperto Networks develops, markets and supports multiservice fixed broadband wireless access systems for global markets. PacketWave products provide point-to-multipoint and point-to-point system solutions, including carriers' infrastructure equipment and subscriber equipment for 2.5 GHz, 3.5 GHz and 5 GHz frequency bands. Aperto addresses service providers' needs for mass market deployment of broadband wireless solutions with products that enable rapid network deployment, multiservice scalability, ease of installation and cost-effectiveness.

Aphelion Communications

http://www.aphelions.com

Aphelion Communications Inc. is a leading mobile wireless networking equipment supplier for various service providers (ILECs, CLECs, WISPs, cellular carriers, government agencies, campus environments, etc.) for public/enterprise, and consumer networks.

Arab Telecommunication

http://www.arabtel.net

Arab Telecommunication (ArabTel) was awarded a wireless license in 1997 as a wireless data service provider in the state of Kuwait. Since then ArabTel has focused on building state-of-the-art networks, consisting of fiber cable as the backbone and cell-based wireless stations to cover nationwide. ArabTel's mission is to provide data connectivity and Internet services to the vertical and horizontal market.

Arasor Corporation

http://www.arasor.net

Arasor develops and manufactures Radio-over-Fiber equipment for efficient transmission of radio signals through fiber for use in next generation Wireless communication, especially WiMAX-enabled networks. It also develops opto-electronics chips and subsystems for Telecom, Power Utility and Consumer applications. Arasor has R&D and international marketing operations in Silicon Valley, United States, integrated production and testing facilities in Guangzhou, China, a marketing and R&D center in Shanghai, China, and a fabrication and R&D center in Yokohama, Japan.

Arcadia Design Systems

http://www.arcadiadesign.com

Arcadia Design Systems, Inc., is an IP and fabless integrated chip supplier providing communications and connectivity solutions for consumers and business.

Areva T&D

http://www.areva-td.com

Our businesses provide the wide range of T&D products, systems and services that cover every aspect of the energy supply chain transforming voltage, switching, protecting, measuring, managing energy flows and interconnecting networks for large or small projects.

ARL Home Communications S.B.

http://www.home.net.my

ARL HomeComm Sdn Bhd is a licensed telecommunications service provider from Malaysia, building a dedicated IP Network designed to deliver Voice, Video and Data over a single seamless interface. Our current major service delivery platform to the last mile is 802.16 FBWA, and we are looking forward to WiMAX to help us complete building a homogeneous, integrated, proven and reliable multimedia and networked services system infrastructure that will revolutionize the way people interact with information, communications, entertainment, and most important of all, with each other.

ArrayComm

http://www.arraycomm.com

ArrayComm, Inc., founded in 1992, is the recognized leader in the commercialization of smart antenna technologies. The company's unique approach to adaptive antenna systems is at work in more than 250,000 wireless deployments worldwide. Having proven the dramatic real-world gains in performance and network economics enabled by smart antennas—in the PHS, GSM, WCDMA, and iBurst protocols—ArrayComm is now partnering with leading equipment manufacturers to bring the same benefits to WiMAX.

ARRIS

http://www.arrisi.com

ARRIS is a leading global provider of broadband access solutions for residential and enterprise markets. ARRIS supplies technologies that enable the delivery of converged video, voice and data services over broadband networks.

AT&T

http://www.att.com

For more than 125 years, AT&T (NYSE "T") has been known for unparalleled quality and reliability in communications. Backed by the research and development capabilities of AT&T Labs, the company is a global leader in local, long distance, Internet and transaction-based voice and data services. Recently acquired by SBC, the newly combined company will soon take on the AT&T name.

ATDI

http://www.atdi.com

ATDI designs, develops and commercializes services and software covering the main areas in the design, planning and use of radio networks operating in a range of frequencies from 30 MHz to 450 GHz.

Atmel

http://www.atmel.com

Atmel Corporation, founded in 1984, is a worldwide leader in the design, manufacturing and marketing of advanced semiconductors, including advanced logic, nonvolatile memory, mixed signal and RF integrated circuits. Atmel is one of the elite new companies capable of integrating dense nonvolatile memory, logic and analog functions on a single chip. Atmel chips are manufactured using the most advanced wafer processes, including BiCMOS, CMOS and Silicon Germanium (SiGe) technologies.

AudioCodes

http://www.audiocodes.com

AudioCodes Ltd. (NASDAQ: AUDC) enables the new voice infrastructure by providing innovative, reliable and cost-effective Voice over Packet technology and Voice Network products to OEMs, NEPs and system integrators. AudioCodes provides its customers and partners with a diverse range of media gateway and media processing technologies, based on VoIPerfect AudioCodes underlying core media gateway architecture. The company is a market leader in voice compression technology and is a key originator of the ITU G.723.1 standard.

AUSTAR Entertainment

http://www.austar.com.au

Austar United Communications Limited (AUSTAR) is one of Australia's leading subscription television providers, offering primarily digital satellite services to customers in regional and rural areas. AUSTAR also offers dial-up Internet and mobile phone services. AUSTAR is listed on the Australian Stock Exchange (AUN).

Award Solutions

http://www.awardsolutions.com

Award Solutions, Inc., is a knowledge-based company rooted in the areas of advanced wireless and Internet technologies. Our exceptional services range from technical training solutions using multiple delivery methods to engineering solutions in various technical disciplines. We have provided successful training and network performance solutions as well as professional services for many telecommunications and Internet equipment manufacturers, service providers and enterprises since 1997.

Axtel

http://www.axtel.com.mx

Axtel is a Mexican telecommunications company that provides local telephone services, national and international long distance services, data, Internet, virtual private nets, and value added services. At present, it is operating in the eight most important cities of Mexico.

Axxcelera Broadband Wireless

http://axxcelera.com

Axxcelera Broadband Wireless is a data networking solutions company, developing technology to deploy networks for broadband wireless communications over the Internet—from the "first leap" to the last mile.

Azaire Networks

http://www.azairenet.com

Azaire Networks' mission is to enable ubiquitous Broadband Mobility. Providing broadband services through macro cellular network using licensed spectrum is prohibitively expensive. Azaire's IP Converged Network Platform (IP-CNP) enables Telecom Operators to create hybrid networks that combine the 2.5G/3G macro cellular network and any fixed or wireless IP network, such as Wi-Fi, WiMax and DSL. Hybrid Networks enable users to receive the Broadband Mobility they desire, and providers to offer Broadband Mobility efficiently and cost effectively.

Azimuth Systems

http://www.azimuthsystems.com

Azimuth Systems is an innovator in wireless data communications test solutions for engineers and test labs qualifying compliance, interoperability and performance of wireless products. The system is designed to deliver a repeatable, scalable and automated tool that dramatically reduces time to test and expenses associated with the test cycle of products. It also provides test engineers and reviewers with objective industry-wide test metrics in a controlled and repeatable environment.

Azonic Systems, Inc.

http://www.azonicsystems.com

Azonic Systems, Inc. is a privately held company located in Orange County, California. Azonic Systems is developing WiMAX-compliant broadband wireless communication solutions for business, industrial, and vertical market applications. We provide complete BWA solutions with high reliability and industry-leading value. Our products are configurable and can be custom tailored to specific customer needs. Our software solutions include bandwidth provisioning, network security, and network management.

Aztech Systems Ltd
http://www.aztech.com
Aztech Systems Ltd is a Singapore publicly listed company providing Electronics Manufacturing Services (EMS) and OEM/ODM design and manufacturing services. Aztech designs and manufactures data and voice communication products such as DSL modems, Analog Modems, Broadband Residential gateway, Wireless 802.11a/b/g, Power Line modems, VoIP, SMS Color DECT/WDCT Phones, Walkie Talkie and Multimedia products.

Bandwidth.com
http://www.bandwidth.com
Bandwidth.com is the single source for data connectivity for businesses worldwide. Bandwidth.com serves businesses by helping them identify, price, and purchase connectivity from telecommunication and broadband wireless carriers, doing for bandwidth what Travelocity and Expedia do for travel.

Barik
http://www.barik.es/castellano.htm
Barik is committed to the deployment of network infrastructure based on next generation wireless broadband standards, like WiMAX, to provide backhaul connectivity to telecom carriers and true broadband services to corporate customers and service providers. Barik can supply scalable networking solutions offering high-speed Internet access and VoIP services.

Beceem
http://www.beceem.com
Beceem Communications Inc. is a fabless semiconductor company developing innovative solutions for the broadband wireless market. The company is formed with a strong foundation in wireless systems, signal processing and software skills.

Bechtel Telecommunications

http://www.bechtel.com

Bechtel Telecommunications, a unit of Bechtel Corporation, has successfully completed more than 140 projects worldwide, including more than 83,000 wireless cell sites; 23,000 kilometers of wireline fiber; and communications centers such as POPs, NOCs, and data centers. Our turnkey deployment services include network planning, RF design, site acquisition, right-of-way, planning and permitting, procurement, construction, equipment installation, testing, optimization and turnover, all serviced by our offices in London and Sydney and our headquarters near Washington, DC.

BelAir Networks

http://www.belairnetworks.com

BelAir Networks provides scalable, wide area wireless solutions with the highest capacity and lowest cost per user for data, voice and video services. BelAir's wireless switch routers are built specifically for outdoor deployments and optimized for high density hot zone and metro deployments. These modular platforms are the foundation of BelAir's multiservice architecture, which includes Wi-Fi, WiMAX and cellular technologies.

Bell Canada

http://www.bell.ca

Bell Canada, Canada's national leader in communications, provides connectivity to residential and business customers through wired and wireless means, voice and data communications, local and long distance phone services, high-speed and wireless Internet access, IP-broadband services, e-business solutions and satellite television services. Bell Canada is wholly owned by BCE Inc.

BellSouth Corporation

http://www.bellsouth.com

BellSouth Corporation is a Fortune 100 communications company headquartered in Atlanta and a parent company of Cingular Wireless, the nation's largest wireless voice and data provider. Backed by award-winning customer service, BellSouth offers the most comprehensive and innovative package of voice and data services available in the market. With over $26 billion in annual revenue and close to 64,000 employees, the company has over 20 million access lines in service, 1.9 million DSL subscribers and 5.7 million long-distance subscribers.

BII Group

http://biigroup.com

Founded in 1999, BII Group developed from BII (Beijing Internet Institute), which was the first private research institute focusing on IT and Telecom in China. BII Group has been the pioneer of China's telecommunication and network industry. BII Group's business field covers consulting, event organization, IT testing and certification and network design/system integration.

Booz Allen Hamilton

http://www.bah.com

Booz Allen Hamilton has been at the forefront of management and technology consulting for businesses and governments for 90 years. Booz Allen, a global strategy and technology-consulting firm, works with clients to deliver results that endure. With more than 16,000 employees on six continents, the firm generates annual sales of more than $2.7 billion. Booz Allen provides services in strategy, organization, operations, systems and technology to the world's leading corporations, government and other public agencies.

bracNet

http://www.bracnet.net

bracNet is a wireless nationwide broadband Internet and data connectivity provider in Bangladesh. It is a joint venture between BRAC of Bangladesh and gNet Defta Development Holding LLC, a group based in San Francisco, CA. bracNet plans to deploy WiMAX technology. bracNet envisions providing connectivity services in cost-effective ways to the masses. bracNet believes by deploying WiMAX technology it will bring digital dividends instead of widening the gap of digital divide. gNet wishes to replicate its success in Bangladesh in other parts of emerging areas of the world.

Bridgewater Systems

http://www.bridgewatersystems.com

Bridgewater Systems provides policy management solutions for dynamic IP services. The Bridgewater Systems product suite includes its market-leading authentication, authorization and accounting (AAA) system and a range of modular products that provide provisioning, mediation and real time management of network resources. With 85% CDMA subscriber market share in North America alone, its AAA systems provide support for deployments of 5,000 to over 50 million provisioned users and for transaction rates from 10,000 to over 1 billion/month. Its customers include Verizon Wireless, Sprint PCS, Bell Mobility, US Cellular, Virgin Mobile USA and more.

British Telecom
http://www.bt.com
BT Group is one of Europe's leading providers of telecommunications services. Its principal activities include local, national and international telecommunications services, higher-value broadband and Internet products and services, and IT solutions. In the UK, BT serves over 20 million business and residential customers with more than 29 million exchange lines, as well as providing network services to other licensed operators.

Broadcom
http://www.broadcom.com
Broadcom Corporation is a global leader in wired and wireless broadband communications semiconductors. Our products enable the convergence of high-speed data, high-definition video, voice and audio at home, in the office and on the go. Broadcom provides manufacturers of computing and networking equipment, digital entertainment and broadband access products, and mobile devices with the industry's broadest portfolio of state-of-the-art system-on-a-chip and software solutions. Broadcom is one of the world's largest fabless semiconductor companies, with annual revenue of more than $2 billion. The company is headquartered in Irvine, California, with offices and research facilities in North America, Asia and Europe.

butlerNetworks
http://www.butlernetworks.com
butlerNetworks has built a national broadband network in order to be Denmark's independent alternative. We are in the process of building out a nationwide net based on the Alvarion WiMAX product. As an independent wholesale business, butlerNetworks offers solutions and access to Telcos, Internet providers, system integrators, ASPs and others who need the right connections. We offer our partners and their end users fast delivery of flexible and future secure connections.

C-DOT (Centre for Development of Telematics)
http://www.cdot.com
C-DOT is the Telecom Technology development center of the government of India. Its objective is to develop telecom technologies and solutions for

fixed-line, mobile, packet-based and converged networks. Its product portfolio includes Digital Switching Systems, Intelligent network solutions, Access Network products, Voice over IP solutions, SDH and WDM technologies, Satellite Communications systems, Network Management Systems and Operation Support Systems. While taking a quantum leap toward the Next Generation networks, C-DOT has kept a significant focus on cost-effective rural network solutions and also leveraged the legacy network. It offers Total Telecom Solutions directly as well as through strategic alliances and partnership.

Cambridge Broadband

http://www.cambridgebroadband.com
Cambridge Broadband has pioneered the development of carrier-class, point-to-multipoint broadband wireless access equipment for network operators wishing to deploy high-capacity, multiservice networks. The company is focused on delivering high quality multiservice networks with the best price performance in the 3.5-GHz band for license holders worldwide. Cambridge Broadband was founded in January 2000 by an experienced team with a strong record of successful innovation in broadband wireless equipment.

Cameo Communications

http://www.cameo.com.tw
Cameo Communications, Inc., is an international Networking products supplier specializing in Layer 2 Management Ethernet Switch, Wireless Client Adapter, Wireless LAN AP/Router, SOHO Router, Ethernet Switches, Media Converter, USB to Ethernet Converter, Web-Smart Switches and Ethernet NIC. Cameo is steadily increasing its market share in the competitive data communications field through innovative product design and marketing. Sales have grown dramatically as a result of aggressive channel development and clear perception of market needs.

CATR

http://www.cttl.com.cn/english
China Academy of Telecommunication Research (CATR) of the Ministry of Information Industry (MII), which is a leading research institution in the telecommunication field in China, integrates the functions of policy research, standard drafting, testing and certification, and consultancy. Owning the most advanced testing facilities in the world, its services are dedicated to the requirement of its clients in Information and Communications Technologies (ICT).

Celestica

http://www.celestica.com

Celestica is a world leader in the delivery of innovative electronics manufacturing services (EMS). Celestica operates a highly sophisticated global manufacturing network with operations in Asia, Europe and the Americas, providing a broad range of integrated services and solutions to leading OEMs (original equipment manufacturers). Celestica's expertise in quality, technology and supply chain management, and leadership in the global deployment of lean principles, enables the company to provide a competitive advantage to its customers by improving time-to-market, scalability and manufacturing efficiency.

Cellcom

http://www.cellcom.co.il/english

The largest cellular operator in Israel, with around 2.5 million subscribers. Technology used since 2002 is GSM/GPRS, with an overlay of TDMA system (from 1994). Recently (May 2004) 3G services have been launched over EDGE and UMTS systems. Cellcom is owned by BellSouth International (35%), Safra Group (35%) and Israeli banking companies (the rest). Cellcom is serving also as a broadband telecom provider with its wide area coverage fiber-optic network.

Cellular South

http://www.cellularsouth.com

Cellular South, headquartered in Jackson, MS, is the largest privately held wireless provider in the United States and is licensed to provide wireless service to a total population of more than five million people on its network stretching from the Memphis Metropolitan Area, throughout all of Mississippi, along Coastal Alabama and the Florida Panhandle through Walton County. Cellular South has over 75 retail locations and operates a telesales call center and a customer care center.

CelPlan Technologies

http://www.celplan.com

CelPlan Technologies, with the CelPlanner™ Suite, is a leading provider of wireless network planning and system optimization software. Wi4Net, a CelPlan subsidiary, introduces a new radio concept for high data rate wireless applications and advanced high-speed wireless data network requirements. Based on open standards and COTS components, Wi4Net now offers advanced radio solutions that offer high performance, outdoor coverage, mobility and flexible wireless connectivity.

Ceragon

http://www.ceragon.com

Ceragon Networks, a pacesetter in broadband wireless networking systems, enables rapid and cost-effective high-capacity network connectivity for mobile cellular infrastructure, fixed networks, private networks and enterprises. The FiberAir product family operates across multiple frequencies, supports integrated high-capacity services over SONET/SDH, ATM and IP networks, and offers innovative built-in add/drop multiplexing and encryption functionality. Ceragon's FiberAir product family complies with North American and international standards and is installed with over 150 customers in more than 60 countries.

CETECOM

http://www.cetecom.es

CETECOM is a Testing and Certification Laboratory and Test Systems solution provider. Main activities are Testing and Certification Laboratory services (conformance, pre-testing and debugging). Some technologies tested at CETECOM are Bluetooth , GSM, GPRS, WCDMA, Wi-Fi, RFID, DECT, SRD. International Radio Type Approval Services, with more than 80 countries covered. Conformance Test Systems (GSM, GPRS, WCDMA, Bluetooth, DECT, RFID). Engineering and Projects in Wireless technologies: Bluetooth, Wi-Fi, GSM, GPRS, WCDMA.

China Motion Telecom

http://www.china-motion.com

Established in 1990, China Motion Telecom International commenced its operations in Hong Kong as a supplier of a wide range of telecommunications products and services with extensive operations in Mainland China, Hong Kong and North America.

Chung-Shan Institute of Science & Technology

Chung-Shan Institute of Science & Technology (CSIST) was founded in 1969 and has more than 10,000 employees working in six research divisions. The organization manufacturers power electronics, microwave, radar and antennas.

Cisco Systems

http://www.cisco.com

Cisco Systems, Inc., is the worldwide leader in networking for the Internet. Today, networks are an essential part of business, education, government and home communications and Cisco Internet Protocol based (IP) networking solutions are the foundation of these networks. Cisco hardware, software, and service offerings are used to create Internet solutions that allow individuals, companies, and countries to increase productivity, improve customer satisfaction and strengthen competitive advantage. The Cisco name has become synonymous with the Internet, as well as with the productivity improvements that Internet business solutions provide. At Cisco, our vision is to change the way people work, live, play and learn.

Clear Channel Broadcasting

http://www.clearchannel.com

Clear Channel Broadcasting, Inc., is a leading radio company focused on serving local communities across the United States with more than 110 million listeners choosing Clear Channel Radio programming each week. The company's operations include radio broadcasting, syndication and independent media representation. Clear Channel Broadcasting, Inc., is a division of Clear Channel.

Clearwire

http://www.clearwire.com

Clearwire is a provider of reliable, wireless, high-speed broadband Internet service to consumers and small businesses. Clearwire is utilizing next-generation non-line-of-sight wireless technology to connect customers to the Internet using radio spectrum, thus eliminating the confines of traditional cable or phone wiring. The tower transmits radio signals from a base site to a small, wireless modem, the size of a paperback book, which easily connects a user's computer to the Internet.

Colubris Networks

http://www.colubris.com

Colubris Networks manufactures and sells an award-winning WLAN product family to service providers and enterprises worldwide. Its WLAN System enables superior customer flexibility and control in the secure delivery of voice, data, and multimedia Wi-Fi applications and services to mobile workers, customers, partners, suppliers and guests. Colubris Networks equipment is deployed by more than 1,000 organizations worldwide.

COM DEV

http://www.saw-device.com

COM DEV SAW Products is a North American producer of high-quality, demanding SAW filters operating in the frequency range 50 MHz to

3 GHz. With exact design software complemented by automated leading edge manufacturing equipment, COM DEV can meet even the most rigorous customer requirements. From niche design needs to high-volume foundry services, we're ready to combine top-notch customer service with competitive pricing.

Comba Telecom Systems
http://www.comba-telecom.com
COMBA Telecom Systems was established in 1997 in Hong Kong with its operation center in the city of Guangzhou, China. Comba is the leading system integration provider of mobile/wireless communication signal distribution and coverage for the telecom industry and holds about 40% of the market share in China. Comba is also engaged in the research, development, and production of application-specific systems for outdoor and indoor mobile/wireless communication coverage. Comba is a big player as a solution provider in today's Asia Telecom market to deliver turnkey systems of signal distribution and coverage for GSM, GPRS, CDMA, WLAN, and 3G systems.

Comcast
http://www.comcast.com
Comcast Corporation is principally involved in the development, management and operation of broadband cable networks, and in the provision of programming content. The Company is the largest provider of cable and broadband services in the United States, serving more than 21 million cable television customers and more than 6 million high-speed Internet customers. The Company's content businesses include majority ownership of Comcast Spectacor, Comcast SportsNet, E! Entertainment Television, Style Network, G4techTV, the Golf Channel, International Channel and Outdoor Life Network.

Compliance Certification Services
http://www.ccsemc.com
Telecommunications Certification Body (TCB) Electronic Filing System.

CompUSA
http://www.compusa.com
CompUSA is the country's leading provider of computers and technology. With over 230 stores under the CompUSA brand and 70 stores under the Good Guys brand, we have become the destination for consumers who want to learn more about technology.

Comsys Communication & Signal Processing

http://www.comsysmobile.com

Comsys develops the industry's leading integrated digital baseband solutions for EGPRS (EDGE), GPRS, GSM and UMTS networks. Ranging from EDGE upgrades to full multimode baseband systems, Comsys solutions combine excellent performance, very low resource requirements, and rapid cost-effective integration into any platform. World-leading chip, handset, and base station manufacturers partner with Comsys to create advanced platforms that support current and future wireless standards. For companies such as Texas Instruments, choosing Comsys means optimizing performance, accelerating time-to-market, and cutting silicon costs.

Covad Communications

http://www.covad.com

Covad is a leading national broadband service provider of high-speed Internet and network access. It offers DSL, T1, managed security, hosting, IP and dial-up services through Covad's network to small businesses and home users via both wholesale and direct channels. Covad operates the largest national DSL network with services offered in 96 of the top Metropolitan Statistical Areas (MSAs), covering more than 40 million homes and business (approximately 45 percent of the United States).

Cushcraft Corporation

http://www.cushcraft.com

Cushcraft Corporation, a world leader in the manufacture and development of communications antennas, has been committed to total customer satisfaction for more than four decades. Cushcraft has become the world leader in antennas for Wireless LAN, ISM band, and small cell applications. Cushcraft also has a strong presence in RFID and Data Collection, Land Mobile Radio, Specialized Mobile Radio, Cellular, Security, Wireless MAN, Amateur Radio and other applications.

CWC

http://www.cwc.oulu.fi

Centre for Wireless Communications (CWC) is a world-class telecommunications research center located near the top of the world in Oulu, Finland. CWC aims to be one of the world's leading research institutes in the field of wireless communication methods from the network level to the transmitter and receiver system level.

Dell

http://www.dell.com

Dell is the world's leading computer systems company. We design, build and customize products and services to satisfy a range of customer requirements. From the server, storage and professional services needs of the largest global corporations to those of consumers at home. We do business directly with customers, one at a time, and believe we do it better than anyone on the planet.

Deutsche Telekom

http://www.t-systems.com

Deutsche Telekom is one of the world's leading telecommunications companies. Our four core strategic divisions—T-Mobile, T-Online, T-Systems and T-Com—cover the entire spectrum of modern telecommunication services and innovation.

Digiweb

http://www.digiweb.ie

Digiweb is Ireland's fastest expanding Broadband Services Provider, deploying Fixed Wireless, two-way Satellite and ADSL technologies to deliver broadband access throughout Ireland and selected European countries. Digiweb was awarded licensed spectrum in the 3.6- to 3.8-GHz range and is currently constructing and operating a national wireless access network for broadband Internet and voice applications. Established in 1997 as an ISP, the company leverages its existing infrastructure and services to offer added-value services for established and new customers in the Government, Business, Educational and Residential sectors.

DiNi Communications

http://www.dini.net

DiNi Communications, Inc., is a full-service global technology service provider based in New Jersey. DiNi specializes in providing solutions to wireless networks to companies around the world. DiNi is certified as wired/wireless, data and voice communication service provider and is staffed by a diverse team of certified communication specialists. Currently DiNi is working on a project to provide infrastructure for wireless networks using WiMax technology in Sri Lanka.

Dishnet Wireless Limited

http://www.dwl.co.in.

Dishnet Wireless Ltd. is now foraying into the Wireless space after its divesting of DSL and dial-up services. Dishnet has a Class A ISP license and plans to provide its subscribers on a Pan-India basis WiFi and WiMAX services. In keeping with the new name of the company, Dishnet is proposing GSM based telecom services covering the north and east of India. Also, Dishnet has a Telecom advisory group which works closely with leading Telcos on setting up GSM/CDMA infrastructure, negotiating with Vendors, etc. Lastly, Dishnet has an in-house software development group, which focuses on developing software based billing, On line education, etc.

Distributel

http://www.distributel.net/

In business since 1988, Distributel Communications is 100% Canadian owned and one of the pioneers of the competitive long-distance industry in Canada. When the company first started providing services in the Toronto area, the founder and president, Mel Cohen, was forced into a ground-breaking battle with Bell Canada. At the time, Bell tried to argue that Distributel's service was illegal. Fortunately, the Canadian Radio-Television and Telecommunications Commission ruled in Distributel's favor, a decision which helped open the door for competition in the long distance market in Canada.

Dyaptive Systems

http://www.dyaptive.com

Dyaptive Systems is dedicated to fundamentally improving wireless network and infrastructure test and optimization technology. The company develops, sells, and supports state-of-the-art wireless load and performance test equipment. We are located in Vancouver, Canada, and were founded in October 2001.

eAccess Ltd.

http://www.eaccess.net

eAccess is a leading ADSL and Broadband service provider in Japan. eAccess's mission is to maximize the value of the customers' lives and the business scene by developing customer needs through our new broadband service. eAccess is determined to become the access service provider of choice for customers. Moreover, we aim to continuously diffuse innovative broadband IP services in Japan by focusing our efforts on broadband IP telecommunications services.

EDX Wireless
http://www.edx.com
Unmatched Accuracy—Unmatched Flexibility. EDX Wireless is the world leader in PC-based wireless network design tools. Our carrier class tools are employed in over 55 countries to design wireless networks, including fixed broadband, MMDS, WiFi, WiMAX, cellular, PCS, and mobile radio of all types from 30 MHz to 100 GHz. With advanced outdoor and indoor design capabilities including 2D and 3D Ray Tracing, SignalPro is the tool of choice for service providers, equipment vendors, and consultants. Identify the potential with EDX Wireless.

Eircom
http://www.eircom.ie
Eircom is Ireland's leading communications company, providing a comprehensive range of advanced voice, data and Internet services in the retail, business and wholesale segments. We are the leading provider in the very fast growing Irish broadband services sector for both business and residential customers across Ireland.

Elcoteq
http://www.elcoteq.com
Elcoteq Network Corporation is a global electronics manufacturing services (EMS) company specializing in wireless communication technology. Elcoteq provides globally end-to-end solutions consisting of design, NPI, manufacturing, supply chain management and after-sales services over the whole life cycle of its customers' products. The company operates on three continents in 12 countries and it has over 12,000 employees. Elcoteq has two business areas, Communications Network Equipment and Terminal Products.

Elektrobit
http://www.elektrobit.com
Elektrobit provides world-class design, testing, production automation solutions and related products and services to the telecommunications and electronics industries. As a leader in wireless technology, Elektrobit supplies the world's foremost brands with the resources and knowledge needed to produce outstanding wireless-based products. From its headquarters in Oulu, the technology center of Finland, Elektrobit has expanded to 30 locations in 13 countries, and has successfully built up a team of 1600 dedicated wireless technology experts. Based on their

skills and knowledge, the company has developed a competence that is difficult to find anywhere else in the world.

Enertel

http://www.enertel.nl

Enertel is one of the largest Dutch telecom operators servicing the business market. Enertel delivers both fixed data and telecommunication solutions with a focus on IP and Wireless Broadband solutions. Apart from business customers and (inter)national carriers, Enertel also services the majority of the independent Dutch Internet Service Providers. The company owns and manages 24x7 an extensive national network and a Datacenter providing Managed IT Services. Enertel acquired WiFi-operator WinQ in June 2004.

Enforta

http://en.enforta.com/

Enforta is a broadband service operator focused on providing Internet, VPN, and telephony services in the regional cities of Russia, using licensed spectrum. Started in 2003, the Company plans to offer services into 28 regional capital cities with an aggregate population of 30 million.

Entel

http://www.entel.cl

Entel Chile S.A. is a leading Chilean telecom operator that provides local and long distance telephony, dial-up and broadband internet, data, wholesale, integration and mobile services (GSM). It has subsidiaries in Peru, Venezuela, Central America and the United States (Americatel). Operates high-quality nationwide networks based in NGN, fiber optics, digital microwave, satellite, copper and broadband fixed wireless (3.5 GHz band).

Ericsson

http://www.ericsson.com

Ericsson is shaping the future of Mobile and Broadband Internet communications through its continuous technology leadership. Providing innovative solutions in more than 140 countries, Ericsson is helping to create the most powerful communication companies in the world.

Ertach

http://www.ertach.com

Ertach, originally Millicom Argentina S.A., started business in 2000. The company installed the first WiMAX network in Latin America; its next-generation wireless network serves more than 70 cities and covers more than 8,000 square kilometers.

ETRI

http://www.etri.re.kr

ETRI (Electronics and Telecommunications Research Institute) was established as a nonprofit government-funded research organization that has been at the forefront of technological excellence for more than 25 years. Our research institute has successfully developed information technologies such as TDX-Exchange, High Density Semiconductor Microchips, Mini-Super Computer (TiCOM), and Digital Mobile Telecommunication System (CDMA). As a recognized leader in the information and telecommunication research institute in Korea, we will strive to be the best in the fields of information and telecommunications.

European Antennas

http://www.european-antennas.co.uk

European Antennas Ltd is a specialist in the development and manufacture of antennas to meet applications within the 0.4-GHz to 18-GHz frequency range, for military and commercial applications, worldwide. All antennas are tested throughout development and manufactured using on-site facilities to ensure compliance with quoted specifications and radiation pattern envelopes. European Antennas is part of the Chelton Group of companies, a subsidiary of Cobham plc.

Euskaltel S.A.

http://www.euskaltel.es

EUSKALTEL is a Telco and CableCo operator in the Basque Country (Spain) with a complete product and services offering as Fixed Voice, Digital TV, Data and Broadband wireline (LL, Cable Modem and ADSL) and Wireless Broadband (WiFi) services.

Filtronic

http://www.filtronic.com

Filtronic is a world leader in the design and manufacture of a broad range of sophisticated and customized RF, microwave and millimeter wave components and subsystems for major cellular infrastructure original equipment manufacturers, network operators and defense contractors. With design and manufacturing facilities in Europe, North America, Australia and China, Filtronic offers flexibility and speed in addressing global telecommunications markets. The organization is composed of five business units that focus on wireless infrastructure, broadband communications, semiconductor, cellular handset and electronic defense markets.

Finnet

http://www.finnet.fi

Finnet Oy is a national telecommunications operator in Finland. It is owned by a group of independent regional operators that constitute the Finnet Group. By joining the Forum Finnet Oy represents all Finnet Group operators and aims to serve them with Forum information. Finnet Group will utilize WiMAX technology in broadband of competition areas where it substitutes the lease of the last mile from the competitor. Finnet Oy is coordinating group activity in WiMAX while regional operators carry out the investments.

Firetide

http://www.firetide.com

Firetide, Inc., is a privately held company that provides equipment for quickly, easily, and affordably deploying large Wireless Instant Networks. Firetide solutions support existing public "hotspots" and the company is developing instant networking technology that will deliver everywhere, all-the-time wireless data communication services to hot zones and hot regions. Firetide's technology is based on advanced wireless mesh routing technologies using standard radio technology. Hot-Point Wireless Mesh Routers replace Ethernet cabling and form a Wireless Instant Network, which eliminates costly and time-consuming provisioning. Firetide has invested considerable intellectual property to develop technology that allows self-configuration, self-healing, and advanced security capabilities within the network.

First Avenue Networks

http://www.firstavenet.com

First Avenue Networks (NASDAQ: FRNS), the holder of one of the nation's most expansive 39-GHz license portfolios, is committed to providing the fastest, simplest, most cost-effective way for telecommunication providers to build reliable, high-speed networks. First Avenue Networks' 39-GHz licensed spectrum leasing products, Express Link and Express Net, simplify and reduce many of the barriers traditionally associated with deploying fixed wireless broadband networks. First Avenue Networks holds over 750 FCC-issued licenses for 39-GHz spectrum, covering virtually the entire United States.

Firstserver

http://www.firstserver.co.jp

Firstserver, Inc., has two main businesses; one is web hosting, and the other is Domain Registration business. We provide a full-scale hosting service for business platforms. We built our own Data Center by our own network technology, and achieve advanced reliability and stability. Now, over 20,000 companies in Japan use our hosting services. And we can provide gTLD domain name like ".com," ".net," and ".org" directly to the customers, as ICANN-Accredited Registrars.

Flextronics Software Systems

http://www.flextronicssoftware.com

Flextronics Software Systems, a global leader in the convergence marketplace, offers its clients licensable technologies and outsourcing services in VoIP, SS7 Signaling, IMS, Broadband, Datacomm, Wireless and Handset domains.

Fortress Technologies

http://www.fortresstech.com

Fortress Technologies is currently the leading supplier of wireless security solutions built to eliminate the vulnerabilities and increase the seamless deployment of high-performance wireless networks. Significant achievements and company milestones include our FIPS certification in early 2001, the U.S. Army's Combat Service Support Automated Information System Interface project and the contract to secure patient-critical wireless applications in the Veterans' Administration hospitals.

France Telecom

http://www.francetelecom.com

France Telecom is one of the world's leading telecommunications carriers, with 117.1 million customers on five continents (220 countries and territories) and consolidated operating revenues of 46.1 billion euros for 2003. Through its major international brands, including Orange, Wanadoo, Equant and GlobeCast, France Telecom provides businesses, consumers and other carriers with a complete portfolio of solutions that span local, long-distance and international telephony, wireless, Internet, multimedia, data, broadcast and cable TV services.

Fujitsu

http://us.fujitsu.com/micro/wimax

Fujitsu Microelectronics America, Inc. (FMA), leads the industry in innovation. FMA provides high-quality, reliable semiconductor products and services for the networking, communications, automotive, security and other markets throughout North and South America. Fujitsu Microelectronics is one of the first silicon vendors to announce its commitment to producing an 802.16a and WiMAX-compliant baseband ASSP.

Funk Software

http://www.funk.com

Funk Software was founded in 1982 in Cambridge, MA. Funk Software develops Odyssey, an end-to-end 802.1x security solution, Steel-Belted Radius, the market-leading RADIUS/AAA server, and Proxy remote control software, which is installed on millions of desktops around the world. Funk Software's customers include some of the world's largest corporations, institutions, telecommunications carriers, and Internet service providers (ISPs); its products are licensed and/or resold by leading manufacturers of Internet hardware and software, communications software, and enterprise call center applications.

Fusion Communications Corporation

http://www.fusioncom.co.jp/

Fusion Communications prides itself as a true pioneer of VoIP telecommunications in Japan. As the first company in Japan to provide large-scale IP (toll bypass) telephone services, Fusion broke new ground by providing voice communications over a private IP network that completely bypassed the conventional telephone exchange network. Today, Fusion has taken the lead in the speedy merger of communications services via IP pathways and offers phone services over a "pure" IP network that completely eliminates exchanges and other legacy systems.

General DataComm

http://www.gdc.ru

General DataComm (GDC), a leading Russian developer and manufacturer of equipment for fixed and wireless network, has applied for membership in the WiMAX Forum as a principal member. GDC designs, manufactures and supplies its wireless solutions to most of the leading carriers throughout Russia and former territories of the USSR. In terms of future perspectives our market should be treated as one of the most attractive for the new high-speed access technologies such as 802.16.

Genius Institute of Technology
http://www.genius.org.br/english/
Genius Institute of Technology is an independent nonprofit institute founded by a private company that focuses its R&D activities in the convergence of electronics, telecommunications and information technology, creating new generations of technologies for both national and international customers. In this way Genius provides its clients and strategic partners the competitive edge they need to outperform their worldwide competitors.

Globalcom
http://www.callglobalcom.com
Globalcom is one of the fastest growing privately held phone companies in the nation. Headquartered in Chicago, Illinois, Globalcom is a next generation Competitive Local Exchange Carrier (CLEC), long distance carrier and Internet Service Provider (ISP). We offer an integrated set of communication products and services designed to put businesses ahead of the competition.

GloBul
http://www.globul.bg/eng/
One hundred percent owned by the Greek mobile operator Cosmote (the mobile subsidiary of the ex-monopoly Greek fixed operator OTE). Primarily a GSM 900/1800 operator, licensed in Q1 2001, which is the second license in Bulgaria. The company has been in commercial operation since Q3 2001, with 1.5 million subs (8 million country population), with about 30% market share and about 40% contract base. Offers the most popular of the GSM "new generation" of VAS like GPRS, MMS, etc.

Golden Telecom
http://www.goldentelecom.ru
Golden Telecom, Inc. (NASDAQ: GLDN), is a leading facilities-based provider of integrated telecommunications and Internet services in major population centers throughout Russia and other countries of the CIS. The Company offers voice, data and Internet services to corporations, operators and consumers using its metropolitan overlay networks in major cities including Moscow, Kiev, St. Petersburg, Nizhny Novgorod, Samara, Kaliningrad, and Krasnoyarsk and via intercity fiber optic and satellite-based networks, including approximately 200 combined access points in Russia and other countries of the CIS. The Company offers mobile services in Kiev and Odessa.

Hanaro Telecom

http://www.hanaro.com

Hanaro Telecom, the second local call service provider in Korea, is providing local telephony, broadband Internet access, and corporate leased line services. As a front-runner in broadband business, Hanaro Telecom also has led the growth of the nation's telecommunication industry by making a great contribution to increase the number of broadband Internet users to more than 10 million within 4 years of its business launching. Hanaro Telecom is currently planning to provide 802.16e-based broadband wireless services.

HCL Infinet

http://www.hclinfinet.com

HCL Infinet Ltd., a CLASS A ISP and leading IPVPN Service provider, is an Internet initiative of HCL Infosystems Ltd. Infinet took corporate networking services to new heights and revolutionized business computing in India, with interconnectivity between multilocation offices, flexibility of platforms, smooth and secure transfer of data/voice/video for corporations. HCL Infinet's managed services include VPN, Global IPVPN, Colocation and DR, Internet Telephony, Wireline and Wireless Broadband Internet Services and contact center solutions.

HCL Technologies

http://www.hcltechnologies.com

HCL Technologies is one of India's leading global IT Services Companies, providing software-led IT solutions, BPO, and Remote Infrastructure Management services. HCL Technologies focuses on technology and R&D outsourcing, working with clients in areas at the core of their businesses. The company leverages an extensive offshore infrastructure and its global network to deliver solutions across select verticals including Banking, Insurance, Retail, Networking, Aerospace, Automotive, Semiconductors, Telecom and Life Sciences.

Hopling Technologies

http://www.hopling.com

Hopling Technologies is an independent software developer and supplier of sophisticated out-of-the-box wireless solutions. With Hopling Technologies indoor and outdoor nodes (mesh routers), access points, bridges, multiclient bridges and the associated management servers, companies are able to instantly create high-capacity metropolitan wireless solutions at lower costs. Hopling Technologies' proven meshed network solutions are suitable for metropolitan area networks, wireless local area networks, the last mile, wireless connectivity, mobile broadband solutions, video surveillance, IP-based cellular phones (VoIP) and event-based solutions.

Huawei Technologies

http://www.huawei.com

Incorporated in 1988 and headquartered in Shenzhen, China, Huawei Technologies specializes in the R&D, production and marketing of telecom equipments, providing customized network solutions in fixed, mobile, optical and data communications networks. Huawei is a key player in China's telecom market and is quickly becoming an active participant in the global market. Huawei focuses on WCDMA, CDMA2000, NGN, xDSL and data communications. Currently Huawei has 22,000 employees, and sales in 2003 reached 3.83 billion US dollars.

Huber+Suhner

http://www.hubersuhnerinc.com

THE HUBER+SUHNER GROUP is a leading global supplier of components and systems for electrical and optical connectivity. We offer technical expertise in radio frequency technology, fiber-optics, cables and polymers under one roof, thus providing a unique basis for continual innovation focused on the needs of our customers all over the world. For the fixed-line and mobile communication markets we offer coaxial and radio frequency components, antennas, fiber-optic components, passive network components and lightning protection components.

Hughes Network Systems

http://www.hns.com

Hughes Network Systems, LLC (HNS), is the world's leading provider of broadband satellite network solutions for businesses and consumers, with more than 800,000 systems ordered or shipped to customers in 85 countries. HNS pioneered the development of high-speed satellite Internet access services and IP-based networks, which it markets globally under the DIRECWAY brand. DIRECWAY terminals are based on the IPoS (IP over Satellite) global standard, approved by TIA, ETSI, and the ITU standards organizations.

Hypres

http://www.hypres.com

HYPRES is engaged in the development, production and testing of next generation high-speed integrated circuits. While transparent to the system designer, HYPRES chips use superconducting Josephson Junction logic to achieve speed and linearity performance that cannot be equaled using semiconductor technology alone. Examples of products produced, demonstrated or under development include ADC and DAC chips, transmitter linearizers, digital signal processing chips and primary voltage standards (used by national laboratories to calibrate other voltage instruments).

IDEA Cellular Limited
http://www.ideacellular.com
IDEA Cellular LTD is a Mobile Telephone Services Operator (GSM) in India. It has licenses to operate in eleven (11) circles in India. With a customer base of over 5 million, IDEA Cellular has operations in eight (8) circles: New Delhi, Maharashtra and Goa, Gujarat, Andhra Pradesh, Madhya Pradesh and Chattisgarh, Uttaranchal, Haryana, UP (West) and Kerala. IDEA Cellular's footprint currently covers approximately 45% of India's population and over 50% of the potential telecom market.

IDT Telecom
http://www.idt.net
IDT Corporation, through its IDT Telecom, Inc. subsidiary, is a facilities-based, multinational carrier that provides a broad range of telecommunications services to its retail and wholesale customers worldwide. IDT Telecom, by means of its own national telecommunications backbone and fiber optic network infrastructure, provides its customers with integrated and competitively priced international and domestic long distance telephony and prepaid calling cards. IDT and Liberty Media Corporation own 95% and 5% of IDT Telecom, respectively. Liberty Media Corporation also owns a 5.6% stake in IDT Media. IDT Media, Inc., is the IDT subsidiary principally responsible for the Company's initiatives in media, new video technologies and print media. Winstar Holdings, LLC is the IDT subsidiary through which we provide broadband and telephony services to commercial and governmental customers through a fixed-wireless and fiber infrastructure. In December 2002, we announced that the services offered by Winstar would begin to be offered under the name "IDT Solutions." Net2Phone, Inc., a subsidiary of IDT Corporation, is a leading provider of high-quality global retail Voice over IP services, either directly or via a partner.

IIT (Institut International des Telecommunications)

http://www.iitelecom.com

The International Institute of Telecommunications (IIT) is a nonprofit organization with more than 70 member companies. Supported by the telecommunications industry since its creation, it focuses on industrial training and technological services in the telecommunications field and, more generally, in the field of information and communication technologies.

InfiNet Wireless Ltd.

http://www.infinetwireless.com

InfiNet Wireless Limited is a global provider of Last Mile solutions utilizing fixed broadband wireless access technology. InfiNet's wireless routing products represent over 10 years of intense engineering efforts by our world-class Russian development laboratories coupled with extensive field experience in design and deployment of wireless carrier-class networks in emerging markets.

Info Quest S.A.

http://www.myQ.gr

Q-TELECOM, a business unit of Info-Quest SA, is the only privately owned Greek Operator that provides integrated telecommunication services mobile telephony, fixed telephony and Internet. Focusing its commercial activities in the large urban centers, Q-TELECOM developed a 2nd generation mobile telephony network with the installation of own Cellular Base Stations, as well as a Broadband Fixed Wireless Access network, using point-to-multipoint advanced technology operating in the 3.5-GHz range. Simultaneously, it develops a national backbone network via leased lines and privately owned transmission systems. Thus, Q-TELECOM ensures true voice quality services, fast call set-up and offers nationwide coverage.

Innowireless

http://www.innowireless.co.kr

Our company develops, manufacturers and sells base station test equipment for mobile teleservices such as CDMA 2000 1x, 1x EV-DO, and W-CDMA.

Inovaware Corporation

http://www.inovaware.com

Founded in 1996, Inovaware Corporation is the leading provider of customer-centric business infrastructure software for Internet service businesses. Through its unique Synchronized Business Infrastructure (SBI), Inovaware integrates the complex billing, customer management, and customer support, as well as sales and marketing aspects of Internet businesses, into one seamless functional unit. Inovaware is powering the Internet Economy by delivering mission-critical billing software and solutions that enable businesses to profitably manage their customers, accelerate new services time-to-market, and maximize revenue generation.

Integrated Devices
http://www.integrated-devices.com
Integrated Devices LLC provides software and hardware design services. We design wireless chips and boards and perform analysis of same.

Intel
http://www.intel.com/netcomms/technologies/wimax/
Intel, the world's largest chip maker, is also a leading manufacturer of computer, networking and communications products. Additional information about Intel is available at http://www.intel.com/pressroom.

Intarlach Wireless
http://www.intarlachwireless.com
Intarlach Wireless was formed in order to break the local landline-based stranglehold on high-speed access Internet services. Intarlach will take advantage of WiMAX technologies to replace the functionality of the PSTN (public switched telephone networks) at a fraction of the cost. There are many underserved markets in America which receive only rudimentary access from the Bells and Cable companies. Intarlach plans on providing customers a total bypass solution including VoIP and high-speed Internet access.

Interpeak
http://www.interpeak.com
Interpeak is a pioneer of networking, mobility and security protocol software for embedded systems. The company's customers span the telecommunications and data communications markets. Headquartered in Stockholm, Sweden, Interpeak operates through a global network of distribution channels and has its own sales and field application force dispersed in strategic locations worldwide, including the United States, Japan, and Europe.

INTRACOM

http://www.intracom.gr

INTRACOM S.A., founded in 1977, is the largest provider of telecommunication systems, information systems and defense electronic systems in Greece. INTRACOM has also established a leading position within the South and Eastern European and Middle Eastern markets. With a presence in more than 55 countries all over the world, INTRACOM is now emerging as a global player. The business sectors of INTRACOM are Telecommunications Systems (P-P, P-MP), IT Systems and Defense Electronic Systems.

Invenova

http://www.invenovacorp.com

Invenova develops instrumentation, test and measurement systems for standards-based Wireless Communication technologies. Invenova takes pride in developing pioneering test solutions and creates highly differentiated best-in-class products. Invenova is currently leading the way in developing test solutions for emerging Broadband Wireless technologies.

Iqara Telecom

http://www.iqaratelecom.com.br

Iqara provides broadband access for operators and service providers in the City of São Paulo plus 10 other state cities. A pioneer in public networking implementing and operating on Metro Ethernet technology, Iqara is the only alternative to unbundling in those areas.

Irish Broadband Internet Services

http://www.irishbroadband.ie/

Irish Broadband is a subsidiary of NTR plc, Ireland's largest developer of privately funded public infrastructure. Established in 2002, Irish Broadband is now the nation's leading provider of fixed wireless broadband services to business and residential users. A subsidiary company (NTR Broadband) is the largest fixed wireless broadband provider in Northern Ireland. Service is focused on major cities in both the Republic and Northern Ireland. Irish Broadband delivers broadband using a combination of license exempt and licensed spectrum. In 2003, the company was awarded licenses for 3.5-GHz spectrum in 7 major cities. Licenses covering an additional 9 cities and towns were awarded in 2004. Irish Broadband is currently deploying pre-WiMAX equipment and will deploy WiMAX equipment across the network as it becomes available.

Iskra Transmission

http://www.iskratr.com

Iskra Transmission is a Slovenian vendor of microwave and fiber-optics transmission systems. With 50 years of tradition this member of Iskra Group with 1,600 employees develops off-the-shelf products as well as customized products for its customers. Main products are divided into four families: SparkWave (microwave), SparkLight (fiber-optics), SparkView (network management), and SparkLine (traditional copper lines).

Ixia

http://www.ixiacom.com

Ixia is a leading, global provider of high performance, highly scalable IP network testing solutions used by Network and Telephony Equipment Manufacturers, Semiconductor Manufacturers, Service Providers, and large Enterprises to generate, capture, characterize, and emulate network and application traffic, and establish definitive performance and conformance metrics of complex network devices or systems under test. Ixia's patented Real World Traffic Suite supports wireless and application testing of networks prior to deployment under realistic load conditions.

Jacket Micro Devices

http://www.jacketmicro.com

Jacket Micro Devices, Inc. (JMD), is a privately held provider of advanced RF integration products for wireless devices. Our patented MultiLayer Organic (MLO) process can replace multiple discrete passive components with significant reduction in size and improvement in performance. By embedding RF filters in packages and substrates, JMD is producing industry leading front-end modules that can support operation over multiple bands in the range of .8 to 5 GHz with rapid electronic reconfiguration.

Juniper Networks

http://www.juniper.net

Juniper Networks is a leading global provider of networking and security solutions that support the complex scale, security and performance requirements of the world's largest and most demanding mission-critical networks, including the world's top 25 service providers and 8 of the top 15 Fortune 500 companies.

Kapsch CarrierCom

http://www.kapsch.net

Kapsch CarrierCom AG is the leading supplier and manufacturer of services and solutions for service providers and carriers. Our service offering comprises the complete range of modern communication networks from fixed, mobile and data networks via broadband communication, Internet Solutions, Next Generation Networks, UMTS up to Service Enabling and Mediation Platforms. Having an R&D department with more than 250 highly qualified engineers, our portfolio includes tailor-made products and services for the Telco market. Relying on about 600 employees with a long-standing excellent knowledge of the markets, state-of-the-art know-how and a first-class service network in Central Europe, we are able to manufacture and implement customized solutions that not only are profitable but also ensure constant value added for our customers. This fact is also supported by our numerous reference projects for major European network operators.

Kathrein Werke KG

http://www.kathrein.com

Kathrein Werke KG is the world's largest antenna producing enterprise and a leading telecommunications company. Know-how and 85 years of experience have made Kathrein one of the market leaders in these product ranges: Antennas for mobile communications, Satellite receiving systems, Antennas for TV and radio, Antennas for cars, trains and buses, Filters and amplifiers. The Kathrein Group employs worldwide more than 4,600 people. In 2004 turnover amounted to more than 1 billion euros.

KDDI

http://www.kddi.com

KDDI is a sole comprehensive provider of virtually every type of telecommunications service from fixed-line and 3G mobile communications to Internet services in Japan. Based on its high-quality telecommunications network and global-leading technologies that serve as the foundation for its services, KDDI is steadily advancing the construction of the ubiquitous network environment. KDDI, by setting "mobile & IP" as a core competency of the business and responding to the customers' further reliance and satisfaction, aims to become a Ubiquitous Solution Company.

KenCast

http://www.kencast.com

KenCast's Fazzt software products enable content delivery of files and streams with unique high reliability. Fazzt Systems are often used for difficult-delivery applications, even one-way in poor environments. Fazzt is currently used in wireless applications on satellite, the Internet and increasingly on terrestrial wireless networks. Fazzt is ideal for wireless delivery of files and live TV to mobile users with handheld devices (PDAs, cellular phones, smartphones) in vehicles or on foot.

KT Corp.

http://www.kt.co.kr

KT (KT Corp.) was established on December 10, 1981. As a total service provider that began operations with a nationwide fixed-line communication network, KT has grown into worldwide Internet and wireless service provider. With KTF (a subsidiary of KT), KT has served customers with converged service through both wired and wireless communication networks. KT recently owned 2.3-GHz licensed spectrum and is planning to launch the commercial mobile broadband service in April 2006.

Kyocera

http://www.kyocera.com

Kyocera Corporation was founded in 1959 as a company specializing in the production of fine ceramic components. Kyocera has expanded its business by effectively developing and applying its ceramics technologies. The company has grown to be a world-leading manufacturer of ceramics, including custom parts and consumer products. Kyocera's materials, components, and finished products are used in virtually all fields of industry. In addition to ceramics, products include information, telecommunications, and optical equipment.

Larsen & Toubro Infotech Limited

http://www.lntinfotech.com

Larsen & Toubro Infotech Limited (established in 1997), a 100 percent subsidiary of the multifaceted and diversified US$2.8 billion Larsen & Toubro Limited, offers comprehensive, end-to-end software solutions and services. Leveraging the heritage and domain expertise of the parent company, its services encompass a broad technology spectrum, catering to leading international companies across the globe.

Lattice Semiconductor

http://www.latticesemi.com

Lattice Semiconductor Corporation provides the industry's broadest range of Field Programmable Gate Arrays (FPGA) and Programmable Logic Devices (PLD), including Field Programmable System Chips (FPSC), Complex Programmable Logic Devices (CPLD), Programmable Mixed-Signal Products and Programmable Digital Interconnect Devices. Lattice also offers industry leading SERDES products. Lattice is Bringing the Best Together with comprehensive solutions for system design, including an unequaled portfolio of nonvolatile programmable devices that deliver instant-on operation, security and single chip solution space savings. Lattice products are sold worldwide through an extensive network of independent sales representatives and distributors, primarily to OEM customers in communications, computing, industrial, consumer, automotive, medical and military end markets.

LCC

http://www.lcc.com

An industry leader in wireless consulting, design, deployment and operations and maintenance services, LCC has been helping wireless operators design and build their networks since 1983. Today, LCC serves the wireless industry in more than 50 nations around the world. This global experience, coupled with the local knowledge of such a diverse employee base, allows us to offer our customers innovative solutions, insight into cutting-edge wireless developments and on time, on budget program delivery. Be it a customized turnkey project or a single service offering, LCC's solutions are tailored for each customer's unique need. In over two decades LCC has advised more than 400 customers in over 75 countries, deployed over 25,000 wireless telecom sites and improved network quality for over 150 million subscribers around the globe.

LG Electronics

http://www.lge.com

LG Electronics provides total solutions ranging from wired and wireless handsets to telecommunication equipment. The company is a leader in the innovation and development of cutting-edge technologies in next-generation wireless telecommunications and is steadily expanding its global market share in 3G(WCDMA/cdma2000) wireless systems.

LitePoint
http://www.litepoint.com
LitePoint Corporation designs, develops, markets, and supports advanced wireless test solutions for today's wireless products, providing complete test solutions targeted to the specific needs of wireless IC manufacturers, OEM/ODM manufacturers and branded product owners.

Lucent Technologies
http://www.lucent.com
Lucent Technologies designs and delivers the systems, services and software that drive next-generation communications networks. Backed by Bell Labs research and development, Lucent uses its strengths in mobility, optical, software, data and voice networking technologies, as well as services, to create new revenue-generating opportunities for its customers, while enabling them to quickly deploy and better manage their networks. Lucent's customer base includes communications service providers, governments and enterprises worldwide.

MWeb
http://www.mweb.com
MWeb supports the development and adoption of industry standards ("W3C Recommendations") enabling multimodal Web access using mobile devices. MWeb includes European outreach activities on first-generation W3C multimodal recommendations as well as support required for developing a second generation of specifications with significant European participation.

The project started on January 1, 2004, and has a duration of 24 months.

The MWeb Project has the following key objectives:

1. Increase the awareness of forthcoming first generation W3C multimodal Recommendations within European research and industry.

2. Raise the level of participation of European research and industry in W3C's second generation multimodal specifications.

3. Support the strategic objectives in IST by ensuring that European research and industry will have competent dialogue partners within the European W3C team during the course of FP6.

4. Establish links with projects funded by the Interface Technologies strategic objective which may have specific requirements to address.

This will be initiated by inviting representatives of such projects to an early workshop funded by MWeb. At this workshop, the invited projects should present their requirements towards standardization, present potential input to standardization their projects could provide, and give feedback on existing W3C solutions.

M/A-COM, Inc.
http://www.macom-wireless.com/default.asp
M/A-COM, Inc., a business unit of Tyco Electronics, is an established industry leader in the design, development and manufacture of radio frequency (RF), microwave and millimeter wave semiconductors, components and technologies for the wireless telecommunications, automotive, aerospace and military industries. Holding hundreds of patents in the field, M/A-COM is internationally known as an innovator and integrator whose technologies are found in today's most advanced signal intelligence and defense systems, as well as in leading automotive navigation, safety, and communications solutions. M/A-COM is also a major supplier of critical communications systems and equipment for public safety, utility, federal and select commercial markets.

Marconi
http://www.marconi.com
Marconi Corporation plc is a global telecommunications equipment, services and solutions company. Our core business is the provision of leading-edge and reliable optical networks, microwave radio, broadband routing and switching, broadband access technologies, multimedia SoftSwitch, network management and services. We are a multiregional business supporting customers in North America, Europe, the Middle East and Africa, Central America and the Asia-Pacific region. The company's customer base includes many of the world's largest telecommunications operators.

Mascon Global Limited
http://www.masconit.com
Mascon Global Limited is an ISO 9001:2000 certified and CMM level 4 assessed global provider of telecommunications and IT services employing more than 1,200 professionals in multiple offices, spread across 3 continents. Through an innovative blend of products, services, and delivery models, we assist companies in building, deploying, and maintaining technology-based solutions as key enablers of their business strategy.

Maxim Integrated Products

http://www.maxim-ic.com

Maxim Integrated Products is a worldwide leader in the design, development, and manufacture of linear, mixed-signal, and RF integrated circuits (ICs). Maxim circuits "connect" the real world and digital world by detecting, measuring, amplifying, and converting real-world signals, such as temperature, pressure, or sound, into the digital signals necessary for computer processing. Maxim's products include data converters, interface circuits, microprocessor supervisors, operational amplifiers, power supplies, multiplexers, switches, battery chargers, battery management circuits, RF wireless circuits, fiber optic transceivers, sensors, and voltage references. The company markets approximately 5,000 analog ICs—more than any other company in the industry.

MediaRing

http://www.mediaring.com

MediaRing is a leading communications company at the forefront of Internet telephony technology. It owns five U.S. patents and has more than a dozen patents pending. MediaRing brings high-quality voice services to carriers, enterprises, service providers, and consumers worldwide. It has its headquarters in Singapore with offices in San Jose (California), Beijing, Shanghai, Hong Kong, Taipei, Tokyo and Malaysia. In 1999 MediaRing was listed on the main board of the Singapore Exchange and is traded under the symbol MRNG.SI. MediaRing's global interconnected infrastructure allows call terminations in more than 200 countries, twenty-four hours a day and seven days a week.

Merrimac Industries

http://www.merrimacind.com

Merrimac Industries Inc. designs and manufacturers a broad line of RF components, integrated micro multifunctional modules (MMFM) and customized precision microwave circuitry (up to 100 GHz) for the wireless industry. Merrimac offers Total Integrated Packaging Solutions by providing integration of both active and passive devices in 3D multilayer structures applicable for small, lightweight, low-cost, high-volume PCS, CDMA, UMTS and WiMAX applications.

MetroBridge Networks

http://www.metrobridge.com

MetroBridge Networks provides businesses in Vancouver, Canada, with 1- to 100-Mbps broadband wireless connections. We cover more than 2,000 square kilometers of urban and suburban areas, serving companies of all sizes. Since 1998, MetroBridge has been building a reputation for speed, reliability and service.

MiCOM Labs

http://www.micomlabs.com

Headquartered in the San Francisco/Silicon Valley area of California, MiCOM Labs provides world-class, accredited RF and EMC testing and compliance certification for products in the global wireless, medical, telecommunications, security and other similar industries. With experience in the development and adoption of standards affecting the wireless communications industry on a global basis, MiCOM Labs is an able partner in researching and interpreting standards and in developing and executing critical-path plans for achieving product compliance.

Microelectronics Technology Inc.

http://www.mti.com.tw

Established in 1983, Microelectronics Technology Inc. (MTI) was Taiwan's first microwave and satellite communications company. For 20 years MTI has pioneered the wireless communications industry in Taiwan and continuously has cultivated the development of microwave integrated circuits, focusing on the design, manufacturing and sales of niche and promising products within the microwave electronics market. MTI's work and contribution have been essential in solidifying Taiwan's position in the global high-tech arena.

Microsoft Corporation

http://www.microsoft.com

Founded in 1975, Microsoft Corporation is the worldwide leader in software, services and solutions that help people and businesses realize their full potential. Microsoft develops, manufactures, licenses and supports a wide range of software products for various computing devices. Microsoft software products include scalable operating systems for servers, personal computers (PCs) and intelligent devices; server applications for client/server environments; information worker productivity applications; business solutions applications; software development tools; and mobile and embedded devices. Microsoft develops offerings in the following product segments: Client, Server and Tools, Information Worker, Microsoft Business Solutions, MSN, Mobile and Embedded Devices and Home and Entertainment. At Microsoft, we work to help people, businesses and communities gain access to the tools, skills and innovations they need to reach their full potential.

Midwest Wireless
http://www.midwestwireless.com
Midwest Wireless was founded on the principle that all people deserve reliable, advanced communication services regardless of where they choose to live and work. Since 1990, we've been building a strong network for the people living in our Minnesota, Wisconsin and Iowa service area, and we back it up with exceptional sales and customer care support. We live and work in the same places as our customers, so we are uniquely positioned to understand their needs. Because of this, answering to our customers comes naturally, and always has.

MITAC Technology Corporation
http://www.mitac-mtc.com.tw
MITAC Technology Corporation (MTC) of Taipei, Taiwan, is a professional wireless communication products design house and manufacturer as well as a manufacturer of notebook computers for use by consumers and for industrial and military purposes.

Mitsubishi Electric
http://www.global.mitsubishielectric.com
Mitsubishi Electric is a major force in communication systems. We develop and install the cable and wireless systems that comprise the planet's space-based, terrestrial and wireless communications infrastructure. To offer high value-added and high performance services in the rapidly advancing mobile telecommunication sector, Mitsubishi Electric creates equipment for base stations, which are expected to improved services by fortifying the technological infrastructure.

mmWave Technologies
http://www.mmwave.com
Active in the wireless industry in general and the Cellular/PCS market most notably, mmWave offers a wide range of communications-related solutions to the Canadian and Mexican markets. The company provides turnkey wireless networks, PCS/Cellular network coverage measurement and remediation, design and implementation consulting, test solu-

tions, and custom hardware and software solutions. mmWave has been involved in the awarding of over 24 community-based broadband wireless projects in Canada, and is an AIR partner of Alvarion, as well as several other WiMAX members.

Mobile Mark

http://www.mobilemark.com

Mobile Mark designs and manufactures antennas for a wide range of applications covering 800 MHz to 10 GHz. WiMAX-specific products include omnidirectional and directional site antennas for network build-out, mobile antennas to facilitate network testing and portability, as well as individual unit antennas for nomadic and personal applications. Antennas are currently available for all WiMAX frequencies under 10 GHz, including 3.5 GHz, 5.8 GHz and 2.6 GHz. Custom designs are available for OEM production. Antennas are also available for other wireless applications including Wireless LAN and ISM using 802.11a/b/g, RFID reader antennas, GPS Vehicle Tracking and Location, Voice/Data including GPRS and 1x-RTT, In-Building Wireless, Fixed Wireless Broadband and Wireless Internet and Remote data monitoring.

MobilePro

http://www.mobileprocorp.com

MobilePro Corp. is a wireless technology and broadband telecommunications company based in Bethesda, MD, with operations in Houston, Dallas and Beaumont, Texas; Coshocton and Cleveland, Ohio; Kansas City, KS; Janesville, WI; Detroit, MI; Stevensville, MD; Tucson, AZ; and Shreveport, LA. The company is focused on creating shareholder value by developing innovative wireless technologies, acquiring and growing profitable broadband telecommunications companies and forging strategic alliances with well-positioned companies in complementary product lines and industries.

Motorola

http://www.motorola.com

Motorola, Inc. (NYSE: MOT), is a global leader in wireless, broadband and automotive communications technologies that help make life smarter, safer, simpler, synchronized and fun. Sales in 2003 were US $27.1 billion. Motorola creates innovative technological solutions that benefit people at home, at work and on the move. The company also is a progressive corporate citizen dedicated to operating ethically, protecting the environment and supporting the communities in which it does business.

Mpower Communications

http://www.mpowercom.com

Mpower Communications is a facilities-based service provider offering an integrated bundle of broadband data and voice communication services including PRI, trunks, integrated and dedicated T1s, DSL, Web hosting and POTS. Mpower emphasizes a personal approach to businesses throughout California, Nevada, and Illinois.

MSV

http://www.msvlp.com

MSV is developing a next-generation hybrid wireless network in North America utilizing powerful new satellites working in unison with MSV's patented ancillary terrestrial component (ATC) technology that will employ thousands of land-based towers in order to deliver seamless service to standard wireless devices on a continental scale. MSV currently operates North America's premier mobile satellite service, providing wireless data, voice and P2T services in spectrum in the L band via its two MSAT satellites.

MTI Wireless Edge

http://www.mtiwe.com

MTI Wireless Edge is the world leader in the development and production of high-quality, cost-effective, flat panel antennas for Fixed Wireless applications. With more than 30 years' experience in both military and commercial applications from 100 kHz to 40 GHz. Subscriber, Base Station and Omnidirectional antennas in both licensed and unlicensed bands. MTI is ISO certified and has in-house test facilities that include antenna test ranges in length from 8 meters to 300 meters.

MTN Group

http://www.mtn.co.za

MTN Group Limited is a leading provider of communication services, offering cellular network access and business solutions. As of March 31, 2005, the Group generated $2.5 billion in revenue and had 14.3 million subscribers across its cellular network operations. To date MTN Group has invested approximately $2 billion in telecommunications infrastructure across the African continent.

Murandi Communications Ltd.

http://www.murandi.com

Since 1992 Murandi Communications has provided market leading wireless designs to clients around the world. With the successful development of broadband wireless access designs at many frequencies we have the design talent, disciplined development processes, and specialized facilities to design superior, low-cost wireless products. Our complete product development services include radio frequency, embedded software, digital and analog hardware, antennas, and automated manufacturing test suites.

Navini Networks

http://www.navini.com

Headquartered in Richardson, Texas, Navini Networks offers a market leading non-line-of-sight wireless broadband technology, Navini Networks RipwaveTM, that delivers multimegabit speeds to customers many miles from the base station. Navini provides nomadic, zero-install T, plug-and-play, NLOS infrastructure to allow for unwired access to the Internet. Navini's Ripwave products consist of a desktop modem or PCMCIA card, base station, and element management system (EMS) and operate in various licensed and unlicensed frequencies including the 2.3-GHz (WCS band), 2.4-GHz (ISM band), 2.5/2.6-GHz (MMDS band), and 3.5-GHz (WLL band).

NEC

http://www.nec.com

NEC is one of the world's leading providers of Internet, broadband network and enterprise business solutions dedicated to meeting the specialized needs of its diverse and global base of customers. Ranked as one of the world's top patent-producing companies, NEC delivers tailored solutions in the key fields of computer, networking and electronic devices, by integrating its technical strengths in IT and Networks, and by providing advanced semiconductor solutions through NEC Electronics Corporation.

Neotec

http://www.neotec.org.br

NEOTEC, the Brazilian Association of MMDS Operators, was created in 2001 to research new technologies for the 2.5-GHz spectrum, create single broadband wireless network throughout the country, assure critical mass for service and equipment providers, and encourage discussions among the participants for a constant improvement of the broadband wireless business. NEOTEC represents 77% of all MMDS homes passed (18 million HH), covering 250 municipalities and a presence in 41 out of the 50 largest cities in Brazil.

Nera Networks ASA

http://www.nera.no

Nera ASA is one of the world's leading companies in the field of wireless telecommunications using microwave and satellite technology. The Nera Group is positioned in growth segments of the international telecommunications market and provides wireless broadband solutions and equipment where products and competence from both radio link and satellite are integrated.

Netgear

http://www.netgear.com

NETGEAR designs technologically advanced branded networking products that address the specific needs of small and medium business and home users. The Company's suite of over 100 products enables users to share Internet access, peripherals, files, digital multimedia content and applications among multiple personal computers and other Internet-enabled devices. NETGEAR is headquartered in Santa Clara, California.

Netopia

http://www.netopia.com

Netopia, Inc., is a market leader in broadband and wireless products and services that simplify and enhance broadband delivery to residential and business-class customers. Netopia's offerings enable carriers and service providers to improve their profitability with feature-rich broadband smart modems, routers and gateways, and software that simplifies installation and reduces ongoing support needs, as well as value-added services to increase revenue generation. Netopia has established strategic relationships with leading carriers and broadband service providers worldwide.

NextGenTel

http://www.nextgentel.no

NextGenTel is a "next-generation telecom company." Since March 2000, NextGenTel has established itself as the clear number two broadband and xDSL player in Norway, the incumbent's main challenger. NextGenTel has acquired the largest number of WiMAX frequencies blocks in Norway. NextGenTel has more than 170 employees in 5 cities: Bergen

(HQ), Oslo, Trondheim, Stavanger and Kristiandsand. NextGenTel is the broadband pulse of Norway and is listed on the Norwegian Stock Exchange (OSE: NEXT).

NextNet Wireless
http://www.nextnetwireless.com
NextNet is the industry's most widely deployed provider of NLOS plug-and-play broadband wireless access systems. Founded in 1998, NextNet quickly moved into a leadership position in broadband wireless after introducing the industry's first non-line-of-sight (NLOS) platform for delivery of high-speed fixed wireless Internet services. Today, the ExpedienceTM NLOS system is deployed in cities throughout Asia, Africa, North America, Latin America, and Mexico, where NextNet is the exclusive NLOS plug-and-play system supplier for Mexico's largest MMDS operator, MVS Comunicaciones. In October 2003, MVS and NextNet announced expansion plans to include 14 new markets in 2004, targeting 41 million people, doubling the current coverage in Mexico City.

NextPhase Wireless
http://www.npwireless.com
NextPhase Wireless is a connectivity company that specializes in delivering integrated Internet, voice and data communication solutions to its customers. The company designs, deploys and operates its own wireless networks and also provides wireless technology solutions to businesses and municipalities. Leveraging its full-service capabilities and world-class infrastructure, NextPhase Wireless offers a comprehensive portfolio of broadband solutions that meet customers' needs today, and can anticipate and grow to meet their needs of tomorrow.

NextWave Telecom
http://www.nextwavetel.com
NextWave Telecom Inc. was formed in 1995 to provide wireless broadband services to consumer and business markets. NextWave intends to operate as a "carriers' carrier" and provide VNOs (Virtual Network Operators) unbranded, open access to our wireless broadband network.

NextWeb
http://www.nextweb.net
NextWeb, Inc., is California's largest fixed wireless Internet Service Provider (ISP) for business. The company utilizes licensed and unlicensed wireless technology to bypass the local telco infrastructure to

deliver cost-effective, carrier-class broadband service that can be installed in hours, rather than weeks.

Nippon Telegraph and Telephone

http://www.ntt.co.jp

NTT is the holding company of the NTT Group, some 430 companies forming a global information sharing corporate group. The biggest mission of the NTT Group is to contribute toward realizing the full-scale broadband, ubiquitous era. In order to bring broadband services to as many people as possible, the Group is drawing on its collective strength to offer a far-reaching broadband service that includes providing a variety of access methods, such as optical-fiber access, third generation mobile telephones and wireless LANs, building a framework to promote the delivery of such content as movies and music, and expanding our content delivery services.

Nokia

http://www.nokia.com

Nokia is a world leader in mobile communications, driving the growth and sustainability of the broader mobility industry. Nokia connects people to each other and the information that matters to them with easy-to-use and innovative products like mobile phones, devices and solutions for imaging, games, media and businesses. Nokia provides equipment, solutions and services for network operators and corporations.

Nortel

http://www.nortel.com

Nortel Networks has designed, installed and launched more than 300 wireless networks in over 50 countries across the globe. Nortel Networks was the industry's first supplier with wireless networks operating in all advanced radio technologies (GSM/GPRS/EDGE, CDMA2000 1X and 1xEV-DO, UMTS and WLAN), and is the only end-to-end provider of all next generation wireless solutions.

North Rock Communications

http://www.northrock.bm

North Rock Communications is a privately held telecommunications company located in Hamilton, Bermuda. At North Rock Communications Ltd. we pride ourselves on offering our customers a better choice. We provide a full range of Wireless, DSL, Long Distance and Local Voice products and services to both business and residential customers. As

Bermuda's premier Telecommunications provider, our team of highly skilled professionals is dedicated to offering the highest level of customer service.

Orbitel S.A. E.S.P

http://www.orbitel.com.co

ORBITEL is an agile, competitive and innovative Company dedicated to providing telecommunications solutions, while exceeding the expectations of our customers. It is the only privately held long distance Company in Colombia and began operations in November 1998. The Company provides long distance, data, broadband and Internet services, and its marketing and commercial strategy is clearly segmented between residential, corporate and international customers in the three countries where it is established: Colombia, the United States and Spain.

Orthogon

http://www.orthogonsystems.com/

Orthogon Systems is a leading provider of high-performance fixed wireless solutions, known for delivering reliable connectivity in the most challenging environments. Based on unique, patented intelligent radio technology, the award-winning OS-Gemini and OS-Spectra products are secure, easy-to-install and self-managing. Since July 2003, Orthogon has installed more than 3,000 wireless links, successfully connecting disparate networks within corporate enterprises, service providers and municipalities in 49 countries worldwide and growing. Orthogon Systems is coheadquartered in Ashburton, England, and Waltham, MA, with offices in Moscow, Dubai, Singapore and Shanghai.

P-Com

http://www.p-com.com

P-Com, Inc., develops, manufactures, and markets point-to-point, spread spectrum and point-to-multipoint wireless access systems to the worldwide telecommunications market. P-Com wireless access systems are designed to satisfy the high-speed, integrated network requirements of Internet access associated with Business to Business and E-Commerce business processes. Cellular and personal communications service (PCS) providers utilize P-Com point-to-point systems to provide backhaul between base stations and mobile switching centers. Government, utility, and business entities use P-Com systems in public and private network applications.

PA Consulting Group
http://www.paconsulting.com
PA Consulting Group is a leading management, systems and technology consulting firm, operating worldwide from over 40 offices in more than 20 countries. Within the group we provide technical consulting and engineering design services in mobile communications, handling DSP, RF and software development in 3G and similar complex systems. We have developed Software Defined Radio systems for 3G and related systems and implemented product level design for our clients.

Pacific Internet Corporation
http://www.pacnet.com
Pacific Internet, or PacNet, is the largest telco-independent Internet Communications Service Provider (ICSP) in the Asia-Pacific region by geographic reach. The company has direct presence in seven markets: Singapore, Hong Kong, the Philippines, Australia, India, Thailand and Malaysia. PacNet runs a round-the-clock IP network with strong international peering relationships, enabling it to offer integrated and secured data, voice, and video services to customers with interests in major commercial centers in Asia and globally.

Panasonic Electronic Devices Europe
http://www.panasonic-eutc.com
As a part of Panasonic Electronic Devices global R&D, the European Technology Center is located near Hamburg in Germany, and our mission is to expand PED's business in Europe by local product development. Our target areas are RF devices such as wireless modules for communication, base station components and antenna application development, as well as support.

Parks
http://www.parks.com.br
Since 1966, Parks has been offering products to the telecommunication brands with the highest technology that are fully tailored to the particularities of the Brazilian market, especially in the segment of broadband Internet access. With solid partnerships with the largest fixed telephony operators in the country, Parks has a dealer's network with more than 800 points of sale. The company provides also a large technical assistance and customer support network.

PCCW

http://www.pccw.com

PCCW is one of Asia's leading integrated communications companies. As the incumbent telecommunications provider in Hong Kong, PCCW is committed to building shareholder value by leveraging synergies among its core businesses and partners to deliver total solutions to corporate and consumer customers throughout Asia, particularly in greater China.

PCTEL

http://www.pctel.com

PCTEL simplifies mobility. We simplify wireless access to the Internet and optimize cellular networks and roaming abilities across carriers. We build specialized antennas to facilitate wireless communication—from public safety applications to wireless broadband. We can help you understand and enhance many aspects of your network's performance, including accessibility, coverage, quality of service, capacity, and security.

Pegasus Communications

http://www.pgtv.com

Pegasus Broadband provides wireless Internet access to residential and enterprise customers. Pegasus Broadband is one of the fastest growing Wireless Internet Service Providers (WISP) in the United States. Pegasus Broadband is a subsidiary of Pegasus Communications Corporation (NASDAQ: PGTV), a publicly traded communications company with a heritage of successfully introducing new digital communication services. Pegasus Communications is a licensee of 700-MHz spectrum covering in excess of 180 million people that will in the future enable the delivery of broadband communications to fixed and mobile users in major markets such as New York, Boston, Philadelphia, Pittsburgh, Cleveland, Detroit, Chicago, Miami, Tampa, Phoenix, San Francisco, Sacramento, Portland and Seattle.

picoChip

http://www.picochip.com/

picoChip provides innovative, flexible wireless solutions to help equipment makers minimize time-to-market, cost, and power consumption for leading-edge wireless systems. The picoArray combines the performance of a dedicated ASIC with the programmability of a DSP, delivering a 10x improvement in price/performance while dramatically accelerating development. As importantly, the platform includes comprehensive tools, boards and reference designs. picoChip technology radically improves ROI for manufacturers of wireless infrastructure, while reducing cost and worry for operators.

Piepenbrock Schuster Consulting AG

http://www.psc-ag.de

Piepenbrock Schuster Consulting AG was founded in March 2004 by the partners of the law firm Piepenbrock Schuster. Both are located in Duesseldorf, Germany. Main topic is the consultancy in economical and technical issues regarding the telecommunications and utilities branch.

PMC-Sierra

http://www.pmc-sierra.com

PMC-Sierra, Inc., is a leading provider of broadband communications semiconductors and MIPS-Powered processors for enterprise, access, metro, storage, wireless infrastructure and advanced consumer electronics equipment. The company is publicly traded on the NASDAQ stock market under the PMCS symbol and is included in the S&P 500 Index.

Portugal Telecom Inovao

http://www.ptinovacao.pt

PT Inovao is a Portuguese Telecom company for the development of innovative value-added services, products and applications contributing to the leveraging of the PT Group companies' competitiveness and business. PT Inovao develops competence covering the various disciplines and sectors of the telecommunications and information technologies market, through the integration of know-how in multiservice networks, information systems and multimedia.

POSdata

http://www.posdata.co.kr/eng/

POSdata Co., Ltd., founded in 1989 and listed on the Korean NASDAQ market in 2000, is an Information Technology Services provider to all kinds of government organizations and commercial enterprises. Its revenue in 2003 was $330 million. POSdata recently launched the Portable Internet (MBWA) business as a new growth engine, while expanding its current businesses of IT Consulting, System Integration, IT Outsourcing, Network Integration, Linux based Parallel Processing system, Digital Video Recorders and VoIP.

PowerNet Global

http://www.powernetglobal.com

Founded in 1992, the integrated communications provider PowerNet Global works with many of the country's top communications agents and affinity groups to offer a wide range of integrated voice, data, wireless, and Internet solutions nationwide to residential and commercial customers. Leveraging its reputation in the industry, a nationwide IP network, and strong carrier partnerships, PowerNet Global offers tremendous opportunities for carriers, resellers, agents, and affinity groups. The company is headquartered in Cincinnati and has offices in Jamestown, New York; Chantilly, Virginia; and Chicago. PowerNet Global has achieved consistent growth throughout the telecom industry downturn by developing and marketing an expanding array of competitive products, as well as through strategic acquisitions.

PricewaterhouseCoopers

http://www.pwc.com/

PricewaterhouseCoopers is an independent member within the international PricewaterhouseCoopers network, drawing on the knowledge and skills of more than 120,000 employees in 139 countries. In Germany, PricewaterhouseCoopers is one of the leading auditing and consultancy companies: 9,000 employees generate a turnover of some $1.2 billion. At 28 locations, experts are working for national and international clients of every size. The focus is on assurance and business advisory services, tax services as well as transaction, process and crisis services.

Prisma Engineering

http://www.prisma-eng.it

Prisma Engineering is a global supplier of hardware and software solutions for telecommunications market worldwide. Since 1992, Prisma has been focused on the development of simulator products for functional, system and load-end stress testing of GSM, GPRS/EDGE, TD-SCDMA, UMTS and Wi-MAX networks.

Pronto Networks

http://www.prontonetworks.com

Pronto Networks, Inc., provides carrier-class Operations Support Systems (OSS) that enable network operators to deploy and manage large-scale, broadband wireless networks. The company's software handles provisioning, configuration, authentication, access control, security, prepaid and postpaid billing, and roaming settlement for large public wireless networks, in addition to remotely managing and updating multi-vendor hardware. Pronto Networks is funded by Draper Fisher Jurvetson and Intel Capital.

Proxim

http://www.proxim.com

Proxim Corporation is a leader in wireless networking. It is the only company exclusively focused on both high-performance indoor and outdoor wireless networking, with the broadest range of wireless infrastructure and client products in the world.

PT Indosat Mega Media

http://www.indosatm2.com

PT Indosat Mega Media or IndosatM2 is the leading Internet, Multimedia and other IP based Services Provider in Indonesia. It provides services such as High-speed/Dedicated Internet, Dial up, Hotspot, TV Cable, VPN (Virtual Private Network), Hosting and Collocation, VoIP (Voice over Internet Protocol), B2B and B2C E-Commerce. IndosatM2 is a full subsidiary company of PT Indosat (the Telecommunication Service Provider in Indonesia), starting to operate in the year 2000 and giving the services for company, organization and personal/residential in Indonesia, supported by a highest capacity network which was connected to the Global Internet. Since 2004, IndosatM2 started to operate Hotspot service all over Indonesia, and at the same time became a member of the Wireless Broadband Alliance (WBA).

PT Telekomunikasi Indonesia, Tbk

http://www.telkom.co.id

TELKOM is the principal provider of local and domestic telecommunications services in Indonesia. TELKOM's objective is to become a leading full-service and network provider in Indonesia through the provision of a wide range of communications services.

Qwest

http://www.qwest.com

Qwest Communications International Inc. (NYSE: Q) is a leading provider of voice, video and data services to more than 25 million customers. The company's 47,000 employees are committed to the Spirit of Service and providing world-class services that exceed customers' expectations for quality, value and reliability.

Radionet

http://www.radionet.com

The Wi-Fi Hotzone company Radionet Ltd. specializes in the development, design and sales of large-scale outdoor wireless broadband networks. Radionet's technology is based on the WLAN standard conforming to IEEE 802.11. Radionet offers comprehensive carrier-class wireless broadband networks for operators, ISPs and wireless ISPs, power utilities, industry and logistics, and system integrators.

Redline Communications

http://www.redlinecommunications.com

Redline Communications Inc. is an innovative provider of second-generation broadband fixed wireless systems.

Redpine Signals

http://www.redpinesignals.com

Redpine Signals is a privately held fabless semiconductor company with expertise in OFDM and MAC protocol processing as well as software and end-to-end wireless system design. Redpine is developing advanced standards-based System-on-Chip and intellectual property platform solutions with differentiation on low power, low system cost and small system footprint. Redpine solutions encompass WiMAX (802.16), Wireless LAN (802.11), and Ultra-Wideband (802.15.3) standards.

ReignCom

http://www.reigncom.com

ReignCom came up with the world's first Multi-CODEC CD Player in December 2000. With that product, ReignCom took the top position in the U.S. market in the short span of six months. Since then, ReignCom has also taken the top position in the domestic Japanese market. Today, ReignCom is known as a global leader in the MP3 player market with the world-famous iriver brand.

Reliance Infocomm Limited

http://www.ril.com

The Reliance Group is India's largest business house. Reliance IndiaMobile, the first Infocomm initiative, was launched on December 28, 2002. Reliance Infocomm is the largest Cellular operator in India and offers a complete range of telecom services, covering mobile and fixed line telephony including broadband, national and international long distance services, data services and a wide range of value-added services and applications that will enhance the productivity of enterprises and individuals.

RemotePipes

http://www.remotepipes.net

RemotePipes, Inc., provides worldwide mobile Internet access solutions to individuals and small and medium-sized businesses and organizations spanning corporate, government, nonprofit, military, and education. The company distributes its globally aggregated network access services directly and via channel partners such as cable MSOs, CLECs, ISPs, and wireless Internet service providers (WISPs). As the founding member of the WiMAX Global Roaming Alliance (WGRA), RemotePipes brings several years of experience in global data roaming to the WiMAX Forum.

Resolute Networks

http://www.resolutenetworks.com

Resolute Networks is the leading provider of circuit emulation gateway technology for integration into OEM networking devices. Resolute solutions enable delivery of high quality E1/T1/T3/OC-3/STM-1 services over newly deployed managed packet networks based on Ethernet, IP and/or MPLS. Resolute products are used in networking solutions in key access and core applications, including WiMAX leased line and backhaul, Metro Ethernet access and core, DOCSIS cable access, PON access and backhaul, and cellular backhaul.

RF Integration

http://www.rfintegration.com

RF Integration Inc. designs and manufactures highly integrated RF/Mixed Signal ASICs for the wireless and broadband communications markets. Strategic foundry alliances provide access to high-performance Silicon (SiGe BiCMOS, CMOS, SOI) and GaAs (Mesfet, pHEMT, HBT) IC technologies, thus allowing RF Integration to choose the IC process that best fits the application's specific requirement.

Rogers

http://www.rogers.com

Rogers Communications Inc. (TSX: RCI; NYSE: RG) is a diversified Canadian communications and media company. Its three primary businesses include Rogers Wireless, Canada's largest wireless voice and data communications services provider and the country's only carrier operating on the world standard GSM/GPRS technology platform; Rogers

Cable, Canada's largest cable television provider, offering cable television, high-speed Internet access and video retailing; and Rogers Media, Canada's premier collection of category leading media assets with businesses in radio, television broadcasting, televised shopping, publishing and sport entertainment.

Rohde & Schwarz

http://www.rohde-schwarz.com

Rohde & Schwarz is Europe's leading manufacturer of electronic test and measurement equipment. Our T&M instruments and systems are setting standards all around the world in research, development, production and service. We are the world's leading supplier of wireless communication T&M equipment. The Rohde & Schwarz group has 5,900 employees worldwide with subsidiaries and representatives in over 70 countries.

Runcom Technologies Ltd.

http://www.runcom.com

Launched in 1997, Runcom Technologies' sole focus is on the development of superior technological standards and product offerings for the emerging Broadband Wireless Access and Digital Interactive TV markets. Runcom is the recognized pioneer of Orthogonal Frequency Division Multiple Access (OFDMA) technology, accepted in 2001 by ETSI as the core component of the DVB-RCT standard, a wireless-enabled platform that facilitates content-rich interactivity between TV broadcasters and subscribers over traditional terrestrial infrastructure. OFDMA has also been incorporated as the preferred solution for the IEEE 802.16.a Broadband Wireless Access (BWA) standard, enabling telecoms to provide customers with enhanced voice and data services.

Samora Digital

http://www.samora-digital.com

Samora Digital is a broad-based integrator of wireless technologies with a specific focus on developing and deploying wide area networks using the WiMAX platform. Samora's main service offerings include: Wireless Integration, Business Development and Consulting for related technologies and deploying Internet Service Providers. Samora is based in Connecticut, with offices in California and Jakarta, Indonesia.

Samsung

http://www.samsung.com

Samsung Electronics Co. Ltd. is a global leader in telecommunication, semiconductor, digital media and digital convergence technologies with 2003 parent company sales of US$36.5 billion and net income of US$5.0 billion. Employing approximately 88,000 people in 89 offices in 46 countries, the company consists of five main business units: Telecommunication Network Business, Digital Appliance Business, Digital Media Business, LCD Business, and Semiconductor Business. Recognized as one of the fastest growing global brands, Samsung Electronics is the world's largest producer of color monitors, color TVs, memory chips, TFT-LCDs and VCRs.

Sanjole

http://www.sanjole.com

Sanjole's Broadband Wireless Tester, BWT, is designed to meet the demanding needs of wireless datacom and telecom product manufacturers. Whether you are interested in Spread Spectrum testing of analog components or Multipath and Doppler testing of digital processors, Sanjole has a system to meet your needs. And for the future WiMax market, Sanjole's architecture will provide a comprehensive PHY Layer tester with future expansion to the MAC Layer.

Sanyo Electric Co., Ltd.

http://www.sanyo.com

Sanyo Electric Co. Ltd. manufactures a broad range of electronic products. The Sanyo Group of companies is multinational, comprising 83 manufacturing companies, 40 sales companies, and 37 other companies around the globe. Sanyo's strategic business focus is on the Digital and Devices and Energy and Ecology fields. In the Digital and Devices fields, Sanyo develops pioneering technologies that drive the digital revolution. The company's digital cameras, liquid crystal display (LCD) Projectors, and cellular and Personal Handyphone System (PHS) phones are highly acclaimed.

Saudi Aramco

http://www.aramco.com

Saudi ARAMCO's operations span the globe and the energy industry. The world leader in crude oil production, Saudi Aramco also owns and operates an extensive network of refining and distribution facilities and is responsible for the gas processing and transportation installations that fuel Saudi Arabia's industrial sector. An array of international subsidiaries and joint ventures, including one of the world's largest and newest fleet of supertankers, deliver crude oil and refined products to customers worldwide.

SBC
http://www.labs.sbc.com

SBC Communications Inc. is a diversified communications company, owning several of the world's leading data, voice and Internet services providers. SBC companies provide a full range of voice, data, networking and e-business services. SBC Communications Inc. owns America's leading high-speed DSL provider and one of the nation's leading Internet Service Providers. SBC companies currently serve 55 million access lines nationwide. In addition, SBC companies own 60 percent of America's second-largest wireless company, Cingular Wireless, which serves more than 24 million wireless customers.

SC Lithuanian Radio & TV Center
http://www.lrtc.net

The stock company Lithuanian Radio & TV Center is the dominant supplier of transmitting on the ground radio and television programs in Lithuania. In 2001 the company started a new activity: wireless data transmission. The successfully implemented advanced wireless technologies of data transmission, the available tower infrastructure as well as high quality personnel comprise a solid basis for rendering quality service of Internet and data transmission in many Lithuanian towns and cities, even in places where other operators are ineffective. The company owns a nationwide license to deploy broadband wireless access networks in 1-GHz, 5-GHz, 26-GHz and 3.5-GHz frequency bands. Also, the company has a license to provide public fixed telephone services. The company is offering the following services: wide range wireless Internet connections; leased line services LAN to LAN connection. The company is focused on the newest BWA, Voice over IP, Video over IP technologies; therefore; we are open for trials and tests. Our goal is to become a leading client-oriented and efficient company providing wireless data transmission service.

Securitas Direct
http://www.securitasdirect.es

Securitas Direct is the alarms division of the worldwide leader company in security: Securitas. As a leader in this area, Securitas Direct is developing new products and services in which communication is a primary component, products based on GSM communication, high-bandwidth video solutions, and new customer interfaces based on mobile and Internet technologies; these products are critical to provide the best services to our customers.

Selex Communications

http://www.seleniacomms.com

Selex Communications, a Finmeccanica company, supplies a complete catalogue of communication products and systems for land, sea and air applications that can be fully integrated and made fully interoperable with each other. The Company's skills encompass civil and military secure communications, avionics, Command and Control, and land, naval and ground-satellite Communications systems. Selex Communications also supplies communications equipments to Railway operators and turnkey Mobile Radio Networks to Police Forces, Emergency Services and Utility Companies.

Semino Communications

http://www.seminocommunications.com

Semino Communications Inc. is a private Canadian company with a mandate to provide economic and reliable wireless communications to Developing Nations. Leveraging a strong business network and a unique combination of 802.1x wireless and VON technologies, Semino is currently positioning itself to enter several international markets.

SES Americom

http://www.ses-americom.com

The largest supplier of satellite services in the United States, SES AMERICOM is recognized as a pioneer in global satellite communications services. Established in 1973, the company currently operates a fleet of 16 spacecraft predominantly providing service throughout the Americas. SES AMERICOM serves broadcasters, cable programmers, aeronautical and maritime communications integrators, Internet service providers, mobile communications networks, government agencies, educational institutions, carriers and secure global data networks with efficient communication and content distribution solutions.

SGS Taiwan Ltd.

http://www.sgs.com.tw/

The SGS Group is the clear global leader and innovator in verification, monitoring, testing and certification services. The organization in Taiwan was established in 1952. The service in Taiwan covers Laboratory Testing, ISO certification and Inspection. SGS has gained a wealth of experience through 50 years of business on the island and has kept up with the tremendous economic development in Taiwan by upgrading our business quality and enlarging our range of services.

Shorecliff Communications

http://www.scievents.com

Shorecliff Communications LLC, a subsidiary of Landmark Communications, is a leading media company serving wireless and wireline service providers and their partners—outsourced infrastructure owners, content developers, and equipment suppliers—through education, information and interactive communities.

Siemens Mobile

http://www.siemens.com

Siemens Mobile offers its customers worldwide solutions and products for the entire spectrum of mobile communications: mobile phones and accessories, cordless phones and telephone systems, smart phones, wireless modules, base stations and intelligent networks, switching systems, applications and comprehensive services.

Sierra Monolithics

http://www.monolithics.com/

Sierra Monolithics Inc. (SMI) is a fabless semiconductor company headquartered in Redondo Beach, California. SMI brings more than 10 years' experience providing field-proven RF Chips and Modules to the wireless and military electronics space. The company specializes in SiGe broadband, high-frequency complex transceiver designs. We have provided numerous solutions in protocols ranging from GPS to OC-768 to 60-GHz transceivers. SMI has a dual band 2.5/3.5-GHz transceiver in development for WiMAX applications.

Sierra Wireless

http://www.sierrawireless.com

Sierra Wireless is a global leader in providing wireless communication solutions that enable mobile professionals to improve their productivity and lifestyle. The Company has a unique ability to design and market the industry's most differentiated and reliable wireless solutions while providing customers and partners with world-class support. Founded in 1993, Sierra Wireless's technical expertise has enabled the company to build highly successful products celebrated for innovation, quality, and reliability.

Sify Limited

http://www.sifycorp.com

Sify is India's pioneer in Internet and e-commerce and offers integrated end-to-end solutions with a comprehensive range of products and services, for both the Business to Consumer (B2C) and Business to Business (B2B) segments, that cover the four critical cornerstones of the Net: Connectivity, Content, Commerce and Community.

SiGe Semiconductor, Inc.

http://www.sige.com

SiGe Semiconductor, Inc., is a leading global supplier of RF front-end solutions for next-generation wireless systems. The company's integrated circuits and chip-scale modules deliver unparalleled performance and power efficiency to Bluetooth-enabled portable devices, GPS and telematics systems, IEEE 802.11a/b/g WLANs, WiMAX broadband access equipment, 2G, 2.5G and 3G cellular handsets, and cordless telephones. SiGe Semiconductor has headquarters in Ottawa, Canada, is registered in Delaware, United States, and has operations in Boston, San Diego, Hong Kong and London.

SingTel

http://www.singtel.com

SingTel is Asia's leading communications company, with a comprehensive portfolio of services that include voice and data services over fixed, wireless and Internet platforms. Serving both the corporate and residential markets, SingTel is committed to bringing the best of global communications to its customers in the Asia-Pacific region and beyond.

SK Telecom

http://www.sktelecom.com

SK Telecom is a leading Cellular Service Provider in South Korea. SK Telecom introduced the first generation analog cellular service in South Korea. Also, we completed a second generation mobile communication technology by successfully commercializing the world's first CDMA cellular service. SK Telecom then launched the world's first commercial 2.5 generation CDMA 2000 1X service, as well as the third generation CDMA 2000 1xEV-DO service and WCDMA service. SK Telecom also acquired a license for WiBro Services in South Korea and has plans to commercialize the service by the year 2006.

SkyPilot Networks

http://www.skypilot.com

SkyPilot Networks designs and manufactures wireless broadband network systems that provide a carrier-grade platform, enabling network operators of all sizes to profitably provide ubiquitous and affordable broadband data, voice, and video services with maximum operational flexibility. SkyPilot is committed to delivering world-class wireless broadband performance to carriers, service providers, enterprises, and network operators around the world through its innovative systems design, unique software expertise, and intelligent integration of industry standards. SkyPilot Networks is a privately held company based in Belmont, California.

SkyTel

http://www.skytel.com

SkyTel Corp., a wholly owned subsidiary of MCI, provides corporations and business customers with wireless access to their mission-critical data. Founded in 1988, SkyTel pioneered early wireless products such as nationwide paging, laptop integration and guaranteed messaging. Today, SkyTel provides a wide range of data services to our enterprise customers, from wireless e-mail and custom data applications, to 2-Way Messaging and traditional paging products.

Skyworks Solutions

http://www.skyworksinc.com

Skyworks is the world's largest company focused exclusively on wireless semiconductor solutions. From basic components and integrated RF modules to complete system platforms, Skyworks offers optimized solutions for any mobile communications application. With over a thousand engineers, dedicated sales, marketing and technical support throughout North America, Europe and Asia, Skyworks will work as a partner to solve any design challenge for WLAN, infrastructure and handsets.

SmartBridges

http://www.smartbridges.com/

SmartBridges manufactures carrier-class outdoor antennas to enhance the RF performance of networking equipment. These rugged antennas assure users their critical Point-to-Point and Point-to-Multipoint links in harsh outdoor environments. These antennas incorporate our Long-Range technology to provide industry-best performance. Simplicity of use, ease of implementation and cost-effectiveness are the cornerstones of our solutions. With offices in North America, Latin America and Asia, our experienced management team is driving the vision of Unwiring Our World.

Softbank

http://www.softbankbb.co.jp/english/index.html
SOFTBANK BB is engaged in the provision of various broadband services and infrastructure coherently from marketing, sales, and support to technical development, centering on Yahoo! BB. SOFTBANK BB also offers IT-related goods, software and service distribution and administers affiliated broadband and e-commerce companies.

SOMA Networks

http://www.somanetworks.com
Integrating the latest advances in wireless broadband, distributed computing, and Internet technologies, SOMA Networks provides a complete last-mile wireless broadband system. The SOMA solution includes large cells for quick and inexpensive market entry, non-line-of-sight access enabling self-installation and self-activation of the SOMA port wireless broadband gateway, and the ability to support multiple next-generation wireless standards on the same platform, which enables service providers to profitably roll out services.

Speakeasy

http://www.speakeasy.net
Founded in 1994, Speakeasy is the nation's largest independent broadband service provider, specializing in residential and small business broadband solutions for those who demand more than just a connection. Speakeasy offers a superior online experience through its private dedicated nationwide network, intelligent customer service and pioneering technologies and product offerings, including unrestricted WiFi, dedicated loop ADSL and VoIP. Speakeasy owns Gamecloud, which is an infrastructure of servers, content repositories, online services (such as GameDaemons), editorial properties and partners that operate on multiple Internet backbones and peering connections in order to deliver the best online gaming experience for broadband-enabled customers. Speakeasy broadband is available in most metropolitan areas within the 48 contiguous United States.

Spirent Communications

http://www.spirentcom.com

Spirent Communications is a global provider of integrated performance analysis and service assurance systems that enable the development and deployment of next-generation networking technology such as Internet telephony, broadband services, 3G wireless, global navigation satellite systems, and network security equipment. Spirent's solutions are used by more than 1,500 customers in 30 countries, including the world's largest equipment manufacturers, service providers, enterprises and governments. Based in Rockville, Maryland, Spirent Communications reported 2003 revenue of $394 million and has 1,800 employees worldwide.

Sprint Nextel

http://www.sprint.com

Sprint is a global integrated communications provider serving more than 26 million customers in over 100 countries. With more than $26 billion in annual revenues in 2003, Sprint is widely recognized for developing, engineering and deploying state-of-the-art network technologies, including the United States' first nationwide all-digital fiber-optic network and an award-winning Tier 1 Internet backbone. Sprint provides local communications services in 39 states and the District of Columbia and operates the largest 100 percent digital nationwide PCS wireless network in the United States.

SR Telecom

http://www.srtelecom.com

SR TELECOM is one of the world's leading providers of Broadband Fixed Wireless Access (BFWA) technology. The Company's unrivaled portfolio of BFWA products enables its growing customer base to offer carrier-class voice, broadband data and Internet services. Its turnkey solutions include equipment, network planning, project management, installation and maintenance. SR Telecom's products have been deployed in over 130 countries, connecting nearly 2 million people.

Starent Networks

http://www.starentnetworks.com

Starent Networks Corporation was founded in August 2000 with a mission to enhance service creation for mobile operators by delivering intelligent infrastructure solutions. Starent Networks has emerged as a market leader in next generation packet core networking. Its solutions enable high-speed data, enhanced voice and multimedia services through an integrated, high-performance network architecture. This architecture delivers new levels of network flexibility that empowers the subscriber and presents the mobile carrier with new revenue-generating opportunities.

Start Telecom

http://www.starttelecom.ru

Start Telecom is a telecommunication company founded to deploy and operate a nationwide wireless network based on WiMax Standard technology. Our goal is to provide a competitive last mile solution for a wide range of communication services for residents, SME and SOHO clients. Our strategic agreements with major players in the Russian telecommunication market among alternative and incumbent operators give us a strong advantage and make it possible to deploy the backbone infrastructure in a time-efficient manner.

Stealth Microwave

http://www.stealthmicrowave.com

Stealth Microwave designs and manufactures linear power amplifiers for single carrier and multicarrier systems. The company's products range from 200 MHz to 20 GHz and can be found in a broad spectrum of applications worldwide. Our proprietary linearization technology allows us to produce some of the smallest ultralinear amplifiers currently on the market, providing the performance needed for current and evolving wireless standards.

Stratex Networks

http://www.stratexnet.com

Stratex Networks, Inc., is an industry leader in the development, manufacture and marketing of microwave radio solutions for point-to-point applications in licensed frequency bands, enabling the development of complex communications networks worldwide.

Stretch

http://www.stretchinc.com

Stretch Inc. is delivering a family of software-configurable processors, the first to embed programmable logic within the processor. Using familiar C/C++ programming tools, system developers automatically configure Stretch's off-the-shelf processors to achieve extraordinary performance, easy and rapid development, significant cost savings, and flexibility to address diverse markets and changing application needs. Founded in March 2002, Stretch is headquartered in Mountain View, California.

Strix Systems

http://www.strixsystems.com

Strix Systems designs, develops, and delivers high-performance wireless mesh networking systems based on the company's unique multiradio, multichannel and multi-RF wireless architecture. Sold globally by a network of integrators and resellers, these solutions address the high cost of hard-to-wire environments while providing the high throughput and low latency needed to support wireless voice, video, and data applications. Strix's Access/One solutions provide scalable, reliable wireless connectivity in both indoor enterprise deployments as well as in the emerging outdoor public safety, municipal, and metropolitan Wi-Fi marketplace.

Symmetricom

http://www.symmetricom.com

Symmetricom is a leading worldwide supplier of atomic clocks and network synchronization and timing solutions. The company designs, manufactures, markets and provides services for products used in wireline and wireless network synchronization; space, defense and avionics systems; enterprise networks; and broadband networks in telecom, government and enterprise markets. Symmetricom is based in San Jose, California, with offices worldwide.

Syntronic AB

http://www.syntronic.se

Syntronic is a prominent design house specializing in services in electronics, electromechanics, and technical and administrative software. As an established design house Syntronic can provide a valuable contribution to our customers and help them to get their products on the market cost-efficiently and at the right time. We offer solutions where we take full responsibility from idea to finished system. The customer will also get access to our modern and complete design and verifying environments. Among our assigners are some of the world's most technique-intensive businesses and organizations in branches such as Telecommunication, Vehicle, Defense, Medicine and Public Sector.

TDC Solutions

http://www.tdc.dk

TDC is a leading provider of communications services in Denmark. We are the leading provider of landline, mobile, and data communications services, and we operate Denmark's largest cable TV business. TDC is also the leading provider of voice and data equipment in the Danish market and is involved in a number of other telecommunications activities.

Tektronix

http://www.tektronix.com

Tektronix, Inc., is a test, measurement, and monitoring company providing measurement solutions to the communications, computer, and semiconductor industries worldwide. With more than 55 years of experience, Tektronix enables its customers to design, build, deploy, and manage next-generation global communications networks and advanced technologies. Headquartered in Beaverton, Oregon, Tektronix has operations in 19 countries worldwide.

Telabria

http://www.telabria.com

Telabria develops and deploys next-generation wireless networks for residential, business, and enterprise markets. Telabria networks utilize multihop NLOS mesh technology operating at 2.4G Hz and 5.8 GHz, offering scalable networking where existing solutions are uneconomical or technically nonviable. Telabria solutions are currently being deployed in private and public sector markets, including schools, public libraries, museums, local government buildings, and public transportation centers.

TelASIC Communications

http://www.telasic.com

TelASIC is an analog/mixed signal radio front-end IC company that offers the world's highest-performance Analog to Digital (A/D) and Digital to Analog (D/A) converters, as well as other semiconductor products that enable next-generation communications systems. The company's chipsets and system-level solutions enable the industry's most power-efficient and cost-effective single carrier and multicarrier cellular base-stations, repeaters and WiMax base stations.

Telcordia Technologies

http://www.telcordia.com

Telcordia Technologies, Inc., is a leading global provider of telecommunications network software and services for IP, wireline, wireless, and cable. As the industry continuously evolves, Telcordia is focused on being the premier transformation partner for its customers. By delivering flexible, standards-based software solutions and consulting services that optimize complex network and business support systems, Telcordia helps customers transform their operations while aggressively reducing their costs and increasing their revenues. Telcordia is headquartered in Piscataway, NJ, with offices throughout the United States, Canada, Europe, Asia, and Central and South America.

TeleCIS Wireless

http://www.telecis.com

TeleCIS Wireless, Inc., is a Silicon Valley–based, fabless IC Company focused on developing highly integrated wireless chipsets for the communications market. The company was founded in January 2000 and has developed IEEE 802.11a/b/g chipsets. TeleCIS is currently developing and commercializing performance-leading WiMAX-compliant chipsets, followed by mobility chipsets based on the emerging IEEE 802.16e standard. Combined TeleCIS solutions will address the Fixed, Stationary and Mobile Broadband Wireless Markets and provide seamless connectivity anywhere and anytime in the most cost-effective manner available.

Telecom Italia

http://www.telecomitalialab.com

Telecom Italia Lab is the R&D branch of the Telecom Italia Group. A thousand researchers work together to increase innovation and deliver value to clients of the Group, developing advanced solutions. A center of excellence since 1964 in networks and services, Telecom Italia Lab took part in the definition and consolidation of the GSM standard, MP3 and optical transmission. Today it goes on creating innovation through direct experience in the planning of fixed and mobile access networks, supporting the evolution of the transport network, developing platforms and services, and prototyping next generation terminals. Through its laboratories Telecom Italia Lab responds to today's needs of users and industries. Telecommunications will be a key factor to be competitive in the world market.

Telecom Technology Center

http://www.ttc.org.tw

"Visions of creating a world-class national certification center to support Taiwan's ICT industry and developing a knowledge-based economy." TTC, a nonprofit organization established by the government in February 2004, is focusing on cutting-edge technology in the information, telecommunications and broadcasting sectors as well as Taiwan's telecom policy and regulatory framework. TTC has established Taiwan's first common criteria testing laboratory with the intention to build up other ICTs' testing and certification capacities, e.g., IOT, WiMAX, and DTV.

Telediffusion de France

http://www.tdf.fr

Group TDF places at the disposal of televisions, radios and operators of telecommunications its competencies as a service provider. It exploits infrastructures dedicated to these activities in France, Monaco, Finland, Spain, Poland and Estonia. TDF also develops services of multimedia information in the field of intelligent transport and Internet broadcasting. TDF exploits and maintains nearly 7,000 sites, including 850 abroad. This requires permanent work for renewal (change of pylons), improvement of customer service (management of access, reliability of energy sources), and maintenance (painting, snow clearance of access). TDF also completes work necessary to the reception of the new points of audiovisual or telecommunications services of its customers.

Telelink AD

http://www.telelink.bg

TeleLink is a leading system and solution integrator in the Bulgarian telecommunications market. Established in 2001, TeleLink has developed significant technological competencies in the turnkey rollout of mobile networks and the integration of strategic network solutions for the national incumbent telecom operator. TeleLink's business strategy focuses on the development and implementation of solutions and services based on Next Generation Network concepts.

Telenor

http://www.telenor.com

Telenor R&D is the research department of Telenor, which is Norway's largest telecommunications group, with 23,450 employees (14,150 of them in Norway) at the outset of 2003. About 200 researchers are currently working in the corporate R&D department. Telenor R&D participates extensively in international as well as national research projects and in international standardization. The R&D activities focus on providing integrated solutions to business, residential and individual markets, with a main focus on broadband and mobility.

TeliaSonera

http://www.teliasonera.com

The Nordic and Baltic telecommunications leader TeliaSonera also holds strong positions in mobile communications in Russia, Eurasia and Turkey. TeliaSonera offers customers services in mobile communications, Internet, data communications and fixed telephony. TeliaSonera International Carrier offers wholesale IP and voice services, as well as high-capacity bandwidth to destinations in Europe and across the Atlantic.

Telkom SA

http://www.telkom.co.za

Telkom SA Limited is South Africa's leading integrated communications group and provides total solutions across the full spectrum of digital communications to a diverse customer base. The network is fully ATM-enabled and can provide voice and data links across a number of technologies both local and in destinations worldwide. The company also offers a wide range of digital services, including data hosting, state-of-the-art network security, full Internet services, an e-marketplace and a full range of PBXs and value-added communication products.

Tellabs

http://www.tellabs.com

Tellabs (NASDAQ: TLAB) delivers technology that transforms the way the world communicates. Tellabs experts design, develop, deploy and support wireline and wireless solutions. Our comprehensive broadband portfolio enables carriers in more than 100 countries to succeed in the new competitive environment. Tellabs is part of the NASDAQ 100 Index.

Telsima

http://www.telsima.com

Telsima Inc. is a leading developer of converged network solutions. Telsima's products provide next generation multimedia capability while fitting seamlessly with legacy network deployments, providing converged broadband for all carriers worldwide that are migrating to a practical unified network model of TDM and multiservice packet delivery in access and metro networks.

Telus

http://www.telus.com

TELUS (TSX: T, T.NV; NYSE: TU) is the largest telecommunications company in western Canada and the second largest in the country, with

$7.5 billion in annual revenue, 4.8 million network access lines and 3.8 million wireless customers. The company provides customers with a full range of telecommunications products and services, including data, voice and wireless services across Canada, utilizing next generation Internet-based technologies.

The Cloud Networks

http://www.thecloud.net

The Cloud is a leading pan-European provider of wireless broadband services. Founded in 2003, it is today Europe's leading Wi-Fi hotspot operator with over 6,500 sites in the United Kingdom, Germany and Scandinavia. The Cloud is a multiservice provider platform that allows providers such as ISPs, mobile operators and cable companies to offer a fully branded wireless broadband experience to their customers across a pan-European footprint. The Cloud also works with the world's leading technology vendors to develop new wireless applications and services for deployment by its service provider customer base.

TietoEnator

http://www.tietoenator.com

TietoEnator is one of the leading architects in building a more efficient information society. TietoEnator has close to 4,500 consultants working with telecom assignments, with customers from all parts of the industry value chain, ranging from content providers to operators and manufacturers of telecom networks and mobile devices. The goal is to be the leading supplier of high-value-added IT and R&D services to the telecom and media sector in Europe, working globally with international customers.

Time Warner Telecom

http://www.twtelecom.com

Time Warner Telecom Inc., headquartered in Littleton, Colorado, is a leading provider of managed network solutions to a wide array of businesses and organizations in 44 U.S. metropolitan areas that require telecommunications-intensive services. One of the country's premier competitive telecom carriers, Time Warner Telecom integrates data, dedicated Internet access, and local and long distance voice services for long distance carriers, wireless communications companies, incumbent local exchange carriers, and such enterprise organizations as health care, finance, higher education, manufacturing, hospitality, state and local government, and military.

TNO Information and Communication Technology

http://www.telecom.tno.nl

TNO is an independent and nonprofit consultancy and product development organization in the Netherlands with about 5,500 employees. TNO Information and Communication Technology is a division (about 450 employees) working on telecommunication issues in the widest sense. Its key competence concerns technological expertise and technology and product development skills. TNO ICT has its own laboratories with various access networks, service platforms and a customer home environment. The expertise covers fixed (xDSL, FTTH, WiMAX, HFC), nomadic (WiFi, WiMAX) and mobile (GSM, GPRS, UMTS, HSDPA) access networks.

Tollgrade

http://www.tollgrade.com

Tollgrade is a leader in access network test and management, testing 150 million POTS and broadband lines and 75% of the HFC plant in North America. Traditional networks are now being leveraged to deliver a full range of IP-based services. With this comes the challenge of managing multilayered network performance and remotely isolating troubles. Tollgrade is extending its leadership position in network service assurance by investments in research to remotely isolate and diagnose service impairments over multilayered IP networks.

TowerStream

http://www.towerstream.com

TowerStream is a fixed wireless broadband provider in the Northeast. TowerStream delivers high-speed Internet access to commercial bandwidth users through its second-generation point-to-multipoint fixed wireless broadband networks.

Trackwise

http://www.trackwise.co.uk

Trackwise is one of the world's leading manufacturers of antennas using printed circuit technology. ISO 9001:2000– and ISO 14001:1996–accredited. From very small chip-sized terminal antennas through patch and panel antennas to the very largest GSM base station antenna or FSS (frequency selective surface), Trackwise is focused on specialized manufacturers using PTFE, FR4 and flexible substrates. Our products are exported worldwide; our service is customer-driven. Trackwise also offers a turnkey antenna assembly service.

TRDA
http://www.trda-inc.com

TRDA Inc. (Taiyo Yuden R&D Center of America) was established in October 2001 by its parent company, Taiyo Yuden Co., Ltd., an industry leader in global standards of passive electronic components, advanced wireless communication module and optical recording media. TRDA Inc. is a world-class, independent R&D organization that provides core technologies and experience to its corporate technology partners. TRDA Inc. draws on the same advanced material science, industry-leading multiplayer fabrication processes and other proprietary technologies that Taiyo Yuden Co., Ltd., pioneered and perfected to help thousands of satisfied customers accelerate their time to market and new product development efforts.

Trillion
http://www.trillion.net

Trillion is a leading provider of wireless broadband services, high-speed Internet access and IP telephony solutions for the public sector, including education, health care, government and libraries. Trillion specializes in designing, installing, operating and maintaining wide and local area network systems that use state-of-the-art wireless technology.

TriQuint Semiconductor
http://www.triquint.com

TriQuint Semiconductor, Inc., is a leading supplier of high-performance products for communications applications. Markets include wireless phones, base stations, optical networks, broadband and microwave, and aerospace and defense. Its products are based on advanced process technologies, including gallium arsenide, indium phosphide, silicon germanium, and surface acoustic wave (SAW). TriQuint has manufacturing facilities in Oregon, Texas, Pennsylvania and Florida and production assembly plants in Costa Rica and Mexico.

Tropos
http://www.tropos.com

Tropos Networks is the leading supplier of systems used to build metro-scale Wi-Fi networks. Tropos's unique Wi-Fi cells enable providers to deliver ubiquitous, citywide mobile broadband to users in any locale. These IP networks are low-cost and easy to install and scale. The Tropos cellular mesh architecture and use of optimized open-standard radios dramatically reduce the need for wired backhaul while eliminating

expensive proprietary clients. Using the patented Predictive Wireless
Routing Protocol, Tropos delivers maximum bandwidth to the user
regardless of conditions, at unprecedented network scale.

Tulip IT Services

http://www.tulipit.com
Tulip IT Services Ltd. is a service provider specializing in providing VPN
connectivity in major cities as well as rural areas of the United States. It
provides intercity bandwidth on fiber, and the last mile is completely on
wireless. It is setting up this network to cover most major cities of the
country. With 600 employees at over 35 locations, Tulip provides the
highest levels of services with near off-the-shelf connectivity.

UNITLINE

http://www.unitline.ru
UNITLINE is the WISP company that provides wireless access to the
Internet. UNITLINE has its own basic cellular network. The company
works in 11 regions of Russia. The company provides end users with
connection to the Internet through radio-based lines, including all
major services commonly provided by all ISPs: e-mail, access, web-site
publishing, hosting, etc. The existing network continues to develop and
improve, and one of the directions being considered is WIMAX technologies.

Unwired Australia

http://www.unwiredaustralia.com.au
Unwired is an Australian company dedicated to building a nationwide
fixed wireless telecommunications network offering carrier-grade Broadband services and voice services in the future.

Urmet Telecomunicazioni Spa

http://www.urmet.it
Telecommunication is Urmet Tlc's core business. The Urmet Tlc mission
is to provide this market with reliable and cost-effective solutions. The
Urmet Tlc strategy is to leverage competence centers (in the form of divisions and companies that specialize in specific product lines/technolo-
gies) as well as the capability to create and deliver both integrated and
open solutions tailored to the Customer's need by focusing on local
requirements. Its product portfolio includes Messaging and Video
Phones, E-Payment, Broadband Modems, Payphones, Kiosks, CO POTS
Splitters, VAS Platforms, Wireless Solutions, and Lawful Interception.

Urmet is directly present with subsidiaries in more than 20 countries and through Partners in more than 25 additional countries.

UTStarcom
http://www.utstar.com

UTStarcom is a global leader in IP-based end-to-end networking solutions and international service and support. The company sells its broadband, wireless, and handset solutions to operators in both emerging and established telecommunications markets around the world. Founded in 1991 and headquartered in Alameda, California, the company has research and design operations in the United States, China, Korea and India.

VCom Inc.
http://www.vcom.com

VCom Inc. (formerly known as WaveCom Electronics Inc.) is a leading designer and manufacturer of high-quality, state-of-the-art products for the Cable Television (CATV), Data over Cable, Digital Video, and Broadband Wireless industries.

Vectron International
http://www.vectron.com

Vectron International (VI) is a world leader in the design, manufacturing and marketing of Frequency Generation and Frequency Control products. Vectron uses the latest technology in both crystal and surface acoustic wave (SAW)-based designs from DC to microwave frequencies. With facilities in the United States, Europe and China, the company manufactures products that fulfill critical functions in the telecommunications, data communications, wireless, military, satcom and multimedia markets in both consumer and industrial applications worldwide.

Venturi Wireless
http://www.venturiwireless.com

Venturi Wireless is the most widely used provider of 3G mobile broadband optimization solutions in the world. Global wireless operators and enterprises rely on Venturi Wireless's patented solutions to increase wireless data speeds by up to 7 times and reduce network traffic by up to 70 percent. Venturi's solution ensures reliable, consistent and high-performance service to all users regardless of network conditions. The company's technology allows users to dependably access email, Web content and business applications at broadband speeds almost anywhere mobile phone service is available.

VeriSign

http://www.verisign.com

VeriSign Inc (NASDAQ: VRSN) operates intelligent infrastructure services that enable people and businesses to find, connect, secure, and transact across today's complex global networks. We operate the systems that manage .com and .net, handling 14 billion Web and e-mail look-ups every day. We run one of the largest telecom signaling networks in the world, enabling services such as cellular roaming, text messaging, caller ID, and multimedia messaging. We provide managed security services, security consulting, strong authentication solutions, and commerce, e-mail, and antiphishing security services to over 3,000 enterprises and 400,000 Web sites worldwide. In North America alone, we handle over 30 percent of all e-commerce transactions, securely processing $100 million in daily sales. By leveraging our world-class infrastructure and robust platform set to deliver our deep portfolio of services, VeriSign can provide unmatched security, interoperability, reliability, adaptability and rapid, scalable deployment around the world, all within an economically efficient business model.

Vivato

http://www.vivato.com

Vivato is a wireless network infrastructure company and manufacturer of Broadband Wireless base stations for service providers. Adhering to the IEEE 802.11 and 802.16 standards, Vivato's PacketSteering technology changes the old rules of Broadband Wireless deployment by delivering unprecedented range and capacity with enterprise-class security.

Warpera

http://www.warpera.com

Warpera is a well-funded start-up based in Silicon Valley that is dedicated to delivering leading-edge products that dramatically lower the cost of entry for new revenue-generating services. Our team has extensive experience and a proven track record of developing quality products for both cable and telecom industries. Warpera's mission is to deliver cost-effective, innovative solutions that enable service providers to offer broadband data, voice, and interactive video services by using their existing cable and wireless infrastructures.

Wavesat Wireless Inc.

http://www.wavesat.com

Wavesat Wireless Inc. is a fabless semiconductor company focused on the development and supply of OFDM modem chips for the Broadband Wireless (BWA) markets, both backhaul and access. The DM110 OFDM chip, based on the recently approved IEEE 802.16a standard, is the first of its kind in the world. It delivers proven non-line-of-sight (NLOS) performance for next generation BWA systems, with a large cyclic prefix, the highest spectral efficiency (5 bps/Hz), the best error correction and the best synchronization, all achieved through patented technology.

WFI

http://www.wfinet.com

WFI is the world's largest independent provider of systems engineering, network services and technical outsourcing for wireless carriers, enterprise customers and government agencies. The company provides the design, deployment, integration, and management of wired and wireless networks that deliver voice and data communication and support advanced security systems.

Wi-LAN

http://www.wi-lan.com

Wi-LAN is a global provider of broadband wireless communications products and technologies. Wi-LAN specializes in high-speed Internet access, data network extension, and wireless data and telephony backhaul, utilizing its high-quality products and industry-leading technologies.

Wi-MAN

http://www.wiman.com.au

Wi-MAN is Australia's premier distributor of carrier-class and WiMAX-class Point to Point and Multipoint systems. Wi-MAN also has coverage in New Zealand, Fiji and Papua New Guinea. We bring a unique range of best-of-breed technologies and techniques to our customers, which include the largest carriers in the country down to the smallest.

WiMAX Telecom AG

http://www.wimax-telecom.net

WiMAX Telecom AG of Switzerland is the parent company of WiMAX Telecom GmbH in Austria. Our Austrian subsidiary acquired through an auction the only nationwide frequencies for WiMAX services in Austria. Other players have acquired locally more limited licenses. All these licenses are in the 3.5-GHz spectrum. WiMAX Telecom GmbH of Austria was scheduled to begin operation in 2005.

WiNetworks
http://www.winetworks.com
WiNetworks is a leading supplier of hybrid 802.16 multimedia systems. The WiNetworks solutions enable broadband network operators to upgrade their existing infrastructure to a full Triple-Play offering, including telephony, data and video services and future mobile service support.

Wintegra
http://www.wintegra.com
Founded in January 2000, Wintegra is a fabless semiconductor company that enables communications companies to build the next generation of access networks around a family of single-chip solutions. Its WinPathT access packet processor family offers best-in-class aspects of network processors, communications processors, communications peripherals and ASICs, creating a new approach to protocol handling. Wintegra products have been shipping into production networks since 2002. Its customer list includes most of the largest communications companies in the world—companies like Ericsson, Tellabs, Marconi and Lucent.

WirelessLogix
http://www.wirelesslogix.com
WirelessLogix is a global leader in providing innovative measurement solutions that allow network carriers to more efficiently enhance performance and maximize network capacity, therefore helping carriers get a quicker return on their investment and increased profitability. Combining years of pioneering experiences and expertise, WirelessLogix provides a full range of comprehensive measurement products and services to help wireless network carriers offer subscribers better quality and more practical communications experience to ensure their satisfaction.

Wong's International (USA)
http://www.wongswec.com
Wong's International Co. Ltd and its affiliates Emerging Technologies Limited (ETL) and Wireless Dynamics Inc. (WDI) are a one-stop solution

provider in the design, development and manufacturing of advanced consumer electronics products based on emerging technologies such as GSM, GPRS, Wi-Fi and Bluetooth. Our mission is to become an innovator in wireless and mobile consumer electronics by increasing the values vested in emerging communication technologies. We are committed to develop differentiating products and becoming the leading company in providing mobile devices such as mobile handsets, smartphones, and Bluetooth headsets for the consumer electronics market.

Xilinx

http://www.xilinx.com

Xilinx leads one of the fastest-growing segments of the semiconductor industry: programmable logic devices (PLDs). Xilinx develops, manufactures, and markets a broad line of advanced integrated circuits, software design tools and intellectual property (predefined system-level functions delivered as software cores). Customers use automated tools and intellectual property from Xilinx and partners to program chips to perform custom logic operations. Xilinx PLDs offer a potent solution to the growing challenges of embedded DSP systems.

Z-Com

http://www.zcom.com.tw

Z-Com, Inc., is a leading global solution provider dedicated to the research, design, development, and manufacturing of wireless data solutions for broadband wireless Internet access as well as various mobile data applications. Headquartered in Science-Based Industrial Park of Hsinchu, Taiwan, or what is commonly known as Taiwan's Silicon Valley, since 1995, Z-Com has outshined the competition by focusing on its goal, which is to deliver quality high-performance and yet cost-effective wireless networking end devices to our OEM/ODM customers.

ZTE Corporation

http://www.zte.com.cn

Headquartered in Shenzhen, China, ZTE Corporation is the largest public telecommunications equipment manufacturer in China. It develops and manufactures end-to-end wireless and wireline equipment, and solutions for various telecommunications markets. With nearly 16,000 employees worldwide, ZTE has several R&D facilities in China, North America and Europe and Sales Offices in over 50 countries.

Summary

All of these companies share a common goal: ensuring the success of WiMAX as a broadband wireless access solution. After reading through the descriptions of their various missions, it is clear that they buy into the WiMAX message and have enrolled to make it a reality. Although WiMAX is not yet mature or widely deployed, trials to date have been successful and equipment certification continues.

WiMAX has had an intriguing history, but its cycle of development is far from finished. Although it enjoys the warm glow of multiple successes from its many trials, a significant cadre of professionals believes that it is overhyped and will never realize its advertised potential. There are definitely challenges ahead. One of the most vexing has to do with spectrum. 700 MHz is one region of the electromagnetic spectrum that has been earmarked for WiMAX use. However, in the United States, that set of frequencies is currently occupied by television and is not available globally. The 2.3-GHz band, also not available globally, is highly fragmented in the United States and therefore less than ideal for an application such as WiMAX, which requires contiguous spectrum for ideal functionality.

The 2.5-GHz band has been completely restructured in the United States for uses such as WiMAX, but it is not widely available on a global basis. 3.5 GHz is preferred on a global basis, but naturally, it is not available in the United States. Finally, the 5.8-GHz band is unlicensed in most of the world and therefore is available, but because it is unlicensed, it cannot be guaranteed against interference in the same way that licensed spectrum can.

Is WiMAX in trouble? All the spectrum challenges might lead one to think so. However, the long list of companies that support its future seems to indicate otherwise. Like any new technology, WiMAX will hit its share of speed bumps along the way to implementation, high-volume deployment, and success. However, as the trials continue and as the standards—and the resulting products—evolve, it will be more widely accepted. Furthermore, as WiMAX takes its place alongside other new technological innovations, most notably IMS, its success will not only be assured but accelerated.

Figure 2-12 illustrates the intended evolution of WiMAX, beginning in 2005. Note that as time passes and the technology advances, a couple of things happen. First, the standard goes from being primarily a fixed solution for backhaul applications to a full-fledged mobility solution in

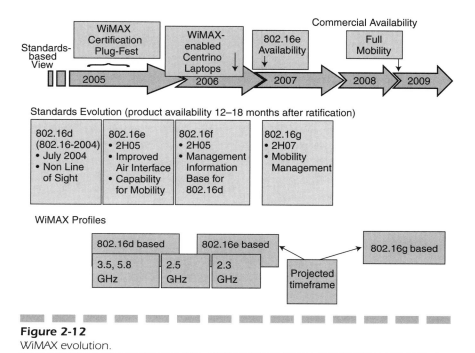

Figure 2-12
WiMAX evolution.

the 2008 time frame. Note also that in addition to the development, ratification, and release of technology standards, IEEE releases standards that deal with service management, OSS, and management information (MIB) delivery. In other words, WiMAX is being viewed not just as a wireless technology but as a full-service solution that demands and deserves management capability.

Stand by. There's more to come.

CHAPTER 3

How WiMAX Works

Fasten your seat belts. In this chapter we dive deeply into the functional workings of Worldwide Interoperability for Microwave Access (WiMAX), beginning with a technical exploration of the 802.16 standard and the group that developed it.

802.16 Development

The organization responsible for the design and development of broadband wireless access standards is the Institute of Electrical and Electronic Engineers (IEEE) 802.16 Working Group on Broadband Wireless Access. As one might expect, the group's original mandate was to develop a collection of new physical layer specifications for broadband wireless service delivery as well as whatever modifications were required to ensure interoperability with the basic media access control (MAC) scheme. Through a series of enhancement releases to the original 802.16 document, that committee has added support for a range of operational frequency domains as well as a specific standard that addresses a fixed wireless option ("Recommended Practice for Coexistence of Fixed Broadband Wireless Access Systems") in the form of 802.16.2.

The 802.16 committee was "born" in August 1998 during a National Institute of Standards and Technology (formerly the National Bureau of Standards) meeting initiated by the National Wireless Electronics Systems Testbed (N-WEST) subcommittee. As a result of the work conducted during that event, the IEEE 802 committee created a new study group for broadband wireless activities: number 16. Incidentally, the 802 committee is called 802 because it was created in February 1980.

Time passed. Since 1999, the 802.16 committee has conducted bimonthly meetings that last approximately a week, with very high interest being shown by the participants—as many as 700 of them, in fact.

Why 802.16?

The original IEEE 802.16-2001 standard, which defined the Wireless-MAN air interface specification for wireless metropolitan area networks, was ultimately completed in October 2001 and published in early April 2002. Its primary purpose as a standard and ultimately as a technology offering is to deliver network access to enterprise and residence customers via a secure broadband wireless facility.

802.16 is quite precise in its description of the intended capability. It specifies that network access will be achieved by means of external antennas connected to central base stations, offering a connectivity alternative to wired broadband options. Because wireless solutions such as 802.16 can provide service to a large geographic area without the need to spend inordinate quantities of capital expense (CAPEX) and operating expense (OPEX) cash in the process, it may turn out to be a less expensive service delivery option than its wired predecessors and may become the solution for broadband delivery in areas that are challenged by distance, population density, or topologic difficulties.

Once the wireless signal has been received at the building that houses the customer, the customer connects its preexisting in-building network to the wireless access point. In the future, however, it will be possible to connect directly to the 802.16 signal since the chipsets ultimately will be cheap enough to install in laptops and perhaps even in personal digital assistants (PDAs). In effect, the base station will connect to the laptop or PDA by relying on a single MAC layer to "erase" the problems associated with different physical layers, thus ensuring adequate quality of service (QoS) and viable connectivity. As later versions of 802.16 emerge, most notably 802.16e, mobility—indeed, *global* mobility—will become a viable usage option.

802.16 Basics

When the 802.16 standard emerged, it had a single clear mission: to define the evolutionary path for a set of air interfaces that would be based on a common MAC protocol that would support multiple physical layer specifications according to spectrum availability, in-country usage restrictions, deployment cost, and so on. The original standard specifies usage of spectrum in the range of 10 to 66 GHz; that range was chosen largely because that particular frequency domain is widely deployed globally. However, because of the short wavelength of the resident signal (this is microwave, after all), the signal at this range of the spectrum band presents unique transmission challenges that must be dealt with; this explains the choice of Orthogonal Frequency Division Multiplexing (OFDM) as part of the developing specification. With the arrival of 802.16a, the air interface was expanded to include frequencies between

2 and 11 GHz, opening the standard to usage options in both licensed and unlicensed (sometimes called *license-exempt*) bands. This lower-frequency range offers a cheaper operating cost, but typically at the expense of bandwidth, although not to the extent that the cost becomes prohibitive.

The technology that underlies 802.16 and ultimately WiMAX is now at a high level of development. Let's spend a few pages on the inner workings of the technology, beginning with the MAC layer. For the purpose of this discussion, I make the assumption that the reader is somewhat familiar with Asynchronous Transfer Mode (ATM) switching, because a basic understanding of what it is and how it works is important for a discussion of service delivery in the 802.16 domain. For readers who are unfamiliar with the technology, contact me and I'll direct you to good resources.

The 802.16 Media Access Control Layer

Actually, let's begin with a definition of MAC. Media access control does exactly what its name implies: It controls access to whatever physical transmission medium is being used by the device that wishes to transmit. The functionality of the MAC layer typically is built into the network adapter device and always includes a unique address (the MAC address) that identifies the machine that houses the network adapter. Typical MAC layer standards include Carrier Sense Multiple Access with Collision Detection (CSMA/CD), Token Ring, Fiber Distributed Data Interface (FDDI), and Manufacturing Automation Protocol (MAP). The MAC layer resides at layer 2 (the data link layer) of the Open Systems Interconnection (OSI) model (see Figure 3-1).

The 802.16 MAC protocol was designed with a number of required characteristics in mind. First, it was created to handle the demands of point-to-multipoint broadband wireless applications. Within that definition, it also was designed to provide very high, full-duplex (i.e., uplink and downlink) bandwidth, with that bandwidth being capable of being parceled out across a collection of channels with hundreds of users in each channel. Additionally, users place varying demands on the channels they are allocated; this translates into a requirement to support traditional voice and data services as well as packet-based Voice over Internet Protocol (VoIP) and other Internet Protocol (IP) data services.

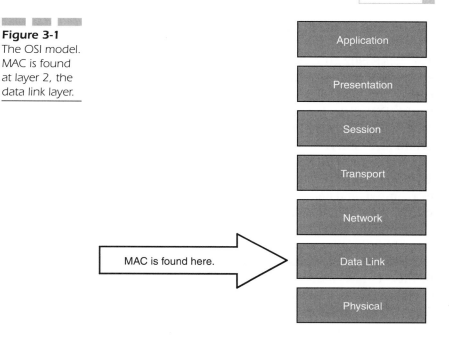

Figure 3-1
The OSI model.
MAC is found
at layer 2, the
data link layer.

Application

Presentation

Session

Transport

Network

MAC is found here.

Data Link

Physical

The MAC, then, must be able to handle the demands of both constant bit rate (CBR) and bursty traffic and must support variable QoS as demanded by the user community. Consequently, the 802.16 MAC offers variable ("definable") service to satisfy the disparate requirements of different traffic types. In many ways it is analogous in its functionality to ATM as well as to Guaranteed Frame Rate (GFR) service. GFR is basically ATM Unrestricted Bit Rate (UBR) with Minimum Cell Rate (MCR), which in effect is "UBR+." It is a frame-based service that relies on traffic shaping and cell loss priority control to achieve the required QoS.

Because it initially was envisioned as a fixed backhaul solution, the MAC protocol supports a range of backhaul options, including packet-based service requirements and ATM. As with ATM, a variety of convergence sublayers map transport-specific traffic to whatever MAC is most appropriate to handle the type of traffic being moved. These convergence sublayers rely on a number of features to ensure the achievement of minimal QoS levels, including Payload Header Suppression, fragmentation, and packing. These features are described in the section that follows. Although this book is not about ATM, the ATM protocol plays a significant role in the deployment of 802.16, as is detailed in *IEEE 802.16.1 Convergence Sublayer for ATM.*

ATM and 802.16

The IEEE 802.16 ATM Convergence Sublayer (CS) sits on top of the 802.16 Media Access Control (MAC) Common Part Sublayer (CPS). The CS accepts ATM cells from the ATM layer and delivers CS Protocol Data Units (PDUs) to the appropriate MAC-CPS service access point. The MAC-CPS creates a MAC header, which facilitates the delivery of appropriate MAC Service Data Units (SDUs) to its peer on the basis of QoS requirements. The CS receives and accepts ATM cells from the ATM layer, classifies them according to performance criteria, processes them as required, and delivers them to the correct service access point. This is illustrated in Figure 3-2.

A few gory details must be mentioned here. First, Figure 3-3 assumes that the subscriber devices are connected to a variety of network types and to a base station that in turn is connected to an ATM-based backhaul facility. It also assumes that an ATM Network-to-Network Interface (NNI) is implemented at the base station, that a User-to-Network Interface (UNI) is implemented at the subscriber terminal, and that some form of interworking function is available if the user is connecting to an ATM network from a non-ATM network. It also should be noted that the

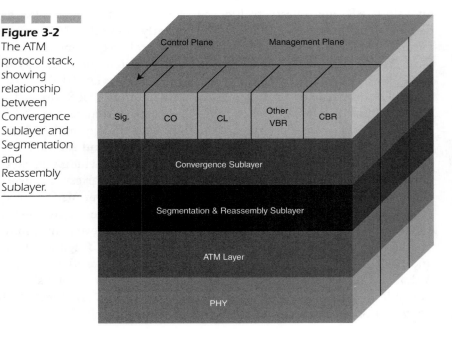

Figure 3-2
The ATM protocol stack, showing relationship between Convergence Sublayer and Segmentation and Reassembly Sublayer.

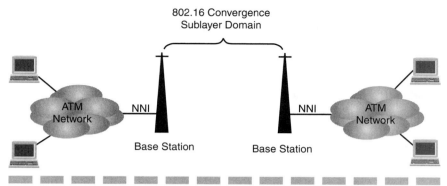

Figure 3-3
Typical network layout showing area of influence of Convergence Sublayer.

type of network to which a subscriber terminal is connecting is implementation-specific and that the protocol that performs switching and routing functions is dependent on the type of network over which it is implemented.

The convergence process described above is shown in Figure 3-4. The ATM layer creates ATM cells and passes them on to the Convergence Sublayer. If Payload Header Suppression is activated, the cell headers are suppressed. Payload Header Suppression is a technique in which repetitive portions of the payload header are suppressed by the trans-

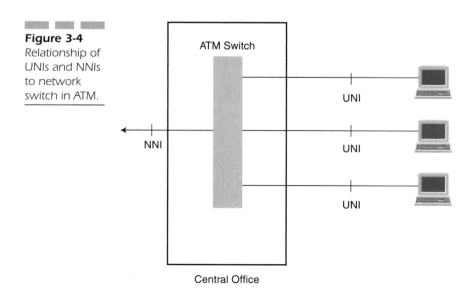

Figure 3-4
Relationship of UNIs and NNIs to network switch in ATM.

mitting device and restored by the receiving device. On the downlink side, the transmitting device is the ATM CS on the base station and the receiving entity is the ATM CS on the subscriber terminal. On the uplink side, the sending entity is the ATM Convergence Sublayer on the SS and the receiving entity is the ATM CS on the base station. To save additional bandwidth, multiple ATM cells from the same connection can be packed within a single MAC PDU payload.

Note also that when Payload Header Suppression is deactivated, no part of an ATM cell header can be suppressed, including error correction. This ensures that there is an option available for protecting the integrity of the cell header.

At any rate, when suppression is activated, the information fields in the cell headers required to reconstruct them on the other end are mapped to the MAC PDU header or encapsulated within the MAC PDU payload.

Service Definitions

The ATM CS supports the convergence of higher-layer PDUs that are created by ATM networks. Since ATM cell flows are generated according to well-accepted ATM standards, no ATM CS service primitive is required.

Service Switching

ATM connections are identified by the combination of a Virtual Path Identifier (VPI) and a Virtual Channel Identifier (VCI). These connections can be switched in either of two ways: They can be Virtual Path (VP) switched or Virtual Channel (VC) switched. In the Virtual Path (VP) mode, all the VCIs contained in a VPI are automatically mapped to another VPI; in Virtual Channel (VC) mode, in contrast, combined VPI/VCI values are mapped to output VPI/VCI values. As a result, when it is performing Payload Header Suppression, the ATM CS must be able to distinguish between these two connection types and perform the suppression accordingly.

In VP switched mode, the VPI field for a subscriber station that is connected to an ATM network is mapped to the 16-bit Connection Identifier

(CID) for a MAC connection. Since the connection parameters for QoS and class of service are set at connection time, this mapping of VPI to CID guarantees that the data will be handled correctly by the MAC layer.

In VC mode, the VPI and VCI fields are mapped to the 16-bit CID for the MAC connection over which they are carried. Because the QoS and class of service parameters for the connection are established when the connection is established, this mapping of the VPI and VCI to the CID guarantees that the data will be managed correctly by the MAC layer.

Payload Header Suppression for Virtual Path Connections

In VP mode, the VPI is mapped to a CID, allowing the remainder of the ATM cell header apart from the VCI, Payload Type Indicator (PTI), and Cell Loss Priority (CLP) fields to be discarded. The VCI is encapsulated within the MAC PDU payload, and the PTI field and the CLP bit are mapped to the CS Pass-Through field and the Payload Discard Eligibility bit of the MAC-CPS PDU header, respectively.

Had enough? No? Figure 3-5 shows the structure of a MAC-CPS PDU that contains a single VP-switched ATM cell with its cell header suppressed. Figure 3-6 shows the alternative structure of multiple VP-switched ATM cells in packed mode with the cell headers suppressed.

Figure 3-5
Structure of a
MAC-CPS PDU
that contains a
single VP-
switched ATM
cell with its cell
header
suppressed.

MAC Header CPT=PTI PDE=CLP	PDU Payload (50 bytes) One VCI + One ATM Payload

Figure 3-6
Structure of a
MAC-CPS PDU
that contains
multiple VP-
switched ATM
cells.

MAC Header CPT=PTI PDE=CLP	PDU Payload (n*50 bytes) N* [VCI + ATM Payload]

Payload Header Suppression for Virtual Channel Connections

In VC switched mode, the VPI/VCI combination is mapped to a CID. This allows the ATM cell header to be disposed of except for the PTI and CLP fields. Those fields are mapped to the CPT (Convergence Sublayer Pass-Through) field and the PDE (Packet Discard Eligibility) bit of the MAC-CPS PDU header, respectively. Figure 3-7 shows a single VC-switched situation, and Figure 3-8 shows the same thing for multiple VC-switched cells.

By now we have determined that you are (1) a glutton for technological self-flagellation or (2) suffering from a serious sleep disorder. You want more? Here it comes.

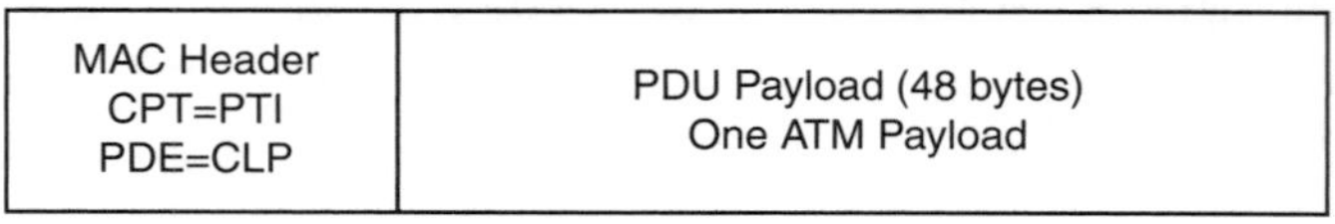

Figure 3-7
Structure of a
MAC-CPS PDU
that contains a
single VP-
switched ATM
cell.

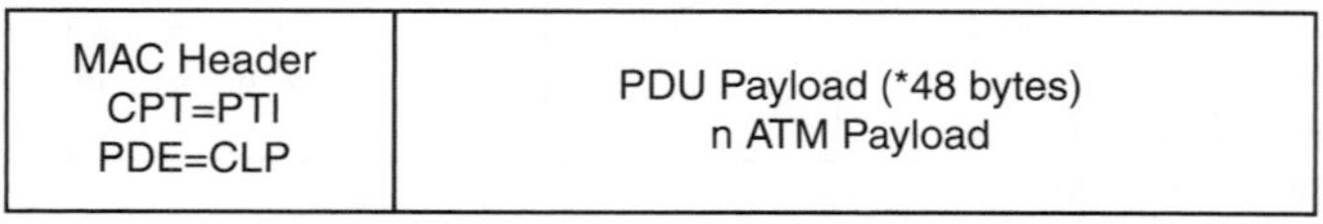

MAC Header CPT=PTI PDE=CLP	PDU Payload (48 bytes) One ATM Payload

Figure 3-8
Structure of a
MAC-CPS PDU
that contains
multiple VP-
switched ATM
cells.

MAC Header CPT=PTI PDE=CLP	PDU Payload (*48 bytes) n ATM Payload

It's amazing that a 3-bit field in any protocol could have so much responsibility, but that is definitely the case in ATM with the PTI field. The second PTI bit, which is located in the cell header, is called the *Explicit Forward Congestion Indication* (EFCI) bit. If an ATM cell carries user data (in which case the first PTI bit will be set to 0), the EFCI bit is used to indicate the presence of congestion in the forward direction. With Payload Header Suppression, the EFCI bit is mapped to the second bit of the Convergence Sublayer Pass-Through. When the packing option is turned on, however, and to determine the value of the second bit of the CPT field when this is the case, the value is the result of applying a logical OR operation on all EFCI bits from all ATM cell headers contained in the MAC-CPS PDU. Put more simply, as long as at least one of the cells in the PDU has an EFCI set to 1, the corresponding bit in the CPT will also be set to 1. This allows ATM cells with different values of EFCI to be packed into a single MAC-CPS PDU to notify the receiver collectively about a congestion condition.

PDU Formats

There are three distinct PDU formats for ATM connections *without* Payload Header Suppression, VP-switched ATM connections *with* Payload Header Suppression, and VC-switched ATM connections with Payload Header Suppression. These formats are illustrated in Figure 3-9. In the case of ATM connections without Payload Header Suppression, the SDU and PDU formats are the same (naturally). For VP-switched ATM connections with Payload Header Suppression, the ATM header is suppressed and the 50-byte PDU payload includes a 2-byte VCI and a 48-byte ATM payload. Finally, for VC-switched ATM connections with Payload Header Suppression, the ATM header is suppressed and no additional information is contained in the PDU payload.

Back to 802.16

802.16 supports a range of backhaul options that include both packet and circuit-type services. As we have described, a variety of Convergence Sublayers map traffic to the appropriate MAC, ensuring efficient and effective transport. When Payload Header Suppression, fragmentation,

ATM Header 5 Octets	ATM Cell Payload 48 Octets

PDU for ATM connections without Payload
Header Suppression.

VCI 2 Octets	ATM Cell Payload 48 Octets

PDU for VP-switched ATM connections with Payload
Header Suppression.

ATM Cell Payload 48 Octets

Structure of a PDU for VC-switched ATM connections
with Payload Header Suppression.

and packing are invoked, traffic often can be carried more efficiently than it was on its home network.

In addition to bandwidth allocation and data transport, the MAC has a privacy sublayer that offers access and connection establishment authentication to avoid service theft and supports encryption and key exchange to ensure data privacy and confidentiality. Because 802.16 is a wireless standard and therefore is subject to the service vagaries of the wireless interface, 802.16a enhances the MAC to offer Automatic Repeat Request (ARQ) for error detection and correction and support for mesh topologies in addition to point-to-multipoint to ensure network survivability.

The 802.16 Physical Layer (1 to 66 GHz)

In early discussions about broadband wireless technology, it was decided that some form of line-of-sight technique was a requirement for many application types. In the range of 10 to 66 GHz, a single-carrier modulation technique was specified, now referred to as *WirelessMAN-SC*. In practical application, the base station transmits a time division multiplexing (TDM) signal, allocating serial timeslots to each subscriber terminal on the point-to-multipoint facility. Uplink access uses time division multiple access (TDMA), and both time division duplex (TDD) and Frequency Division Duplex (FDD) burst modes are supported across the access facility. Half-duplex FDD is also supported.

The 802.16 Physical Layer (2 to 11 GHz)

Both licensed spectrum and unlicensed spectrum are found in the range of 2 to 11 GHz, and both are discussed in detail in the IEEE 802.16a documentation. The overall design of the 2- to 11-GHz physical layer is based on the clear demand for a non-line-of-sight option. This came about because of a realization on the part of standards developers that residence application of 802.16 would encounter multipath propagation issues because of trees and other signal obstacles.

Three air interface specifications for 802.16a are described in the original standard. They are WirelessMAN-SC2, which relies on a single-carrier modulation scheme; WirelessMAN-OFDM, which relies on OFDM with a 256-point transform scheme with TDMA access, which is mandatory for unlicensed bands; and WirelessMAN-OFDMA, which uses OFDMA with a 2048-point transform. Here, multiple access is provided by targeting a subset of the various subcarriers to individual receiving devices.

Because of the high frequencies selected for 802.16 and the resulting propagation issues that occur that high in the microwave world, 802.16 supports the use of advanced antenna systems. This technique, which sometimes is called diversity reception, is a method in which the signal is transmitted over different propagation paths. This is done by using multiple receive antennas or multiple transmitting antennas. For the best results, the antennas typically are located one wavelength apart, and because of the wavelength of signals below the microwave band, this technique typically is not used for systems that operate in the submicrowave domain as a result of the distance required between antennas.

The Physical Layer

The 10- to 66-GHz physical (PHY) layer relies on a single-carrier modulation scheme with adaptive burst profiling; this means that the modulation and coding schemes can be adjusted individually for each user device on a frame-by-frame basis. The standard also specifies both TDD and burst FDD operating schemes.

In the United States, the standard specifies channels of 20 or 25 MHz, whereas 28-MHz channels are defined for European operators. Forward error correction (FEC) operations rely on Reed-Solomon GF(256), with this function's inherent variable block size and error correction capabilities. This is combined with a convolutional code to guarantee the transmission of critical data content such as frame control parameters and initial access queries. FEC operations are combined with Quadrature Phase Shift Keying (QPSK), 16-state Quadrature Amplitude Modulation (16QAM), and 64-state QAM (64QAM) to control transmission efficiency. If the final FEC block is not filled at the time of transmission, it can be shortened by the base station in both the uplink and downlink directions. If this operation is performed, it is communicated to the other end in the Uplink Map (UL-MAP) and the Downlink Map (DL-MAP).

The 802.16 PHY specifies a frame duration of 0.5, 1, or 2 ms. It is divided into timeslots for bandwidth allocation and identification of PHY transitions. A timeslot is defined by four QAM symbols; when TDD is used, the uplink subframe follows the downlink subframe (see Figure 3-10) on the same carrier frequency. In FDD operations, the uplink and the downlink coincide in time but use separate transport frequencies.

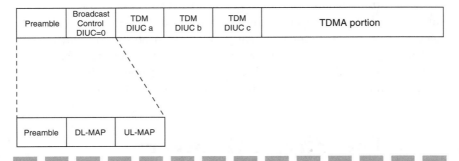

Figure 3-10
The downlink subframe structure.

▓▓▓ The Downlink Subframe

The downlink subframe begins with a frame control region that includes the DL-MAP for the current downlink frame as well as the UL-MAP for some specified future period. The DL-MAP specifies when modulation and FEC changes occur in the downlink subframe. Typically, the downlink subframe includes a TDM-specific portion immediately after the frame control section.

Data on the downlink are transmitted to each subscriber station by relying on a negotiated burst profile. The data are transmitted in decreasing "robustness" to permit the station to receive the data correctly, minimizing the possibility of receiving a burst profile that could cause the station to lose downlink synchronization.

In situations in which FDD is employed, the TDM portion of the frame can be followed by an additional TDMA preamble field that provides additional support of half-duplex terminal devices. This is necessary because in some circumstances in which numerous half-duplex terminals are deployed in an efficiently scheduled FDD environment, a station may be required to transmit earlier than it receives. In normal systems, this could result in the loss of link synchronization because of the half-duplex nature of the facility. The additional TDMA preamble field allows the device to regain synchronization, thus avoiding the need to retrain it on the carrier.

Because of diverse application requirements, the breadth and duration of burst profiles (as well as the lack or presence of the additional TDMA preamble) may vary widely from frame to frame. Because the receive device is implied in the MAC header rather than in the DL-MAP, subscriber devices "listen" to or monitor all components of the downlink subframe they are capable of receiving. In full-duplex mode, this requires them to receive all burst profiles with robustness equal to or greater than their own.

An uplink subframe for the 10- to 66-GHz PHY is shown in Figure 3-11. Here the UL-MAP assigns bandwidth to individual subscriber stations; this is different from the procedure followed on the downlink. Stations transmit within their allocated space by using the burst profile defined by the Uplink Interval Usage Code (UIUC) in the UL-MAP that gave them access in the first place. The UIUC is used to allocate timeslots on a case-by-case basis.

The uplink subframe also can include contention-based allocations for initial access and to handle requests for broadcast or multicast band-

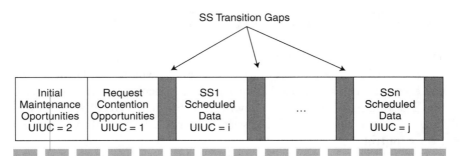

Figure 3-11
The uplink subframe structure.

width. For initial system access, opportunities are sized in such a way that they allow additional time for subscriber devices that have not yet resolved the transmit time advance required to overcome the round-trip delay between the user station and the base station.

Transmission Convergence Sublayer

Described in detail earlier in this chapter, the Transmission Convergence Sublayer lies between the MAC and the PHY. It converts variable-length MAC PDUs into fixed-size FEC blocks within each burst. The Transmission Convergence Sublayer PDU fits within the FEC block that is in the process of being filled. It begins with a pointer that indicates the start of the next MAC PDU header in the FEC block (see Figure 3-12). If unrecoverable errors result in loss of synchronization, the format of the Transmission Convergence Sublayer PDU allows it to synchronize itself with the next MAC PDU. Without the capabilities of the Transmission Con-

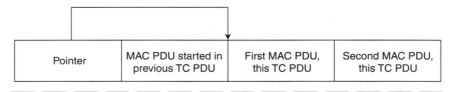

Figure 3-12
Format of Transmission Convergence Sublayer PDU.

vergence Sublayer, an unrecoverable error could result in the loss of the rest of a burst upon arrival at either the base station or the user's device.

Medium Access Control— and Friends

Are you crying uncle yet? No? Then let's continue. Within the MAC is a function called the Common Part Sublayer that is responsible for performing the critical MAC functions. However, the MAC also includes service-specific convergence sublayers that talk to higher-layer services that reside above the Common Part Sublayer. *Below* the Common Part Sublayer is the previously mentioned Privacy Sublayer.

Service-Specific Sublayers

802.16 defines two service-specific convergence sublayers that are used to map services to MAC connections. The first is the ATM Convergence Sublayer that was described earlier, and the second is a Packet Convergence Sublayer that is used for IP, Ethernet, and virtual local area network (VLAN) service environments. The goal of this particular sublayer is to categorize or classify SDUs and point them at the proper MAC connection, ensure that QoS requirements are met, and ensure that proper bandwidth allocation takes place. This mapping process varies with the type of service being handled. As was described in an earlier section of this chapter, a collection of additional capabilities such as Payload Header Suppression, packing, and fragmentation can be employed to boost link efficiency when required.

The 802.16 Common Part Sublayer

The MAC for 802.16 deployments is designed to handle the requirements of point-to-multipoint network environments in situations in which a central base station handles multiple simultaneous transmission regions. On the downlink side, data transmitted to user devices are multiplexed by using traditional TDM techniques. On the uplink side, the uplink is shared among user devices that wish to transmit by using a "round-robin" TDMA mechanism similar to that used in the early digital cellular phone systems.

The 802.16 MAC is a connection-oriented mechanism. All the services it is capable of dealing with—including those which are connectionless in nature, such as IP—are mapped to a specific connection. This ensures the availability of a procedure for requesting bandwidth, associating specific QoS requirements with a particular connection, and routing data to the appropriate convergence sublayer. Connections are identified with 16-bit connection identifiers and in some cases may require either continuous bandwidth or bandwidth on demand. Both work.

As one would expect, every subscriber station has a standard 48-bit MAC address that is used as a device identifier, since the primary address is the CID. Once the user's device is connected to the network, it is assigned three management connections in each direction that represent the three different QoS requirements of the various management levels. The first is a basic connection that is used for the transfer of short, time-critical MAC and facility control messages. The second connection is used to transfer management messages such as those from Dynamic Host Configuration Protocol (DHCP), Trivial File Transfer Protocol (TFTP), and Simple Network Management Protocol (SNMP) applications. The third (primary) connection is used for longer, delay-tolerant messages such as authentication and connection setup signaling.

Subscriber stations are also allocated connections for subscribed services. Transport connections are designed to be unidirectional to improve the granular control and distribution of various uplink and downlink QoS and traffic parameters and typically are assigned to subscribed services in pairs.

The MAC also can reserve connections for other purposes. One connection is reserved for contention-based initial access. Another is reserved for broadcast across the downlink and to broadcast signaling requests in contention-based polling environments.

The MAC PDU Format

From basic data communications, you will recall that the PDU is the data that are passed between the communicating entities, in this case

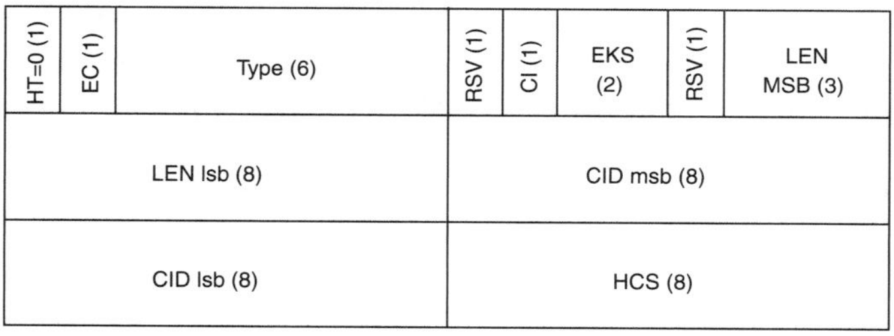

Figure 3-13
Header for
MAC PDU.

HT=0 (1)	EC (1)	Type (6)	RSV (1)	CI (1)	EKS (2)	RSV (1)	LEN MSB (3)
LEN lsb (8)			CID msb (8)				
CID lsb (8)			HCS (8)				

between the base station and the user terminal. In 802.16, the MAC PDU (see Figure 3-13) consists of a fixed-length header, a variable-size payload field, and a cyclic redundancy check (CRC) field that is optional. Two header formats are available and are differentiated by the Header Type (HT) field. The first is the standard header, and the second is the bandwidth request header. Other than the bandwidth request PDUs, all MAC PDUs transport either convergence sublayer data or management messages.

In addition to the standard headers, three MAC subheaders have been defined. The *grant management subheader* communicates bandwidth management requirements to the base station. The *fragmentation subheader* carries information that indicates the presence of SDU fragments in the payload. The *packing subheader* indicates whether multiple SDUs have been "packed" into a single PDU.

The grant management and fragmentation subheaders can be inserted immediately after the generic header if the Type field indicates that they should be present. The packing subheader can be inserted before each SDU if the type field indicates a need for its presence.

PDU Transmission

As we have seen, 802.16 supports a variety of higher-layer protocols, including ATM and IP. Inbound SDUs are formatted according to the format requirements of the PDU, with fragmentation or packing if required, before they are transmitted as dictated by the MAC protocol. After crossing the access "facility," the PDUs are reconstructed into the original SDUs to ensure that the format changes that were performed by the transmitting MAC are not seen by the receiving process.

It is interesting to note that 802.16 combines the packing and fragmentation processes with the bandwidth allocation process to take the greatest advantage of the flexibility, efficiency, and effectiveness of all these processes. Fragmentation defines the process by which an SDU is divided into one or more MAC SDU fragments; packing is the process by which multiple MAC SDUs are carried within a single MAC PDU payload. Both processes can be invoked by either a base station on the downlink side or a user station on the uplink side.

Frame Structure

The 802.16 MAC, which supports both TDD and FDD, supports a variety of transmission modalities. In FDD operation, both continuous and burst mode downlinks are available. Continuous downlinks facilitate the availability of a variety of transmission enhancement techniques, whereas burst downlinks allow the use of more advanced techniques, including capabilities such as subscriber-level adaptive burst profiling and the use of advanced antenna systems, as was described earlier in this chapter.

Building the Frame

The MAC constructs the downlink subframe, beginning with a frame control section that contains the DL-MAP and UL-MAP content. These maps indicate PHY transitions on the downlink and bandwidth allocations and burst profiles on the uplink. The DL-MAP always applies to the current frame and is always a minimum of two FEC blocks long. The first PHY transition is carried in the first FEC block to allow adequate processing time. In both TDD and FDD environments, the UL-MAP facilitates allocations that begin no later than the next downlink frame. In contrast, the UL-MAP can begin its allocation process in the current frame as long as processing times and round-trip delay limitations are met.

Radio Link Control in 802.16

Link control in 802.16 is somewhat complex if for no other reason than the fact that PHY must transition constantly between disparate burst profiles.

Link control starts with an occasional base station broadcast of the burst profiles that have been selected for uplink and downlink. The profiles that are used on any specific channel are selected on the basis of known environmental conditions, equipment limitations, and so on. The profiles for the downlink are labeled with a *Downlink Interval Usage Code* (DIUC), and the uplink profiles are tagged with an *Uplink Interval Usage Code* (UIUC).

When network access begins, the user device engages in a series of activities that include power leveling and signal ranging by using a series of RANGING-REQUEST messages. The results of these exercises are returned to the terminal through the use of using RANGING-RESPONSE messages. The base station also may occasionally transmit RANGING-RESPONSE messages to the user's terminal, ordering it to make adjustments to its power or timing settings.

During the initial ranging process, the user terminal requests downlink service by using a specific burst profile and transmitting its selected DIUC to the base station. The device selects its DIUC on the basis of the results of the testing done during the initial start-up phase. The base station has the option of confirming or rejecting the request.

The base station also monitors the uplink signal quality from each user's device. If that quality declines, the base station has the ability to direct the user terminal to use a specific uplink burst profile by including the profile's UIUC with the user terminal's grants contained in the UL-MAP messages.

Once the initial burst profiles have been selected by the combined efforts of the base station and the user terminal, the link control process continues to monitor and control the selected burst profiles, because network conditions could change, resulting in an inferior communications environment or in some cases better conditions that result in the ability to use (at least temporarily) a better, more efficient profile. Because the base station is the primary device in the connection between the two, the procedure for modifying the uplink burst profile is straightforward. The base station simply specifies the profiles that are associated with a UIUC whenever it grants bandwidth to the user device in a frame. This removes the requirement for an explicit acknowledgment since the user device will always receive the UIUC and grant together—or receive nothing at all. There is therefore no chance that a burst profile mismatch can occur between the base station and the user device.

On the downlink side, the user device monitors the quality of the received signal and as a result knows when its selected downlink burst profile should be modified. However, the base station is the primary device and is therefore in charge of whatever changes take place. Two techniques can be used by the user device (the subscriber station) to request a burst profile modification, depending on whether the user device operates in Grant per Connection (GPC) or Grant per Subscriber Station (GPSS) mode. In GPC mode, the base station occasionally allocates a *station maintenance interval* to the subscriber station. During that interval, the user device can transmit a Downlink Burst Profile Change Request (DBPC-REQ), which causes the base station to respond with a Downlink Burst Profile Change Response (DBPC-RSP) that either confirms or denies the change, similar to the procedure described earlier.

Change Control

Messages can be lost irretrievably as a result of serious bit errors, and so the procedure for requesting a change to a downlink burst profile must be designed and monitored carefully. The order of events used in changing to a more robust profile is quite different from the chain of events employed to go in the other direction. The 802.16 standard relies on the fact that the user device is always required to listen not only to its own profile but to any profiles on the downlink that are more robust. This is shown in Figure 3-14.

Scheduling Services

In the uplink direction, each connection is mapped to a scheduling service, and each of those services is associated with a set of rules that the base station scheduler is required to use for allocating uplink facility capacity and controlling the request-grant protocols between the end user device and the base station. When connection setup is negotiated between the two endpoints, the specific rules are applied. Interestingly, the scheduling services used in 802.16 are the same scheduling services specified in the Data over Cable System Interface Specification (DOCSIS) standard for cable modems.

Occasionally applications emerge that generate fixed volumes of data on a repeating, periodic basis. *Unsolicited Grant Service* (UGS) is designed for these types of applications. In UGS environments, the base

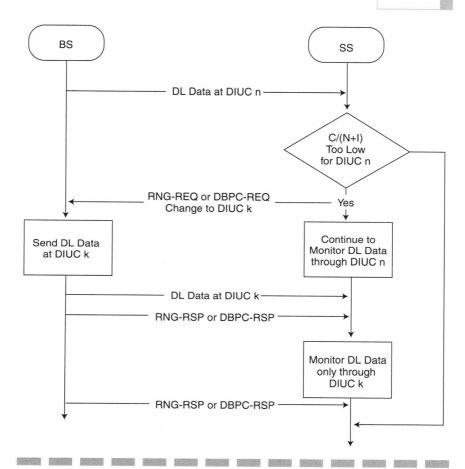

Figure 3-14
Transition between burst profiles.

station schedules service grants on a periodic basis according to the details negotiated at the time of the initial setup. This removes the overhead and delay associated with repeated setup procedures in a situation in which the requirements do not change and are completely predictable. Applications that fall into this domain include TDM over ATM and ATM CBR service.

When UGS is invoked, the Grant Management Subheader includes the poll-me bit and the Slip Indicator Flag. The flag allows the subscriber station to tell the base station that there is congestion on the upstream side of the facility. When the base station receives a Slip Indicator Flag, it has the option to allocate additional capacity to the user device, giving it the breathing room it needs to recover from what one hopes is a transient event.

The *real-time polling service* is designed for dynamic services but also offers occasional dedicated request opportunities to meet the requirements of real-time situations such as VoIP, streaming video, and streaming audio. The *non-real-time polling service* is virtually identical to the real-time polling service except for the fact that connections can use random access transmission opportunities to send bandwidth requests. Services and applications that rely on this service are typically less sensitive to delay and jitter than are their real-time counterparts.

The standard also defines a "best effort service" that makes no guarantees about delay or throughout. When required, the subscriber station transmits a bandwidth request in random access slots or in one of the dedicated transmission opportunities. However, because the frequency of dedicated opportunities is a function of network load, the user device cannot count on their availability.

Support for Grants and Bandwidth Requests

The 802.16 MAC supports two classes of subscriber stations. These device classes are based on their ability to accept bandwidth for a single connection or for the overall subscriber device. Both classes request per-connection bandwidth to permit the base station uplink scheduling rules to consider QoS requirements correctly when allocating requested bandwidth. The GPC class implies that bandwidth is granted explicitly to a connection, and the subscriber station uses the granted bandwidth for that connection only.

Under the rules of the GPSS class of devices, subscriber terminals are granted bandwidth as well, but it is aggregated into a single large grant for the entire device. This implies that the terminal operating in GPSS mode must be able to allocate bandwidth intelligently as required to the various connections it supports.

These differing classes of subscriber stations allow a balance to be maintained between the simplicity of the GPC class and the bandwidth management efficiency of the GPSS class.

It should be noted that GPSS is the only class of subscriber station that is allowed to be used with the 10- to 66-GHz PHY.

For both grant classes, the 802.16 MAC relies on a "self-correcting protocol" rather than the more common acknowledged protocol simply because the former requires less bandwidth. Acknowledged protocols also introduce considerable delay. Although this discussion seems to assume that requests for bandwidth always are granted, that is not the case. Reasons for failure to allocate requested bandwidth include the possibility that the base station did not have the requested bandwidth available or failed to see the request because of a PHY error or collision, the subscriber station failed to see the grant because of a PHY error, and the subscriber station, operating in GPSS mode, used the bandwidth for another purpose.

The self-correcting protocol described above works like any other protocol. After a period of predetermined delay, the connection times out and the subscriber station simply resubmits its request.

Bandwidth can be requested by the subscriber station in a variety of ways. For applications with continuous bandwidth requirements such as ATM CBR service, the station is not required to solicit bandwidth; it is granted without question. For reasons of efficiency, a station that is operating in UGS can take advantage of the poll-me bit in the header to notify the base station that it needs a bandwidth allocation on another connection. If it is set up properly, the base station may conserve bandwidth by choosing to poll stations *only* when they have set the poll-me bit.

A more traditional technique for bandwidth requests is to transmit a bandwidth-request MAC PDU to the base station that consists of nothing more than the bandwidth request header and an empty payload field. Stations operating in GPSS mode can transmit this request by using any bandwidth allocation they receive. Terminals in GPC mode can transmit the request in a request interval or in a data grant interval that is granted to their connection. Similarly, a grant management subheader can be used to "piggyback" a bandwidth request for the same connection within a MAC PDU.

The base station also has the option of sending a broadcast poll instead of a single station by allocating a request interval (as described earlier) to the broadcast CID. 802.16 supports the formation of multicast groups to increase the granularity of station selection for contention-based polling environments.

Because of the unpredictable delay caused by traffic-generated collisions and retries, contention-based requests are permitted only for connections with a lower class of service requirements.

Channel Initialization and Acquisition

Because manual configuration is a time-consuming and error-prone process and because 802.16 is by definition a highly dynamic environment, the MAC protocol defines an initialization procedure that eliminates the need for such configuration. When a subscriber station is installed, it begins scanning its known frequency list to find a functional channel. On the basis of the configuration, it may have instructions to register with a specific base station by seeking a base station identifier that each base station broadcasts. After selecting a channel or channel pair, the station attempts to synchronize to the downlink facility by listening for and synchronizing with the periodic frame preamble signatures. Once synchronized, the subscriber station listens for the Downlink Channel Descriptor (DCD) and Uplink Channel Descriptor (UCD) messages that are transmitted periodically as broadcasts and tell the station the details it needs to know about the modulation and error correction schemes that are in use.

Once it learns the details it must have for its initial ranging efforts, the station seeks initial ranging opportunities by scanning the UL-MAP messages that arrive with every frame. The subscriber station uses an algorithm that is similar in function to that used for collision control in CSMA/CD to determine which initial ranging timeslot it will use for its initial ranging message. The station will send the burst of information by using a low-power setting and will continue to transmit at higher and higher power levels if it fails to receive an immediate response to its ranging requests. Then, based on the arrival time of the initial ranging request and the power of the signal, the base station issues a timing advance and a power adjustment to the subscriber station specified in the ranging response. The response also provides the station with the basic and primary management CIDs it needs to be minimally functional from a network management perspective. Finally, the station uses ranging to tweak the power, perfecting the parameters of the channel.

Next on the list is efficiency setting. Until now, all transmissions have used the least efficient burst profile. To avoid wasting capacity on an ongoing basis (it's fine for start-up, but after that, efficiency in networks is everything), the subscriber station reports its PHY capabilities, including the encoding and modulation schemes it supports and whether it operates in half-duplex or full-duplex (assuming that the station operates in an FDD environment). The base station then responds, accepting or denying the request for service as the situation demands.

▰▰▰ Security Considerations

Needless to say, any wireless access methodology, particularly a broadband solution, requires strong security protocols to keep customers happy and comfortable with regard to the privacy and confidentiality of their transmitted data. 802.16 incorporates very robust security protocols. Each subscriber station is associated with a manufacturer-installed X.509 digital certificate as well as the unique certificate of the manufacturer. Those certificates are sent to the base station by the subscriber station in the Authorization Request and Authentication Information messages and are used to establish a connection between the subscriber station's 48-bit MAC address and its public Rivest, Shamir, and Adleman (RSA) key.

The network can verify the identity of the device by checking the validity of the certificates and then verify the access level authorization of the device. As long as the device is authorized to join the network, the base station responds to the request with an authorization response that includes an Authorization Key (AK) that is encrypted with the subscriber station's own public key and that will be used to secure all future transactions. Once authorized, the station registers with the network. This establishes the secondary management connection that is used to determine connection requirements and MAC operation details. At the same time, the IP version information is exchanged to ensure compatibility. After registration, the subscriber station receives an IP address via DHCP, which also provides the address of the TFTP server from which the station can request the configuration file that provides the vendor-specific information it requires for full functionality.

To guarantee that network resources are used in the most efficient manner possible, 802.16 uses a two-stage activation technique. With this technique, network resources are not committed until the service flow is fully activated, at which point each active flow is mapped to a MAC connection through the use of a unique CID.

For the most part, service flows in 802.16 are preprovisioned, and service flow setup is initiated by the base station during initialization of the subscriber station.

Service flows also can be established dynamically by the base station and the subscriber station, although the subscriber station typically initiates service flows only in situations in which there is a dynamically signaled connection such as an ATM switched virtual circuit (SVC). 802.16 also supports dynamic service modifications in which negotiated service flow parameters are renegotiated.

The privacy capabilities of 802.16 are based largely on the Private Key Management (PKM) protocol that is inherent in the DOCSIS BPI+ specification. PKM is based on a series of Security Associations (SAs), which are cryptographic techniques and their associated keys. During initialization, the subscriber station uses at least one SA, and each connection (except for the basic and primary management connections) is mapped to an SA at start-up or dynamically.

PKM relies on X.509 digital certificates and RSA public key encryption for authentication and authorization. Traffic is encrypted by using a 56-bit (or greater) Data Encryption Standard (DES), and keys are exchanged using 3DES.

The PKM protocol messages are authenticated with the Hashed Message Authentication Code (HMAC) protocol, using Secure Hashing Algorithm (SHA-1). Finally, message authentication, when required, relies on the PKM protocol.

Summary

In this chapter we first took a look at the birth of the original IEEE 802.16 committee before discussing the series of 802.16 standards that the committee published. We then went into the workings of the air interface that makes the protocol (and WiMAX) work. After reading this chapter, you should have a good idea how elegant a protocol it is.

In Chapter 4 we examine applications. After all, this protocol stuff is interesting, but what good is it if it doesn't do something useful?

CHAPTER

4

WiMAX Applications and Services

Demand for broadband services is growing at an increasing rate, and broadband rapidly is becoming a necessity for the enterprise and residence markets. Wireless delivery of broadband is introducing a new degree of flexibility and universal connectivity, ushering in the new era of "personal lifestyle" technology applications.

One of the newer technologies that are seen as central to the ongoing success of service delivery via broadband wireless is Worldwide Interoperability for Microwave Access (WiMAX). Although still early in its development and deployment, it shows promise as a cost-effective, flexible, globally applicable, and relatively future-proof technology that will integrate well with other new entrants, such as wireless fidelity (WiFi), Internet Protocol television (IPTV), and Internet Protocol Multimedia Subsystem (IMS), all of which are centered on the delivery of anywhere, anytime content to mobile enterprise and consumer users.

Judging from manufacturers' directions, it is widely anticipated that WiMAX initially will be deployed as a delivery mechanism for high-end enterprises, offering Digital Subscriber Line (DSL) and cable modem–like service over a wireless facility (Figure 4-1). It will also have initial usage as a backhaul technology for wireless hotspots, a role currently played primarily by DSL. By mid-2007, the role of WiMAX will expand to what has come to be known as personal broadband services that can be tailored to lifestyle choices, meeting the demands of an increasingly mobile and content-dependent society. Personal broadband deployments will deliver bandwidth to mobile devices at levels ranging from 2 to 10 Mbps and will have follow-me capability that will make distance and location immaterial. This is the promise of both WiMAX and IMS, and the market is primed and ready.

Other applications for WiMAX are equally intriguing. Cellular telephony sites have always relied on conventional point-to-point microwave facilities (Figure 4-2) for signal backhaul to the central office and connectivity to the wireline network. These facilities have always been designed and deployed on the basis of full radio line-of-sight (LOS) between the towers, because traditional microwave is too easily interrupted by foliage, buildings, and weather. As functional as it is, it needs all the help it can get. WiMAX can be deployed in a cellular-like fashion that includes small regions called microcells and picocells. These regions typically are used in situations in which overcapacity exists or there are service holes that need to be filled. WiMAX also can be used for backhaul traffic management, in which case a traditional copper or optical backhaul facility can offload traffic to an 802.16 facility as the need arises. Third-generation (3G) mobile systems, which rely on a combination of

Internet Protocol (IP) routing and a T1 or E1 backhaul, can use a WiMAX point-to-multipoint connection, the deployment of which can be a very cost-effective alternative.

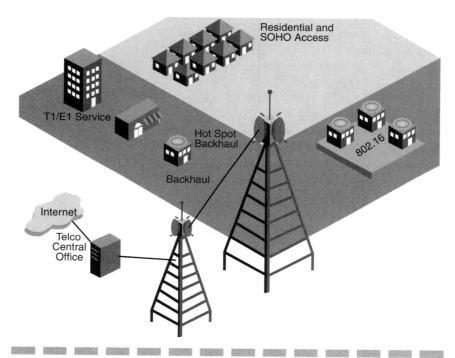

Figure 4-1
Delivering broadband services over WiMAX.

Figure 4-2
Using conventional microwave for backhaul.

Many of the WiMAX products that are appearing on the market for early deployment have both T1/E1 and IP interface support and are therefore ideal for enterprise applications. For example, a WiMAX base station with support for both interfaces can be used to provision time division multiplexing (TDM) bandwidth quickly for enterprise voice applications [such as connectivity requirements for a corporate private branch exchange (PBX)] and high-speed data applications, both of which represent potentially lucrative profit centers or highly effective cost-reduction opportunities.

Perhaps the most visible WiMAX opportunity is the ability to offer what has come to be known as "wireless DSL." Using primarily 802.16d-based devices, service providers are beginning to offer wireless broadband by taking advantage of compliant devices that offer full broadband connectivity with the performance of DSL and the flexibility of WiMAX, a very interesting combination, indeed.

Finally, let's not forget about WiMAX's predecessor, WiFi. Service offerings that combine the best of WiFi and WiMAX are beginning to appear, with WiFi providing hotspot connectivity for mobile users and WiMAX providing high-speed backhaul between the hotspot and the central office. The most intriguing aspect of this scenario is the potential for the creation of a new form of service provider. Consider the following: A WiMAX service provider (let's invent a new acronym, BISP, for broadband Internet service provider) hires a market analysis firm to determine the ideal location for its product or service. The result of the analysis is that the BISP should set up shop across the street from the airport. Why? Because clustered around the airport is a collection of business traveler–oriented hotels, all of which offer broadband connectivity in their guest rooms and all of which must pay for a wired connection, either a T1/E1 or a DSL line, to connect them to the wireline carrier. Along comes our BISP with the promise of equal or greater bandwidth, lower cost, and greater flexibility. By putting up a WiMAX base station in the area (Figure 4-3), the BISP can provide connectivity to the hotels as an alternative to their captive relationship with the local service provider, but just as important, it will be in place when WiMAX-enabled laptops start to appear and travelers begin looking for broadband wireless connections.

The residence market will see equally intriguing applications of WiMAX as a first-mile solution. Consider SBC's fiber-to-the-curb optical buildout. When a WiMAX base station is put in place and connected to the optical termination point, broadband wireless becomes an alternative to DSL and cable for residents in the area (Figure 4-4). Furthermore,

Figure 4-3
A WiMAX
antenna
mounted on a
spire can
provide service
to a large area.
Courtesy
MaxRad
Corporation.

Figure 4-4
WiMAX can
easily serve as
an alternative
local loop.

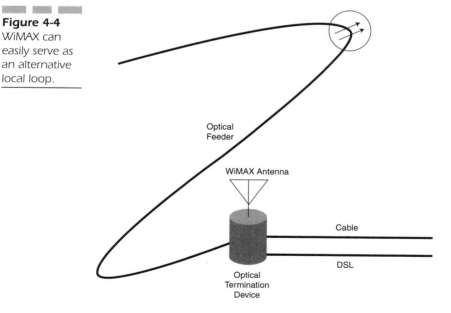

Optical
Feeder

WiMAX Antenna

Cable

DSL

Optical
Termination
Device

manufacturers selling WiMAX-capable routers such as the AirSpan
device shown in Figure 4-5 will be able to network all the home devices
over the broadband connection.

Figure 4-5
A WiMAX
router.
Courtesy
AirSpan Corp.

The Arrival of Mobility

Imagine being able to drive at a high rate of speed while staying connected to a broadband facility. Okay, that would be illegal. Imagine instead being a passenger in a car moving at high speed while still being connected, as I was in my description in Chapter 1 of my first experience with WiMAX in Raleigh-Durham. With the arrival of 802.16e, which adds mobility and roaming to the existing WiMAX standard, the rules of the wireless road change in a big and significant way. Bandwidth at levels as high as 10 Mbps will be available to roaming devices, allowing them to support applications such as gaming, interactive video, broadband content download in real time, and high-quality music delivery, along with a host of other so-called lifestyle choices. As long as we are on the subject of lifestyle choices, let's discuss the most powerful lifestyle change agent to come along in a long time: the Millennials. I discuss them here because they, more than any other sector of the population, will drive the success of WiMAX. Defined as people born between 1982 and 2004, they are a technology-centered yet inordinately social generation.

The Millennials

Millennials are strongly influenced by and dependent on communications technologies. They are the first generation in history to grow up in a world that has always had the Internet, the World Wide Web, and mobile telephony. To this generation a wired telephone is a hindrance, and they are disconnecting them at a frightening rate (especially if you happen to be a service provider), relying instead on mobile devices. Predictably, Millennials' preferred communications techniques are Short Message Service (SMS) and Instant Messenger (IM), along with e-mail; if they absolutely have to, they'll talk on a phone, but it better not be tethered.

Millennials enjoy group activities and in fact perform best in cooperative teams. As individuals they do not test well in problem-solving situations, yet they test *off the charts* in groups. Even in social situations they prefer larger groups. If you ever have the opportunity to attend a Millennial high school dance, do so just for the experience. They don't dance in couples; they dance in *clusters*. They don't date in pairs either; they date in large groups, enjoying the camaraderie of their peers.

This grouping phenomenon has considerable implications in the workplace. Millennials are remarkable problem solvers when allowed to do so in groups. They often subconsciously use a mobbing theme to resolve conflicts and problems that to biologists is reminiscent of the technique used by honeybees to make collective hive decisions about nest locations, flower availability, predator avoidance, and the like. When confronted with a problem, Millennials collectively analyze the problem, individually analyze the data, and then gather to make the decision collectively. All ideas "go into the discussion pot," and the discussion ensues. If an idea is deemed invalid, irrelevant, or simply wrong, it is discarded instantly and emotionlessly. It can always come back into the discussion later. As a result, the "fact tree" is pruned rapidly, and a decision is reached equally rapidly. Individuals may peel off at a moment's notice to call or SMS a friend or colleague to ask a question, extending the knowledge web that produces the most accurate answer.

This behavior is a living example of Metcalfe's law, which states that the value of a connected network increases exponentially as a function of the number of nodes in the network. If the network is a Millennial decision-making process, it is easy to see why this technique is so functional. It is also easy to see why a Baby Boomer or Generation-X manager watching this process might wonder what in the world is going on, because to the unschooled eye it looks an exercise in unbridled chaos. Baby Boomers and Gen-Xers were taught to respect the laws of linear thinking, whereas Millennials are nonlinear problem solvers. Managers beware: Just because they don't approach a problem the way you would, that doesn't mean they're ineffective or off-track. It also means that their behavior as customers and competitors will be substantially different from the norm to which we have become accustomed. They will use every means at their disposal, most of them electronic and immediate, to employ their knowledge web to gather intelligence about a product or service. Recognize also that this behavior of using the web of connectivity that is an inextricable component of their lives feeds directly into the IMS concept: anywhere, anytime access to content and computing, with services delivered to any device recognizable by the network.

It is also interesting to note that the Millennials are members of the first generation in the 54-year history of television that is watching *substantially* less of it than any previous generation, choosing to get their entertainment content elsewhere. As you might imagine, this is a serious, vexing concern for television advertisers, forcing them to place ads elsewhere, for example, in video games.

One other observation while we are on the subject of technology: To a Millennial, computers and the connections that give them to access the Web are *not* "technology" any more than the telephone and television were technologies to earlier generations. Perhaps most important, they are not optional.

I include this brief discussion about Millennials because they, more than any other segment of the population, will drive the ultimate success of technological innovations such as WiMAX and IMS simply because those technologies enable them to live their lives the way they want to live them: always on, always connected, always with access to the content they desire—on their terms, not the provider's.

Where does all this lead? It leads to what many players in the industry are calling "personal broadband." Eerily reminiscent of the words that many are using to describe IMS, it means bandwidth that is available anywhere, at any time, in any amount, to the right user, using any device, for the right price. Simple, huh?

WiMAX Is Great, But...

Whenever a new technology emerges, its arrival reminds me of the game kills I have seen in Africa (the final moments of one are shown in Figure 4-6). At the immediate center is the victim, being gnawed on by the primary predators on the scene, in this case wild dogs that ran down a gazelle. Wandering back and forth behind them are hyenas, waiting for the opportunity to dash in and grab a piece of the action. Then, behind

Figure 4-6
African wild
dogs on a kill.

the hyenas are the birds, storks and vultures, patiently waiting their turn at the carcass.

WiMAX is at the center of the herd here, and arranged around it in concentric circles are would-be customers, standards bodies, component and device manufacturers, service providers of all types, and application developers. Somewhere within the pack are the mavens, the people who herald the arrival of a new technology that will cure the world's network ills. With them, of course, are the naysayers who decry the hype surrounding WiMAX, claiming that it will never fulfill its promise, that the hype about its capabilities is overblown, that it is too expensive, too complex, too little, too late. Somewhere between the rantings of the two groups lies the truth.

There is no question that WiMAX has a way to go before it is ready for prime-time action. The standards remain in a state of flux, there are questions about the global availability of universal spectrum, and there are concerns about its ability to compete and interoperate with preexisting technologies. However, there must be something there if the list of companies that want to play in that space is any indication.

Because of the efforts of the WiMAX Forum and other interested groups, WiMAX has become much more than a wireless technology. Over 200 component manufacturers, application developers, trade organizations, system and device manufacturers, service providers, and professional services firms have joined forces to drive WiMAX into being and help it take up a position as an alternative technology for broadband service delivery. Initially the technology will see play among wireless Internet service providers (WISPs), service providers, and state and city governments that will use it for wireless backhaul, gap management, and point-to-point microwave-like connectivity. Around the world, particularly in greenfield and emerging markets, the technology will see accelerated play as it finds use as a service delivery medium for rural areas and in urban and metropolitan areas that suffer from facilities exhaustion or outmoded, incapable plant.

Although these applications represent the initial "bread-and-butter applications" that will help WiMAX carve out a toehold in a very competitive broadband access market, most strategic-level attention is being showered not on the fixed version of the technology but on the mobile version.

In light of the competitive tension between cable companies and traditional service providers for the broadband marketplace and given the observation that the triple play and quadruple play are the competitive edge they are striving for, WiMAX begins to look attractive as an addition to the access technology stable.

Key Applications

Let's take a few minutes to discuss the key applications that WiMAX addresses. This is by no means a complete list, but it will give you a good sense of where it fits in the thinking of the companies that are looking to deploy it.

Internet Access

DSL and cable dominate this market today, having wrenched it from the hands of dial-up. The bad news is that this is an extraordinarily competitive market segment, and thus it is difficult to make progress in it. The good news is that the United States has one of the lowest broadband penetration rates in the developed world, meaning that there are serious large-scale opportunities for the provider that comes to the market with the right strategy. Of course, current estimates place the global broadband user number at 450 million by 2010—not a number to sneeze at. Since the margins for telecom services are small to begin with and are shrinking rapidly, an option that requires comparatively little in the way of capital expenditures (CAPEX) and operating expenditures (OPEX) is highly attractive. This is certainly the case with WiMAX. Since roughly 80 percent of network start-up fees are OPEX dollars because of the need

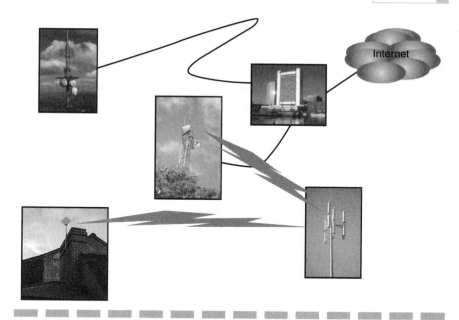

Figure 4-7
Cost components of a broadband wireless installation.

to install delivery infrastructure (outside plant for the most part), WiMAX, with its minimal infrastructure requirements, begins to look very good (see Figure 4-7).

The small and medium business (SMB) market and the small office, home office (SOHO) space are also viable targets for WiMAX. They are often found in areas that are underserved by existing broadband providers and are therefore hungry for high-grade service. WiMAX also works well in rural areas that have a scattered population of would-be broadband customers that cannot be served cost-effectively by traditional means.

Local Loop Alternative

What was that phrase about striking fear and terror into the hearts of criminals everywhere? Let's dispense with the criminals part and think about the fear and terror that a viable alternative to the traditional local loop causes for the traditional service provider. In North America alone wireline providers are losing access lines at the rate of 10,000 a day. Yes, a percentage of these losses involve second line disconnects because of DSL, and yes, some of this is wireless substitution, but the danger of stranded assets in the form of all that soon-to-be-underutilized outside plant is a very real threat, at least to telephone company accountants.

Consider the case of a medium-size to large business with a large corporate PBX. Every month that company pays a large sum to the local telephone company for the high-bandwidth facilities that connect its PBX to the telephone company's central office and, by extension, the outside world (see Figure 4-8). Speaking of the outside world, it's a big place (although the comedian Steven Wright says, "It's a small world, but I wouldn't want to have to paint it"), and copper or optical facilities provided by the telephone company are charged for by the mile. If the enterprise is any distance from the central office, its cost per month for connectivity increases dramatically. With WiMAX, however, there is no added cost component. Furthermore, the enterprise could reduce its cost of doing business further by moving to a Voice over Internet Protocol (VoIP) service provider and using WiMAX instead of a copper local loop.

WiFi Backhaul

Hotspots continue to be installed on a global basis at an accelerating rate, and for every hotspot there is a DSL or otherwise dedicated broadband facility used to backhaul the hotspot traffic from the wireless access point to the telephone company central office for connection to the Internet. WiMAX serves brilliantly as a backhaul solution, but there's more to

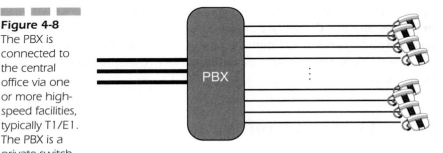

Figure 4-8
The PBX is connected to the central office via one or more high-speed facilities, typically T1/E1. The PBX is a private switch that offers features to local users at an enterprise location.

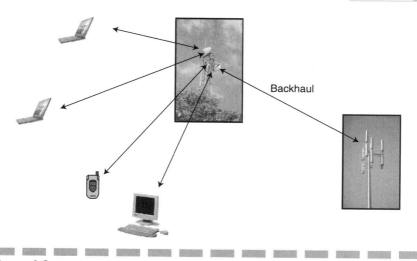

Backhaul

Figure 4-9
In addition to serving as a backhaul solution, a WiMAX base station can serve as a connectivity point for WiMAX-equipped laptops and PDAs.

the package than that, as Figure 4-9 shows: In addition to serving as a backhaul solution, the WiMAX base station can serve as a connectivity point for the growing number of WiMAX-equipped devices [laptops and personal digital assistants (PDAs)] that are expected to be arriving on the market. Thus, in this particular application WiMAX performs double duty.

Cellular Backhaul

Similar to the situation described in the WiFi scenario above, cellular backhaul is an equally likely candidate for WiMAX deployment. Most backhaul for cell towers is via either a dedicated T1 facility or the like or a microwave hop, as shown in Figure 4-10. By deploying WiMAX as an alternative, wireless carriers enjoy a number of benefits. First, they reduce their OPEX by limiting the monthly fees for fixed line service. Second, they begin the incorporation of new technologies into their networks that will support broadband roaming once application sets that can take advantage of it are developed. Finally, they go a long way toward "disaster-proofing" the access network. Although wireless connections certainly are disrupted by natural disasters such as floods, fires, earthquakes, and landslides, they are far easier to restore than are their

Figure 4-10
Cellular
backhaul using
traditional
microwave.

wireline counterparts. Wireless, then, is a major contributor to the disaster recovery capabilities of a modern broadband network.

Cable Bypass

This application is certainly not popular among mobile switching offices (MSOs), but so be it—reality can be painful. In the same way a telephone company's local loop can be bypassed by WiMAX, a cable company's broadband distribution facility can be bypassed. With the arrival of applications such as IPTV, it is possible to deliver cable-like content (broadcast television, video on demand, and other media types) under the control of an IP network. For example, if I have IPTV, I can be sitting in my favorite chair watching a show, and if the phone rings, I can pause the television program, display caller ID data on the television screen, and answer the telephone through the television. This is convergence at its best, and it's real. With WiMAX, a traditional telephone company easily could get into the content delivery game by forming alliances with content providers while at the same time deploying WiMAX base stations throughout its operating region (see Figure 4-11).

Figure 4-11
A service provider with a WiMAX node on any one of the buildings shown in the photograph could easily deliver content to businesses (foreground) and residential customers (background).

Throughout this discussion it would appear that the deck is stacked against the incumbent providers. However, this is not the case. There is a significant cadre of doom speakers out there who are quick to proclaim the imminent demise of the legacy telephone companies, but ask yourself this: What percentage of cellular telephone calls traverses the wireline telephone network? Answer: virtually 100 percent. And what percentage of Internet traffic is carried on the phone company's network? Answer: roughly 100 percent. Remember that the only part of the cellular network that is actually wireless—that is, uses no wires—is the link between the customer's handset and the local tower. After that the call jumps onto the wireline network for switching and transport. We often forget that the Internet consists of a large collection of private line connections that for the most part are leased from the local telephone company; this means that Internet traffic by and large is carried over the wireline infrastructure.

Thus, although the services offered by incumbent players may be somewhat marginalized as a result of commoditization, rumors of their imminent death are overblown. The idea that a telephone company will shut down because it isn't as profitable as it used to be is as ludicrous as shutting down a country's airlines because they aren't profitable. Both are critical, nonoptional components of a country's economy and will not disappear.

The key to success with regard to WiMAX is this: The technology is as available for deployment to the incumbent legacy providers as it is to new players and therefore can be as much a part of their success strategy as it can be for the success of new entrants. Most important to the success of *all* players is this: Service providers of every ilk must recognize that when customers buy access from them, those customers are not, as many believe, buying access to the network; they are buying access to *their stuff*. Technology, including WiMAX, is a means to an end, and that end is satisfaction of customer demands using telecommunications solutions as the facilitative resource. I have long argued that for the most part customers are not looking for the next great killer application but are looking for the next great killer way to get to the applications they already have. When questioned about application demand and requirements, the market as a whole typically responds en masse. They want mobile voice, messaging (SMS or IM), and *occasional* access to e-mail while mobile; far less often they express a need for Web access from a mobile device such as a PDA or a mobile phone. Think about it: These are applications they already have. There are of course exceptions, but they are far and away a small minority of the population.

Central to this realization is the need for mobility on all fronts, and right behind the need for mobility is the need for mobile broadband. Needless to say, WiMAX begins to appear rather attractive as a facilitator of both. A service provider can satisfy the requirements of a very large segment of its customer population by deploying WiMAX as part of its overall strategy for service delivery. The service provider benefits not only because of the revenue uptick that the technology's deployment brings about but also because the incorporation of the technology in its network topology and its resultant use make customers stickier, reducing churn and providing guaranteed revenue.

Making the Case for WiMAX

The value of a broadband wireless solution such as WiMAX is linked directly and fundamentally to the degree to which pervasive access and pervasive deployment are demanded. At the lower end of the available spectrum, setting up a broadband wireless network using WiMAX is largely a function of setting up a base station. Since the cost of WiMAX chipsets is expected to decline precipitously over the next couple of years, widespread deployment and widespread use are anticipated.

However, there are always challenges in network design and deployment, and they are legion in the wireless domain because of inability to control the environment. Wireline networks are bounded domains whose behavior can be controlled or, if not controlled, at least anticipated. In wireless, the capacity or bandwidth of the network is a function of its topology: in effect, the number of base stations deployed throughout the operating region. The more base stations there are, the more customers can be allowed into the network. Of course, the output power of the base stations must be controlled carefully to avoid crosstalk among collocated radios, but this can be done easily by radio frequency (RF) engineers.

One challenge is cost. Base stations are not cheap, and rooftop space typically comes at a price, often a recurring monthly price that is not trivial. To be truly competitive with alternatives such as cable and DSL, a station also must be equipped with intelligent, adaptive antenna arrays if it is to serve large numbers of subscribers. The point here is that wireless bandwidth does not a solution make. Keep in mind that during the mid-1990s a tremendous amount of attention (and money) was showered on wireless cable systems using local multipoint distribution system (LMDS) and multichannel, multipoint distribution system (MMDS) technology, and none of those initiatives survives today in spite of the fact that the underlying technology was quite good. Therefore, WiMAX has to offer more than ubiquity and speed if it is to be a successful alternative to legacy infrastructures.

Another challenge facing WiMAX deployment, particularly in the upper ranges of the allocated microwave spectrum, is getting to the customer base. These higher-frequency systems must be operated in line-of-sight mode; this means that any building or facility that cannot be "seen" by the base station cannot be served by it, as shown in Figure 4-12. Because these devices are costly, the need to reach all possible customers is tempered by the cost of the capital required to outfit the network to do that.

Equally important is the manner in which the customer connects to the network. WiMAX systems that operate in the higher frequencies

Figure 4-12
The transmitter on top of building A can reach the buildings in B, but will not reach building C. This is a line-of-sight (LOS) issue.

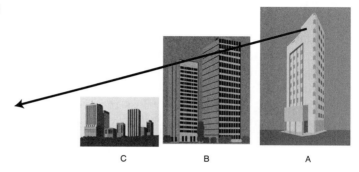

generally are designed to serve business customers rather than residence markets. Because business customers by and large are congregated in metro areas and are further aggregated within tall office buildings, service providers strive to overcome the line-of-sight limitations by hitting as many customers as possible by creating connections between buildings and then running a riser cable down a building's cable conduit, providing Ethernet connectivity on a floor-by-floor basis. This saves on the cost of providing a WiMAX connection for each customer. In the process, however, it creates an ironic competitive twist.

It would seem that the wireless provider would have an advantage in this situation because of its ability to "bathe" the building in WiMAX signal, providing connections to everyone who wants them. However, in the case of metro deployments, the incumbent telephone company may have the advantage for the simple reason that it already is in the building (telephony typically comes from the incumbents, after all) and for historical reasons does not have to pay any kind of access fee for the right to have risers in the building. Thus, in fact, although wireless broadband can cover a broad service footprint, it does not necessarily provide a significant competitive advantage.

Keep in mind that it was the telephone industry that gave the world that wonderfully prophetic observation "If it ain't broke, don't fix it." Service that is being delivered today via a wireline solution and that is perfectly functional over that medium should not be considered for replacement simply because a wireless alternative is available. T1, DSL, cable, and optical alternatives provide highly secure, high-bandwidth connectivity and will do so for some time to come. Other considerations must be taken into account, including the economics, the survivability, and the freedom that a wireless solution brings to the table.

From the perspective of the enterprise, it is critical to perform an analysis of the total cost of ownership inherent in building or using a wireless broadband solution. Also, the nature of the environment in which the technology is being deployed—greenfield versus preexisting, for example—will have a significant bearing on the overall cost, as we'll see in a moment. In fact, certain characteristics of the wireless environment unquestionably result in cheaper prices overall, largely because of the logistics of installation.

There is no question that wireless requires less CAPEX and OPEX because of the lower cost of initial deployment. The laying or stringing of cable (trenching and putting up poles) can cost thousands of dollars per mile in rural territory to millions in a city, particularly when stringent permitting requirements and the delays inherent in scheduling a dig in a major thoroughfare are costly realities. Of course, to a large extent DSL relies on existing access infrastructure and may not require any additional installation work other than the "tweaking" of end-user equipment—customer premises equipment (CPE), if you will. Consequently, the advantage that WiMAX has because it does not require huge labor efforts may be moot.

Nevertheless, WiMAX does have the potential to offer a broad array of services and service types. Although its physical layer is subject to the service interruptions that plague all physical layers—and this problem is exacerbated by its wireless nature—the technology's data link layer has the ability to detect and overcome many of the radio-related frailties that plague service delivery over broadband wireless. Because WiMAX supports IP as a fundamental transport modality, any service that is deliverable over IP can be delivered over WiMAX. Bandwidth on demand, multiparty conferencing, storage area network access, VoIP, IPTV, video on demand, and machine-to-machine signaling (sometimes called by its old name, telemetry) are viable applications for WIMAX installations.

The Cost of Deployment

Once again we dive into the less-than-trivial issues associated with network implementation decisions, this time by taking a look at the cost elements of network deployment. One of the most serious considerations is the design of the capital budget that will guide the actual deployment. CAPEX details cover a large number of elements, including the infrastructure elements that must be purchased and amortized, not the least of which are the base station radios that must be deployed, often in significant quantities. Equally significant can be the cost of spectrum that may or may not have to be licensed for operation in a particular area, assuming, of course, that the spectrum is available in the first place.

Another element that often rears its head has to do with the intended line or lines of business. If the service provider intends to operate as an Internet service provider (ISP) in addition to being a traditional voice carrier, it will encounter expenses from the need to acquire virtual private network (VPN) equipment, routers, firewalls, various types of software, and other ancillary expenses associated with administering an Internet access domain. There will also be interconnect charges and miscellaneous costs associated with application hosting, server availability, and component redundancy.

Typical operating expense elements are shown in Table 4-1.

Table 4-1
Operating expense elements.

OPEX Cost Element	Legacy Network: Investment?	Greenfield Network: Investment?
Roof or tower space lease	*	Yes
Base station maintenance	*	Yes
CPE maintenance	Yes	Yes
Network operation and maintenance	*	Yes
Network management	*	Yes
Private line rental fee	*	Yes
Facilities and office space	*	Yes
Advertising, churn reduction, customer acquisition	*	Yes
Facilities management and maintenance	*	Yes

*Indicates that this cost may or may not be incurred; if it is, it may be shared among multiple sites.

Typical capital expense elements are shown in Table 4-2.

Table 4-2
Capital expense elements.

CAPEX Cost Element	Legacy Network: Investment?	Greenfield Network: Investment?
CPE	Yes	Yes
CPE installation	Yes	Yes
Radio and network design and planning	*	Yes
Base station	Yes	Yes
Roof space or tower setup	Yes	Yes

(continued on next page)

Table 4-2
Capital expense elements (continued).

CAPEX Cost Element	Legacy Network: Investment?	Greenfield Network: Investment?
IP infrastructure	*	Yes
Backhaul	Yes	Yes
Network management, operations support systems, operations, administration, maintenance, and provisioning	*	Yes
Billing, basic service set	*	Yes

*Indicates that this cost may or may not be incurred; if it is, it may be shared among multiple sites.

Summary

Perhaps the most important thing in this chapter is the idea that WiMAX is not offering anything new to enterprise or residence users. What it does offer is a well-designed and highly functional alternative to traditional "tethered" broadband solutions. For customers with a need for mobility or the flexibility that wireless solutions offer, WiMAX may be the answer. There is no question that it offers tremendous utility and, if deployed intelligently, can provide a significant competitive advantage. However, the fact that it is wireless does not necessarily make it better than long-standing solutions. When making decisions about WiMAX deployment, do so carefully and always be aware of what I call the Jurassic Park effect. Originally cited by Jeff Goldblum in the movie, the Jurassic Park effect observes that "just because you *can* make dinosaurs doesn't mean that you should." The same thing is true here: The fact that WiMAX is available doesn't mean that it's the best solution for your particular situation. It may be the best thing that a provider could offer or that a company could invest in, but as in all such situations, investing in technology for the sake of investing in technology is not good business.

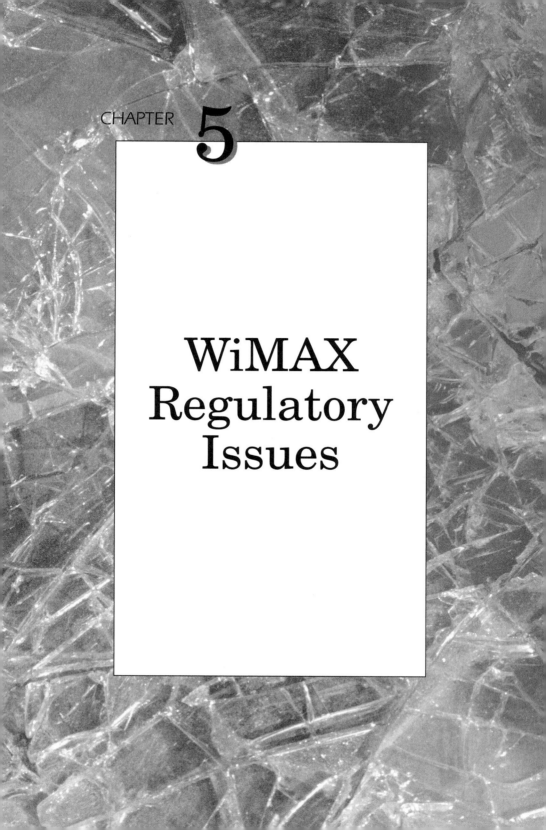

WiMAX Regulatory Issues

Whenever I mention regulation in the talks I give (except when I'm speaking to groups of regulators), a generalized grumble and/or groan typically flows around the room as people begin to think of every reason they can come up with to study their Blackberries very seriously and then leave the room looking worried, as if the fate of the world rested on their shoulders and staying in the room would be irresponsible. Although regulatory drama may not be the most exciting thing to read and follow, it is crucially important, and it is the responsibility of everyone in the industry to follow it closely. These are times when telecom regulatory policy is more important than it has ever been. The technological changes that are happening on what seems to be a daily basis and the lack of appreciation for and understanding of the impact of things such as Voice over Internet Protocol (VoIP) on the part of legislators mean that we all have a responsibility to educate them and spread the word about the importance and magnitude of the changes that are imminent.

A subtle change is occurring among regulators. For the longest time it appeared that regulators had come to believe that their primary responsibility was to create competition. In fact, the primary goals of regulation are twofold: first and foremost, to ensure that the users of a regulated service (whether telecommunications, power, or airlines) have the best possible experience while using the service, and second, to "fill in the gaps" where the market fails to create the appropriate environment. Regulators can use competition as a way to achieve these goals, but competition is a means to an end, not the end itself.

Furthermore, regulators should not be in the business of regulating technology per se; instead, they should be regulating the application of technologies according to the mandates listed above. Today significant regulatory attention is being paid to VoIP, but consider this: VoIP is a technology, not a service. What comes out of the phone is the same voice that has always come out of the phone. Although VoIP today enjoys a certain amount of immunity from regulatory forbearance, that is a temporary situation: The time will come, and not all that long from now, when VoIP providers will reach "critical mass" and find themselves under the same degree of regulatory scrutiny as other, more traditional providers.

To understand the impact of regulatory change on Worldwide Interoperability for Microwave Access (WiMAX) and vice versa, let's spend a few pages on recent regulatory decisions so that we can develop an appreciation for what has happened before looking at what is yet to come.

Relatively Recent Regulatory Decisions

Early in 2003 the Federal Communications Commission (FCC) rewrote the basics of U.S. telecom regulation. After the 2003 Triennial Review that concluded in February of that year, the FCC released a series of high-impact decisions that pleased everyone and no one. In an effort to resolve the question of which unbundled network elements (UNEs) the incumbent providers were required to make available to their competitors, the FCC essentially turned the issue over to the states for local resolution. It also ruled that incumbent local exchange carriers (ILECs) no longer had to provide switching as an unbundled element to competitive local exchange carriers (CLECs) for business customers unless state regulatory agencies could prove within 90 days of the order that this resulted in an overly onerous impairment to the ability of the CLECs to do business.

In the residence market, the FCC outlined specific criteria that each state had to use to determine whether CLECs were impaired without unbundled switching. They also concluded that ILECs did not have to provide competitors with Synchronous Optical Network (SONET)-level transport services Optical Carrier Level-N - OC-N) but shifted responsibility to the states to determine whether ILECs should be required to unbundle dark fiber and Digital Signal Level 3 (DS3) transport on a route-by-route basis.

For broadband, the FCC's decision was clearer: It ruled that all new broadband buildouts, including both fiber builds and hybrid loops, were exempt from unbundling requirements as well. It also ruled that line sharing no longer would be classified as an unbundled network element, a decision that put considerable pressure on competitive carriers that rely on line sharing.

The decisions reached by the commission were far from unanimous. Commissioner Kevin Martin was the only member who agreed with the entire order. Then-Chairman Michael Powell and Commissioner Kathleen Abernathy disagreed with the decisions about line sharing and unbundled switching, and Jonathan Adelstein and Michael Copps disagreed with the broadband decision.

The feedback from various industry segments about the decisions was, as would be expected, varied. CLECs grudgingly agreed for the most part that it was about as good as it could have been and that it could have been far worse. Incumbents, in contrast, saw the decision to turn much of the decision making over to the states as a step in the wrong direction, concluding that it would extend the period over which definitive decisions would be made.

What we do know is this: Although the decisions made by the fragmented FCC were not ideal for all the players (how could they be?), they did move the industry forward and shook up the players in a positive way. ILECs now had a renewed incentive to invest in broadband infrastructure, and competitive providers had an incentive to invest in alternative technologies such as cable and wireless (both fixed and mobile) in their competitive efforts. Digital Subscriber Line (DSL) rollouts were accelerated, and as penetration climbed, alternative solutions were invoked. Thus, although the results were not as comfortable as they could have been for the industry players, they led to the appropriate marketplace behavior, and that's a good thing.

Consider the following simple scenario. Regulators, after a great deal of wrangling, remove unbundling requirements, providing the appropriate degree of incentive to incumbent providers to accelerate broadband deployment. ILECs publicly commit to universal broadband (DSL) deployment throughout their operating areas. In response, cable and wireless players accelerate their own rollouts, preparing for the price wars that inevitably will come.

The broadband deployment effort involves infrastructure; shortly after the service announcement, ILECs issue requests for proposals (RFPs) and requests for quotes (RFQs) for Digital Subscriber Line Access Multiplexers (DSLAMs), optical extension hardware, and DSL modems and begin to jockey for content alliances since DSL provides the necessary bandwidth for television signal delivery in addition to voice and high-speed data. Customers, meanwhile, excited by the prospect of higher-speed access and all that it will bring them in the way of enhanced capability, buy upgraded personal computers (PCs) and broadband service packages. Hardware manufacturers and service providers applaud the evolution because they know that the typical broadband user generates 13 times the traffic volume that a dial-up user generates, and although service providers rarely charge by the transported megabyte, the increased traffic volume requires capability upgrades to the network: capital expenditures (CAPEX), in other words.

Meanwhile, software manufacturers, mobile appliance makers, and content owners scramble to develop products for wireline and wireless broadband delivery. Upgrades occur, innovation happens, and prices come down. Cable and wireless players march along with their own parallel efforts, and soon this great dynamic money engine known as the telecom industry starts to turn again, slowly at first but building rapidly as it feeds on its own self-generated fuel. That is the ultimate end state: a self-perpetuating industry that evolves and changes in concert with market demand, sustained by a forward-thinking, reasonable regulatory environment.

What this boils down to is the FCC's ultimate goal: to force the industry at large to become facilities-based in terms of its competitive model. The fact is that the local loop is a natural monopoly; there's no getting around that. The UNE rules are basically unnatural and simply do not work as well as they were envisioned to work. Want to compete with the incumbent service providers? Use a different technology, such as cable or broadband wireless. Clearly this strategy is working in the cable industry's favor.

Other Regulatory Activity

On May 12, 2003, the FCC commissioners were presented with a proposal to modify the existing rules that govern media ownership. On the surface, this does not appear to affect the technology sector per se, but in fact it potentially has a significant impact because of a blurring of the lines between the sectors. Under the terms of the proposal, ownership of broadcast rights could change dramatically.

Among the changes is a proposal to allow a single company to own television stations that reach as many as 45 percent of U.S. households, today capped at 35 percent. Needless to say, the major networks are in favor of eliminating the existing 35 percent cap. This decision would favor companies such as News Corporation (the owner of Fox) and Viacom (the owner of CBS and UPN), which are already in violation of the 35 percent limit because of mergers and acquisitions (M&A) activity that has put them slightly over the top. There are some inviolable restrictions to the decision: The four major networks (CBS, NBC, ABC, and Fox) are prohibited from merging, and ownership of more than eight broadcasting stations in a single market remains prohibited.

Under the terms of federal communications law, the FCC is required to consider reasonable changes to the rules it oversees that affect the communications marketplace and the public it serves. Since some of these laws were written over 50 years ago, they are in dire need of revision. In many cases the changes are driven by the growing influence of the cable- and Internet-dominated sectors.

Recent Events

In March 2004, an appeals court struck down FCC rules for the way regional telephone companies must open their networks to competitors. Federal law originally required regional phone companies to lease parts of their networks (the UNE-P mandates) to competitors at reasonable rates set by the states. The ILECs have long contended that they have been forced to give competitors rates that are below their actual cost.

In its decision, the appeals court found that the FCC wrongly gave power to state regulators to decide which parts of the telephone network had to be unbundled. The court also upheld an earlier FCC decision that ILECs are not required to lease their high-speed facilities to competitors at discount rates the way they lease their standard phone lines.

In April 2004, regulators rejected AT&T's petition to eliminate the requirement that it pay long-distance fees on calls transported partially over the Internet.

That decision means that AT&T may be required to pay hundreds of millions of dollars in unpaid retroactive fees to the ILECs.

Earlier in 2004 the FCC had ruled that calls that originated and terminated on the Internet, such as those made using Skype, Vonage, and other VoIP service providers, are free from the fees and taxes that traditional phone companies are required to pay, such as support for E911 and the Universal Service Fund. The FCC said that because calls that travel over the Internet do not provide anything in the way of enhanced features, standard rules apply. Furthermore, in a recent decision, the FCC consolidated all regulatory power over VoIP service at the federal level, wresting it from the states.

The key here is that regulatory agencies are trying to balance the need for a regulated telecommunications marketplace with the need for an unfettered development environment in which companies can innovate technologically without fear of onerous fees and taxes. The FCC wants to engender a spirit of facilities-based competition rather than the UNE-based environment that has not worked as well as hoped. Of course, recent events have shown that VoIP is growing far faster than anyone anticipated, and pure VoIP providers such as Vonage are now required to make 911 service available even though they may not provide immediate service the way a wireline telephone does. Nevertheless, regulatory change continues, and as we have seen, it affects broadband wireless as much as it affects wireline options.

▰ Spectrum Considerations

WiMAX spectrum, like wireless fidelity (WiFi) spectrum, is a funny beast from a regulatory perspective because it involves both licensed and unlicensed spectrum components. Early in the process, the FCC allocated 300 MHz of licensed spectrum in the 5.150- to 5.250-GHz, 5.250- to 5.350-GHz, and 5.725- to 5.825-GHz ranges, followed by an additional 255 MHz of spectrum in the 5.470- to 5.725-GHz band in November 2003. However, the siren song of unlicensed radio was appealing to the players in the broadband wireless game, and they lobbied loudly for its inclusion.

One argument was that because unlicensed spectrum has no cost component associated with it, equipment that operates there is inexpensive and therefore has an advantage over that of its licensed cousin. However, this argument does not necessarily make sense. Equipment that operates in the licensed domain, though expensive, can achieve similar levels of cost-effectiveness and economies of scale if the volume sold is high enough.

There are also a significant number of downsides to operating in the unlicensed bands. First, those bands are limited by law to low output levels, making it difficult to use them over any distance. Second, because they are unlicensed and therefore in the public domain, they are subject to unfettered interference from other operators, and when that happens, there is no recourse as there is when one is operating within the licensed domain.

In contrast, technologies such as WiFi that operate quite handily in the unlicensed realm work exceptionally well for small coverage area situations such as wireless local area networks (LANs) and hotspot deployments. Thus, although there are clearly downsides to operating in the unlicensed spectrum, there are also compelling positive reasons to do so.

In regard to the issue of unlicensed spectrum, there is quite a bit of it available that has not been released. Oddly, there are both proponents and opponents of opening it up. The proponents include wireless Internet service providers (ISPs) and other providers that depend on unlicensed spectrum for the delivery of their services. The opponents, in contrast, typically represent the cellular industry, the National Association of Broadcasters, and other organizations that stand to lose revenue from the increased availability of unlicensed spectrum.

One area that has the attention of regulators is the potential value of WiFi and WiMAX in the rural marketplace. The cost to deploy these solutions is comparatively low compared with wireline alternatives, and the time needed to set them up is significantly lower. For these and other reasons, these technologies are garnering significant interest from legislators and regulators alike.

Ultimately, there is great demand for flexible, cost-effective wireless broadband access. 802.16 and the WiMAX technology that is based on it were designed to support a wide range of services, including T1/E1-like transport and "wireless DSL." The standard also dictates specific requirements with regard to quality of service (QoS) so that delay-sensitive services such as voice and video can be carried without a problem. Because the technology is designed to be extremely flexible, service providers can deploy it in multiple service tiers, charging increasingly higher prices for increasingly capable service levels.

From a long-term point of view, the value of these technologies will be realized most visibly when they are deployed in emerging markets in the third world, where telecom service is viewed as a basic requirement for economic growth and national success. Earlier in the book I wrote about Tom Friedman and his book *The Lexus and the Olive Tree*. If you haven't read it yet, put this book down and go get it (come back and finish this one afterward, though). In that book Friedman writes compellingly about the role of technology:

> Microchip Immune Deficiency Syndrome (MIDS) [is a] disease that can affect any bloated, overweight, sclerotic system in the post-Cold War era. MIDS is usually contracted by countries and companies that fail to inoculate themselves against changes brought about by the microchip, and the democratizations of technology, finance and information—which created a much faster, more open and more complex marketplace, with a whole new set of efficiencies. The symptoms of MIDS appear when a country or company exhibits a consistent inability to increase productivity, wages, living standards, knowledge use and competitiveness, and becomes too slow to respond to the challenges of the fast world. Countries and companies with MIDS tend to be those run on Cold War corporate models—where one or more people at the top hold all the information and make all the decisions, and all the people in the middle and the bottom simply carry out those decisions, using only the information they need to do their jobs. The only known cure for countries and companies with MIDS is "the fourth democratization." This is the democratization of decision-making and information flows, and the deconcentration of power, in ways that allow more people in a country or company to share knowledge and innovate faster. This enables them to keep up with a marketplace in which

consumers are constantly demanding cheaper products and services tailored specifically for them. MIDS can be fatal for those companies and countries that do not get appropriate treatment in time.

Thomas L. Friedman, *The Lexus and the Olive Tree*, p. 76.

The impact of pervasive low-cost communications technology in a new market is compellingly powerful. I have seen its impact firsthand in my work in Africa, Asia, and Latin America, and technologies such as WiMAX can and will play a major role when it comes to the responsibility for connecting these countries to the world. Here we are talking about much more than FCC-like regulation: We are talking about global regulatory requirements. One of the most important requirements as far as WiMAX is concerned is the need to ensure global agreement on the issue of spectrum availability. The universal allocation of spectrum for WiMAX is crucial to lowering overall equipment costs because the radios represent a significant component of developing a global WiMAX system. To maximize base station radio performance and minimize costs, radios must operate within each of the allocated WiMAX bands.

Near-Term Predictions

Most industry analysts believe that global broadband wireless set-asides will occur in the next few years on a widespread basis, leading to lower equipment and deployment costs and therefore faster rollout schedules. Most organizations, including the WiMAX Forum, believe that the most movement will take place as follows.

There will be strong activity in the unlicensed 5-GHz band, particularly between 5.25 and 5.85 GHz. This particular range of spectrum is used most commonly for low-power indoor applications and is therefore not ideal for WiMAX. It will play a significant role in emerging markets in which innovators will take advantage of license-free spectrum to develop homegrown (and often quite successful) systems. As far as WiMAX is concerned, much activity will take place in the upper reaches of the 5-GHz band, particularly between 5.725 and 5.850 GHz. There is a good reason for this: Many countries allow devices to operate at much higher power in this spectrum, thus facilitating the development of longer-range systems. For example, the lower bands typically are limited to 1-watt operations, whereas the higher bands can broadcast at 4 watts, which is far better for the wide coverage of a WiMAX deployment. In fact, there is serious consideration for allowing limited deployment of systems operating at output power as high as 25 watts.

In the licensed domain there will also be a great deal of activity as the market jockeys for competitive position. Most of the spectrum that is licensed for broadband wireless systems lies between 3.4 and 3.6 GHz, as well as between 3.3 and 3.4 GHZ and 3.6 and 3.8 GHz. Regulatory efforts will be designed largely to minimize the bureaucratic impact of regulation to ensure that the service deployed within these spectral ranges is not unduly burdened. This will also be the case in the 2.5-GHz operating range, particularly between 2.5 and 2.7 GHz, which has been made available primarily in Brazil, Mexico, the United States, and a number of Southeast Asian nations. In Southeast Asia, including New Zealand, Korea, and Australia, the 2.3-GHz range of frequencies is available.

One bone of contention that has plagued the wireless world in general and the broadband wireless world specifically is the significant amount of spectrum that is controlled (but massively underutilized) by the television industry. There is quite a bit of spectrum below 1 GHz that could be redeployed for broadband wireless applications if the television industry released it, and at this juncture it appears that that industry is primed to do so as its migration from analog to digital continues. Already, the U.S. FCC has made spectrum available between 699 and 741 MHz (formerly UHF channels 52 to 59) and between 747 and 801 MHz (UHF channels 60 to 69). Even though current legislation does not require television broadcasters to vacate redirected spectrum until 2010, the FCC continues to issue reassignment orders, including the range of spectrum between 512 and 698 MHz (channels 21 to 51).

Summary

They may not be the kind of things you want to curl up with in front of a roaring fire on a snowy winter afternoon, but regulatory decisions are among the most powerful shaping forces the telecom and information technology (IT) industries face. As services become more clearly defined and as the various technologies available to deliver them become more broadly deployed, service providers, network designers, and application developers will begin to combine their efforts to reach greater portions of the available market than ever before, at the same time wrestling with the need to define the bounds of the market more clearly. Regulators will find themselves running to keep up, working hard to do what they are paid to do: ensure universal availability of advertised services throughout the coverage area and guarantee that customers get what they pay for. As WiMAX matures, Internet Protocol Multimedia Subsystem (IMS) arrives, and applications such as Internet Protocol Television (IPTV) become commonplace, the role of the regulator will become more complex; it will grow even more complex as service delivery becomes more global in scope. Stand back and watch: This space is going to get very interesting very fast.

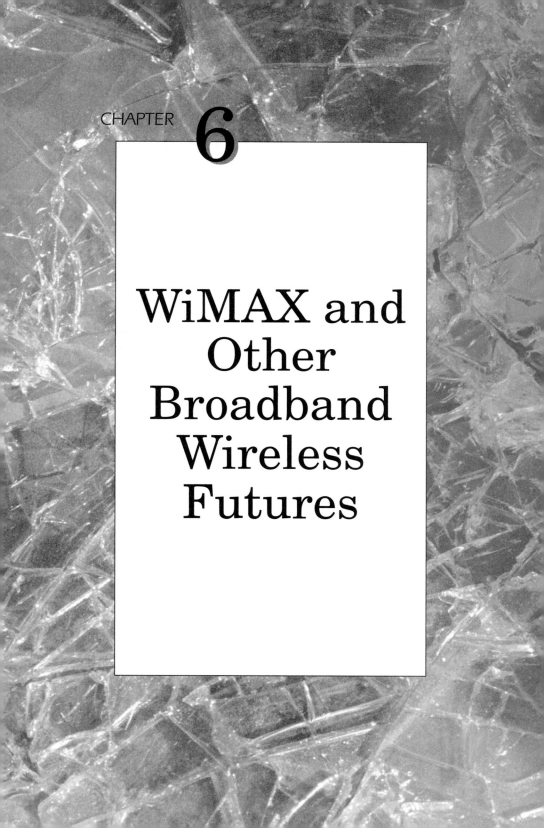

CHAPTER **6**

WiMAX and Other Broadband Wireless Futures

The telecom industry is at one of the most important, challenging, and exciting crossroads in its 130-year history. Computing power has reached an all-time high, with analysts predicting that the average laptop will have a terabyte of memory in 2010. Networks have reached a zenith of functionality with pervasive broadband just around the corner. Presence- and location-based services make it possible not only to know where customers are at any time but to deliver services to them whenever and wherever they like, regardless of the network to which they are attached or the device they are using.

Worldwide Interoperability for Microwave Access (WiMAX) has come along in the middle of this process, offering pervasive standards-based wireless broadband access. Depending on which authority you ask, it's a big market. According to the WiMAX Forum, it will be a $20 billion market by 2015; the Telecommunications Industry Association (TIA) says $30 billion by 2008. Either way, it's big dollars and getting bigger.

The availability and relevance of broadband are growing rapidly in both existing and emerging markets. The fixed broadband side of the house is still dominated by cable and Digital Subscriber Line (DSL), although various forms of broadband wireless and optical are growing as well. A number of factors affect the degree to which these warring technologies gain ground, including competition, growing customer expectations, and declining profitability. For many companies the focus has shifted from providing high-speed universal technology to providing capabilities that enhance a company's ability to do business and be competitive. Some of the emergent trends include a focus on mobile high-speed data, the availability of the triple or quadruple play, Internet Protocol Multimedia Subsystem (IMS), Internet Protocol television (IPTV), and Voice over Internet Protocol (VoIP).

In the wireless space, WiMAX and third-generation (3G) devices are on something of a collision course. Convergence, largely brought to life by IMS, is erasing the lines of demarcation that have always divided the wireline and wireless worlds, forcing service providers and customers alike to accept the fact that it is just "access." 3G is clearly a major component of IMS, since most of the IMS standards and in fact the original design came out of the Third-Generation Partnership Project (3GPP). However, 3G is somewhat limited in terms of the bandwidth it can provide and its coverage area. WiMAX covers a broader area and offers higher bandwidth, but is still somewhat nascent in its development cycle, although not for long if things continue the way they are going. Driven largely by economics at this point, WiMAX represents a technology that can provide cost-effective broadband network access to sparsely populated rural areas and add economic strength to the telecom marketplace.

As a consequence, convergence is taking on another face: Not only is the line between wireless and wireline blurring, so too are the lines between 3G, wireless fidelity (WiFi), and WiMAX. Once again we see that the focus is not so much on any particular technology but rather on what one can do with it. If roaming, mobile nomadic broadband services require the deployment of a patchwork quilt of technologies—WiFi, 3G, Universal Mobile Telephony System (UMTS), WiMAX—so be it.

A significant series of changes are coming with regard to broadband wireless, and they go beyond (but are closely related to) the evolution of WiMAX. In Arthur C. Clarke's *Space Odyssey* series, astronauts who were caught up in remarkable events described them by saying, "Something's about to happen. Something wonderful." We could play *Also Sprach Zarathustra* in the background as we describe what's about to happen, but that would be a bit over the top. IMS, IPTV, WiMAX, WiFi, 3G, and a few other technologies such as High-Speed Downline Packet Access (HSDPA) are on a collision course with one another, and the resulting big bang will be something to behold.

First and foremost, none of these innovations amounts to much on its own; each is nothing more than a clever innovation of a preexisting clever thing. However, when they are put together, it's a very different story. They epitomize everything that convergence was, and is, supposed to be. However, in addition to all the great things these technologies portend, uncertainties abound that leave a lot of technological dust in the air and blur the horizon, making it difficult to predict suitable directions for companies that are planning their futures. Some of these developments are directly related to WiMAX; others are peripherally related but important nonetheless.

Progress on WiMAX

One of the first major events that will occur in the near term will be the arrival of certified WiMAX equipment that is based on the now largely complete 802.16-2004 standard. Following closely on the heels of product rollouts will be the arrival of a small number of devices that are based on the 802.16e standard and that demonstrate mobility in the broadband wireless arena. 802.16-2004 will see a great deal of attention as trials and products that are based on its mandates continue. However, competition for attention from 802.16e and Korea's wireless broadband (WiBro) activities will lead to a certain amount of market distraction, slowing the pace of penetration of 802.16-2004.

Critical to the continuation of WiMAX's forward momentum is the need for vendors offering 802.16-2004 hardware to prove the ability of that hardware to support 802.16e as it arrives. Most vendors of 802.16-2004 equipment already make this claim, but the field will be winnowed rapidly as vendors that don't make that claim emerge.

Network Design Considerations

The tendency of city governments to get into the network business seems to ebb and flow. Lately it seems that every city, as well as many private companies, has decided to deploy a mesh WiFi network; consider what Google has decided to do throughout the city of San Francisco and, potentially, beyond it. In response, vendors all over the landscape have announced mesh products, and though they have done this with the best intentions and though the organizations looking to deploy these networks in their environs are doing so for what appear to be the right reasons, there is a major flaw in the logic: *Show me the money*. It is highly likely that the market, good though it may be, will not be able to support as many vendors (or deployments) as currently exist.

The good news is that there is once again vibrancy and a degree of excitement in the telecom industry, and start-ups are flourishing and venture money is flowing—cautiously this time but flowing nonetheless. Equipment vendors and providers alike will rub and bump against one another for the foreseeable future, but inevitably a couple of things will occur. Consolidations will take place as the reality of the marketplace sinks in, and some of the many vendors that are extant will fade away; these are normal behaviors for this kind of market.

Core IP

It seems that only yesterday there was a huge "ah-ha" moment when the industry made the psychic connection between the mobile world and

Internet Protocol (IP). As adjacent technologies have developed, including SoftSwitch and IMS, IP has emerged as a core component in the mobile space, particularly in light of its role in the early standards developed by the 3GPP. As the application set develops, particularly any application that involves interactivity (video, screen sharing, gaming), the role of IP will increase in importance.

Closely related to the increasingly important role of IP is what I refer to as the ongoing "inversion of the network." Historically, the telecom network consisted of a relatively small number of very large service access points (switches) buried deep in the core of the network. Today that model is being supplanted rapidly by the opposite situation: a very large number of small service access points (switches *and* routers) located at the very periphery of the network, a demonstration of the edge-based model of service delivery. One result of this is that the closer the service delivery point is placed to the customer (meaning the person with the money), the more granular the service delivery process becomes and the more customized the makeup of that which is being placed into the hands of customers becomes. This also translates into a need for increased intelligence at the edge of the network, where service differentiation takes place. When network intelligence is distributed, it can be applied far more effectively and immediately, resulting in the identification and realization of new revenue opportunities.

Moving Forward: Redefining the Customer

A critical realization has begun to dawn on the companies that make up the global telecommunications realm. For years they have enjoyed massive market share, in some cases because of a long-standing monopoly position and in other cases simply because the cost barrier to entry is so prohibitive that new entrants are effectively blocked. With the move to an IP-based network and the attendant drop in cost for both hardware and services, new entrants have come in with a strong focus on customer service. And the realization that has come about? In this new game, companies have to accept the fact that they will have two choices in the future: They can have *some* of the customer's money or *none* of the customer's money. They can no longer have it all. This translates into a new business model that is described in the pages that follow.

This is particularly true as new technologies such as WiMAX, IMS, and IPTV come into the market. Service providers and manufacturers alike must learn that successful market service is about content, not about the technology that delivers it.

Beginnings

Faced with declining market share as a result of increasing competitive pressure, reduced service provider revenues [and therefore capital expenditure (CAPEX) spending], commoditization of product capabilities, and an increasingly lethargic response from the marketplace to claims of technological superiority as a differentiation scheme, telecommunications equipment manufacturers find themselves in a tenuous place. On the one hand, they are unmatched at designing and creating technology-based hardware and software products that address themselves to service provider challenges. It is what they have always done, and they do it exceptionally well. On the other hand, they are less accustomed to creating broad-brush solutions that provide a turnkey response to client business issues. Today's customers are asking for a single bundled technology solution that addresses every aspect of their business so that their revenues are increased, their operating expenses (OPEX) and CAPEX expenses are reduced, and their competitive position is assured if not enhanced.

Unfortunately, it does not fall within the purview of the telecommunications manufacturer (or any vendor, for that matter) to offer such a wide-spectrum solution to its customers. This is not a criticism of the sector; these companies previously were been called upon to be "soup-to-nuts" players and are therefore ill equipped to do this on such short notice. As a result, their efforts often fall short of customers' expectations. This perceived failure on their part, however, is not a failure at all. In fact, it is a case of the right capability being delivered to the wrong customer. Realignment on the part of the manufacturing sector can eliminate this perceived shortcoming quickly and effectively.

The Legacy Model

For many years the technology industry has been structurally characterized by the stack shown in Figure 6-1. At the bottom layer are the component makers, companies that manufacture semiconductors and optoelectronic devices that they sell to the systems manufacturers above them. Component companies include Agere, Intel, AMD, Texas Instruments, and IBM.

Systems manufacturers build switches, routers, multiplexers, and other infrastructure components; they include, among others, Lucent, Nortel, Ericsson, Alcatel, and Fujitsu. They sell their complex devices to service providers. These providers include local telephone companies, long-distance providers, Internet service providers (ISPs), independents, and corporations large enough to have their own infrastructure (multinational banks, health consortia, universities). Systems manufacturers are technologically visionary and technically adept and typically have large research and development (R&D) organizations that push the limits of technology to determine its applicability in customer environments.

Service providers develop and offer a wide array of access and transport options that include voice and data, wireline and wireless, and additional services such as diverse billing models, converged voice and data solutions, Internet access, and other technology-dependent offerings. Like the manufacturers, they are technically savvy, but they tend to have a better understanding of the end users because they are in direct contact with them.

The end user is a multifaceted creature. End users include everything from individual residence customers with simple telecommunications requirements to massive, complex corporations with locations in multiple countries and tens of thousands of employees. The service requirements of these corporations vary greatly with many factors.

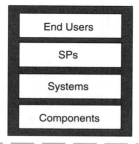

Figure 6-1
The service hierarchy, from the fundamental component (optoelectronic and semiconductor) layer up to the end user layer. All are interdependent.

Taking Stock: Where Are You on the Value Chain?

In terms of the value chain continuum, companies want to be as close to the top of the chain as they can get because that is where the customer (with the money) dwells. Regardless of whether a company manufactures components, systems, or services, the ability to offer an integrated, innovative solution that exceeds customer requirements is a cornerstone of long-term success. The reality of the situation, however, is that no single company has the ability to do this. Some form of alliance is necessary, and the best way to craft an alliance is by identifying strengths that must be reinforced and weaknesses that must be strengthened. Equally important, but beyond the scope of this book, is the fact that companies entering into an alliance must enter it with the appropriate motivation: The goal of an alliance partner should *not* be to enter into the relationship as a way to control the partner. That's not an alliance; that's hegemony, and it doesn't work.

Consider the diagram shown in Figure 6-2. Voice is a largely undifferentiated service characterized by specific features that certainly have value, but the value is largely commoditized: Everyone offers the same features because those services are for the most part standardized. Traditional data such as T1, local area networks (LANs), frame relay, and Asynchronous Transfer Mode (ATM) offer both features and functions on the value chain but little else. They too are largely commodities.

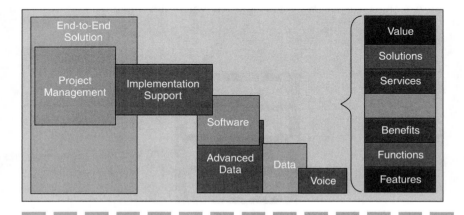

Figure 6-2
As the offered service becomes more complex, the ability of a single entity to satisfy the increasingly complex demands becomes difficult.

Advanced data, including switched Gigabit Ethernet, IP services, and certain forms of wireless, add a few benefits as they claw their way upward, but they too are dangerously close to the commodity level. Software offers benefits and applications, but software providers do not have the ability to deliver the underlying infrastructure and do not offer further differentiation to carry them higher up the value chain.

Implementation support is an example of an offering that provides further differentiation. Project management also does this, but neither offers seriously differentiable value on a stand-alone basis, and neither provides infrastructure.

The point of this diagram is that no single technology company offers a complete end-to-end solution. However, if one company finds its "sweet spot" on the continuum shown in the diagram and if it takes the time to understand the customer's requirements, it can identify the company or companies with which it should ally to deliver a complete solution that is crafted on the customer's terms. Such strategic relationships create unique and compelling value that is much greater than any single vendor can offer to its customers; stated another way, the whole is greater than the sum of its parts. This is the model for success in the future.

Changing Times

Ten years ago manufacturers were able to rely on a very different set of differentiators than they rely on today. The year was 1996, and the Internet was just beginning to appear in the public consciousness. For the most part, "access" was analog, except for the Integrated Services Digital Network (ISDN). There was no DSL, and Ethernet had not yet escaped from the desktop environment to become a valid high-speed access and transport option. Transport was T1 and Digital Signal Level 3 (DS3), although the Synchronous Optical Network (SONET) had made its appearance and was beginning to be rolled out by the major long-haul carriers. Switched broadband technologies were limited to ATM and frame relay, which were used exclusively for the transport of data. The Communications Act of 1934 would be rewritten in response to all the changes.

The telecommunications business environment was different as well. Competition for long distance was mature, having been mandated shortly after the 1984 divestiture of AT&T. Local competition remained spotty at best, a nascent concept that only a few companies could demonstrate. The Regional Bell Operating Companies (RBOCs), now called incumbent local exchange carriers (ILECs), were for all intents and purposes local monopolies, a model that would not change for another three years, when the Telecommunications Act of 1996 redefined the responsibilities of major industry players.

During this early stage in the development of a close relationship between communications technology and the end user, the key differentiator for both manufacturers and service providers was the technology. Because of the lack of competition, it was reasonable for these companies to place a great deal of focus on and invest large amounts of money in technology development because that was their differentiator. They investigated communications technologies, pushed them to the limits of their capabilities, built networking systems around them, and sold them to service providers, which in turn built networks with the devices, from which they derived services for sales to end users. That model worked. It was stable, and every player had a clearly defined role in the hierarchy of technology and delivery of services. The final factor that made this model a success was the customer. In 1996 customers' requirements were much less demanding and typically isolated to a single application or department. Information technology (IT) and telecommunications requirements were focused largely on improving "back office" internal operations.

Things Get Complicated

As time went on, technologies standardized and the industry matured. Competition became more real as services became more diverse, opening the door for specialization and the resulting waves of competition. Customers demanded more from the service provider, and the service provider demanded more from the manufacturer. With full-blown mature competition came a migration of influence from the technologists to the end users, who quickly flexed their muscles and began to redefine the technological rules of engagement. Instead of technology, they wanted applications. Instead of applications, they wanted services. Instead of services, they wanted full-blown end-to-end solutions that reflected a deep awareness of the end user's business model and competitive challenges.

A great deal has been written in recent years about the need for companies to sell to the "customer's customer," sometimes referred to as the "third tier." For example, systems manufacturers sell their products directly to the service provider sector. In that relationship they compete directly with other manufacturers largely on the basis of price. However, if they position their products by selling the advantages those products bring to the service provider's customer, they will find themselves at a higher position in the food chain. Instead of being one of several potential vendors, they become a trusted business advisor that enjoys a position within the inner circle because of their ability to affect the service provider's relationship with its own direct customer.

Many things flow downhill, including panic. As competition grew and revenues [average revenue per user (ARPU)] shrank, service providers began to put pressure on the manufacturers to do something they had never before been called on to do: create full-service solutions, in effect an entire network in a single, low-cost box with management and billing built in. And one more thing: It had to be targeted at the needs of the end user.

Thus began the great quandary that characterized service provisioning in the waning years of the twentieth century and continues to characterize it today. Customers became more technologically adept and demanding because they knew what the new technologies were capable of doing. Service providers faced a changing regulatory environment, a legacy network that was built at a time when economic design efficiencies were not as critical as they are today, a broad spectrum of predatory competitors, falling ARPU, and application demands that changed faster than they could track or build networks to support.

As the process cycled through to its inevitable conclusion, several things became clear. First, demands from the customer were not going to slow down and could not be ignored or denied because with competition, those customers had a choice and believed they could go elsewhere for what they wanted. Second, service providers faced the realization that the "service" in "service provider" had become a very different thing from what it had been in the past, and they were ill equipped to deliver it. Third, manufacturers, driven by service provider demands, tried to become solution providers, but without a clear understanding of the issues facing the industry verticals served by their own service provider customers, they didn't have what it took to be effective.

The first response on the part of the manufacturers (in many cases this continues to be the only response) seemed to make sense. They formed alliances with other manufacturers. Lucent, for example, formed alliances with Cisco and Juniper. In the final analysis, this type of relationship adds footprint, but in the eyes of customers it does not add differentiation—or value. In fact, it reinforces the image of commodity status. Consider the wheat or soybean business. Because their products are commodities, farmers grow as much as they possibly can by forming enormous farming cooperatives. Commodity selling is a price game, and the way to have the lowest price is to have the most product. Their differentiator isn't better wheat; it's more of it. In the technology sector, the key to differentiation is added value, not added capacity.

The Answer

Manufacturers sell technology. It's what they have always done, and they are extremely good at it. They have massive R&D infrastructures, employ thousands of design engineers, and have an intimate understanding of the inner workings of the service provider world *from the perspective of technology*. Unfortunately, manufacturers are allowing themselves to be dragged into a role they are not designed to play. They do not understand their customers' customers (the vertical enterprise space) because for the most part they do not sell to them.

Manufacturers need to recognize that a fundamental change is needed in their value chain if they are to remain robust and viable and provide value in the technology food chain. The change, as shown in Figure 6-3, involves the introduction of a new layer in the value chain called the *architects*. In this new model, the architect becomes the manufacturer's primary customer, replacing the service provider.

Manufacturers will be quick to react negatively to this concept because it implies that they are being disintermediated. In this model, they no longer sell directly to the service provider; instead, they have been "demoted," selling to an intermediate company. In their minds, they lose the customer.

Figure 6-3
The service hierarchy, this time with the architect layer inserted between the system and service provider layers.

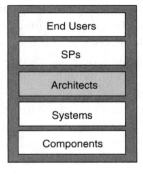

End Users

SPs

Architects

Systems

Components

This, however, is not the case. As the hardware and software that manufacturers sell move closer to commodity status—an inexorable outcome—it is critical that manufacturers move up the food chain, providing services that add unique value to the enormously valuable commodities they sell. One way to move up the chain is to redefine the customer. By selling to an architect, a manufacturer assures its role as a technology innovator. This role is fundamental to the overall process of selecting a valid technology combination, designing a solution, and selling the solution to a service provider. The architects, often called a professional services firm, are strong on the business side of the equation. They do not have technology prowess, but the manufacturer does.

The combination of a firm that understands the end user and a firm that offers superior technology is powerful. Furthermore, by adding the architect to the value chain, the manufacturer suddenly becomes the trusted advisor to the architect about the technology issues that face the service provider. Nobody knows the service provider as well as the manufacturer does. Suddenly, the third tier (the customer's customer) for the manufacturer is the service provider, not the end user. The manufacturer's value to the architect is enhanced by the fact that it understands not only the technology-based products it delivers but also the strategic intelligence it now can share with its architect partner.

In this model, the manufacturers are not "demoted" to a position of less importance. Instead, they realign themselves with a more strategic customer. Think about it: Network systems rapidly are becoming commodities on the open market; indeed, many already have done this. Furthermore, the services offered by telecommunications service providers are already commodities, as evidenced by the fact that they are price-arbitraged every minute of every day. This model of a commodity being sold to a commodity provider is a long-term recipe for true disintermediation of both the buyer and the seller. In the new model, however, the architect sits in a position to aggregate diverse capabilities and offer specific business-oriented solutions to enterprise customers.

A manufacturer's multiservice box may be a solution, but in the final analysis it is a solution to a technology problem, not a business challenge. Under the terms of the new business model, however, the architect aggregates the functional components required to offer a solution to a legitimate business challenge, one component of which is the multiservice box described above. The manufacturer takes on a linchpin role as technical advisor to the architect, providing the network substrate over which the final solution is delivered.

Each layer of the value chain, then, does what it does best. The component manufacturer sells components to the system manufacturer, which in turn works closely with the professional services firm to craft a technology solution that is based specifically on the business challenge identified by the professional services firm in its discussions with the service provider. The manufacturer also provides advice and counsel to the architect in its role as an expert on the issues facing the third tier. The professional services firm researches and understands the business issues facing the end user and serves as the key interface between the end user and the technology that runs the end user's applications.

In local area networks, there is a standards-based concept known as *logical link control* (LLC). LLC allows disparate access techniques (Ethernet, token ring, wireless, etc.) to reach higher-layer applications, as shown in Figure 6-4. In effect, it serves as a universal translator between the user's applications and the network, making the complex underlying technology invisible to the end user. The business model suggested here is identical to the LLC concept: When the customers are isolated from the technology and are offered a business-oriented solution that is *based* on technology, the customers' requirements are served better.

This model can be applied to other companies in the technology industry as well. For example, there is no reason why the architect cannot aggregate products and services from a wider array of providers, as shown in Figure 6-5. The architect could assemble solution components from systems manufacturers, software developers, network management system developers, billing and invoicing service providers, local and long-distance providers, cable companies, ISPs,

Figure 6-4
The Logical Link Control Layer (LLC) makes it possible for any physical layer to work seamlessly with any upper layer service.

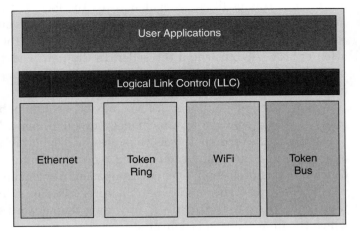

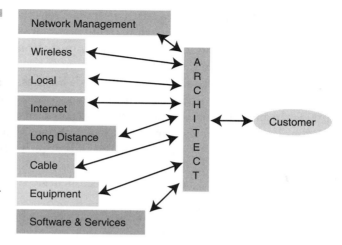

Figure 6-5
The "architect" sits between the diverse offered services and the end user, making the complexity of the services layer invisible to the customer.

and wireless providers. These services could be combined into a targeted solution to customer business challenges. Like the Roman god Janus shown in Figure 6-6, the architect has two "faces:" One is pointed toward the technologies on the left, the other toward the customer on the right. The left-facing half of the company has great technological expertise: It understands what each technology does, what its strengths are, how it works, and how it interacts (if appropriate) with the others. The right-facing side of the firm understands the customer's business challenges.

Consider the following example. A strategic customer engages a services architect; the customer in this case is a large bank. In the last decade deposits have fled the banking industry in favor of mutual fund investments, most of which are transacted either through a financial services broker or over the Internet. As a result, the banking industry has fewer deposits and, by definition, less revenue, forcing it to raise rates to maintain operating revenue. This causes more customers to flee, resulting in a vicious downward spiral.

The customer-facing side of the architect understands this phenomenon from a business perspective. Working closely with the left-facing side of the business, the architect crafts a technology solution that addresses

Figure 6-6
The two-faced Roman god, Janus.

the banking death spiral: perhaps a greater Web presence, perhaps financial consulting services, perhaps converged investment instruments that better position the bank within its marketplace. This results in several outcomes. First, it delivers to the customer a solution that uniquely and immediately addresses the bank's business issues. Second, it shields the bank from the need to have expertise in technologies that lie outside the banking industry. Under the terms of this model, the companies that provide technical services to the architect also serve as consulting resources, allowing them to deliver on-target technology-based solutions jointly. The customer is left to focus on banking issues, freed from the need to support an overly robust technical services organization of its own.

This approach is in many ways radically different from the designs of prior customer relationship modalities and requires a significant realignment of thought relative to the evolving roles and responsibilities of the players in the alliance. However, the model has a direct and quantifiable impact on service-level agreements and revenue models and speaks directly to the four things that customers—*all* customers—want today: CAPEX and OPEX reduction, increased revenues, protection and advancement of the firm's competitive position, and mitigated marketplace risk. The intermediate architect model complements all four of these drivers.

Final Thoughts

I live in northern Vermont, 30 minutes south of the border with Quebec, three hours north of Boston, and five hours from New York City. In Chittenden County where I actually live, I have access to three different forms of broadband, three major wireless carriers, and countless ISPs. I can get pretty much anything I need here, yet the joke most Vermonters make about Chittenden County is that "the nice thing about it is that it's so close to Vermont." Indeed. I need drive only about 10 minutes in any direction (okay, let's leave out west; if I drive 10 minutes in that direction, I'll be in the middle of Lake Champlain) to be in rural countryside where the infrastructure delivers voice but little else. The population is sparse at best, and there are often many miles of wilderness between neighbors. With most of the affluence concentrated in and around Burlington (Chittenden County), the mean income in most of Vermont is very low, in many areas well below the poverty level.

When I work in South Africa, Paraguay, or Thailand, I find eerily similar conditions. Outside of major population centers are vast underserved areas supporting sparse populations that earn little money but that could in many cases benefit economically from the availability of affordable broadband. The point is that I don't have to go to the third world to find technological and social conditions that mimic this situation. There are plenty of first world countries with dark corners that have third world infrastructures, and there's no excuse for that. It is a well-known fact that telecommunications, like roads and power, is a critical element and change agent when it comes to economic growth.

WiMAX and the technologies it will find itself in partnership with will become a major component of global connectivity efforts. Together with IMS, IPTV, and VoIP, it will facilitate the delivery of cost-effective, high-quality communications services to the world, not only enabling greenfield markets but enriching existing ones. Its ability to make broadband available to rural areas and overcome the prohibitive cost of bringing service to sparsely populated areas is one of the greatest advantages it offers.

That being said, I caution readers not to get caught up in the hype that surrounds WiMAX at the moment. It isn't a perfect solution: No technology is. WiMAX is what it is, no more and no less. Does it have value? Absolutely, when deployed properly. In combination with other technologies, it becomes even more powerful, illustrating one of the key tenets of success: Collaboration is everything. Companies that want to deploy WiMAX should look carefully at the facts, watch the standards development efforts, pay attention to the companies manufacturing WiMAX equipment, keep an eye on the regulators, and listen to the market. The winner of the WiMAX service game will be the company that learns to deploy the best that all these sectors have to offer.

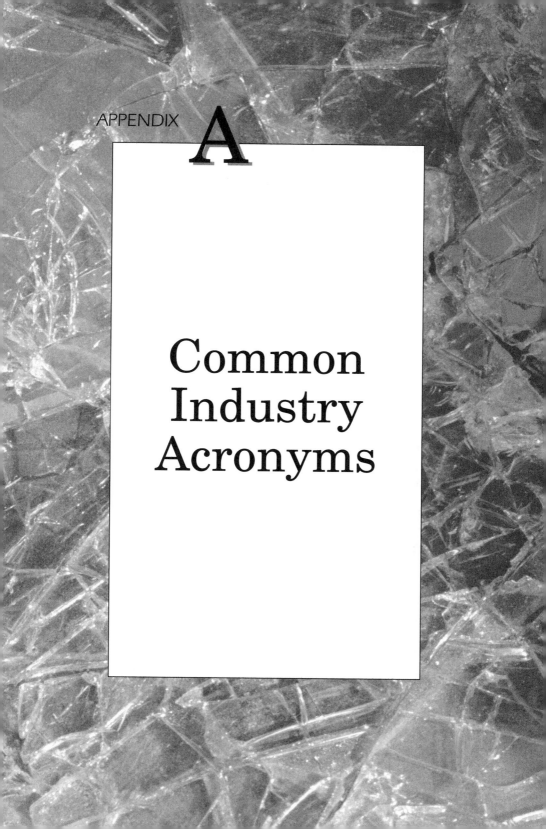

APPENDIX A

Common Industry Acronyms

AAL   ATM Adaptation Layer

AARP   AppleTalk Address Resolution Protocol

ABM   Asynchronous Balanced Mode

ABR   Available Bit Rate

AC   Alternating Current

ACD   Automatic Call Distribution

ACELP   Algebraic Code-Excited Linear Prediction

ACF   Advanced Communication Function

ACK   Acknowledgment

ACM   Address Complete Message

ACSE   Association Control Service Element

ACTLU   Activate Logical Unit

ACTPU   Activate Physical Unit

ADCCP   Advanced Data Communications Control Procedures

ADM   Add/Drop Multiplexer

ADPCM   Adaptive Differential Pulse Code Modulation

ADSL   Asymmetric Digital Subscriber Line

AFI   Application Family Identifier (RFID)

AFI   Authority and Format Identifier

AI   Application Identifier

AIN   Advanced Intelligent Network

AIS Alarm Indication Signal

ALU Arithmetic Logic Unit

AM Administrative Module (Lucent 5ESS)

AM Amplitude Modulation

AMI Alternate Mark Inversion

AMP Administrative Module Processor

AMPS Advanced Mobile Phone System

ANI Automatic Number Identification (SS7)

ANSI American National Standards Institute

APD Avalanche Photodiode

API Application Programming Interface

APPC Advanced Program-to-Program Communication

APPN Advanced Peer-to-Peer Networking

APS Automatic Protection Switching

ARE All Routes Explorer (source route bridging)

ARM Asynchronous Response Mode

ARP Address Resolution Protocol (IETF)

ARPA Advanced Research Projects Agency

ARPANET Advanced Research Projects Agency Network

ARPU Average Revenue Per User

ARQ Automatic Repeat Request

ASCII American Standard Code for Information Interchange

ASI Alternate Space Inversion

ASIC Application-Specific Integrated Circuit

ASK Amplitude Shift Keying

ASN Abstract Syntax Notation

ASP Application Service Provider

AT&T American Telephone and Telegraph

ATDM Asynchronous Time Division Multiplexing

ATM Asynchronous Transfer Mode

ATM Automatic Teller Machine

ATMF ATM Forum

ATQA Answer to Request A (RFID)

ATQB Answer to Request B (RFID)

ATS Answer to Select (RFID)

ATTRIB Attribute (RFID)

AU Administrative Unit (SDH)

AUG Administrative Unit Group (SDH)

AWG American Wire Gauge

B2B Business to Business

B2C Business to Consumer

B8ZS Binary 8 Zero Substitution

BANCS   Bell Administrative Network Communications System

BBN   Bolt, Beranak, and Newman

BBS   Bulletin Board Service

Bc   Committed Burst Size

BCC   Block Check Character

BCC   Blocked Calls Cleared

BCD   Blocked Calls Delayed

BCDIC   Binary Coded Decimal Interchange Code

Be   Excess Burst Size

BECN   Backward Explicit Congestion Notification

BER   Bit Error Rate

BERT   Bit Error Rate Test

BGCF   Breakout Gateway Control Function

BGP   Border Gateway Protocol (IETF)

BIB   Backward Indicator Bit (SS7)

BICC   Bearer Independent Call Control

B-ICI   Broadband Intercarrier Interface

BIOS   Basic Input/Output System

BIP   Bit Interleaved Parity

B-ISDN   Broadband Integrated Services Digital Network

BISYNC   Binary Synchronous Communications Protocol

BITNET   Because It's Time Network

BITS   Building Integrated Timing Supply

BLSR   Bidirectional Line Switched Ring

BOC   Bell Operating Company

BPRZ   Bipolar Return to Zero

Bps   Bits Per Second

BRI   Basic Rate Interface

BRITE   Basic Rate Interface Transmission Equipment

BSC   Binary Synchronous Communications

BSN   Backward Sequence Number (SS7)

BSRF   Bell System Reference Frequency

BTAM   Basic Telecommunications Access Method

BUS   Broadcast Unknown Server

C/R   Command/Response

CAD   Computer-Aided Design

CAE   Computer-Aided Engineering

CAGR   Compound Annual Growth Rate

CAM   Computer-Aided Manufacturing

CAMEL   Customized Applications for Mobile Networks Enhanced Logic

CAP   CAMEL Application Part

CAP Carrierless Amplitude/Phase Modulation

CAP Competitive Access Provider

CAPEX Capital Expenditure

CAPEX Capital Expense

CARICOM Caribbean Community and Common Market

CASE Common Application Service Element

CASE Computer-Aided Software Engineering

CASPIAN Consumers Against Privacy Invasion and Numbering (RFID)

CAT Computer-Aided Tomography

CATIA Computer-Assisted Three-Dimensional Interactive Application

CATV Community Antenna Television

CBEMA Computer and Business Equipment Manufacturers Association

CBR Constant Bit Rate

CBT Computer-Based Training

CC Cluster Controller

CCIR International Radio Consultative Committee

CCIS Common Channel Interoffice Signaling

CCITT International Telegraph and Telephone Consultative Committee

CCS Common Channel Signaling

CCS   Hundred Call Seconds per Hour

CD   Collision Detection

CD   Compact Disc

CDC   Control Data Corporation

CDMA   Code Division Multiple Access

CDPD   Cellular Digital Packet Data

CD-ROM   Compact Disc-Read Only Memory

CDVT   Cell Delay Variation Tolerance

CEI   Comparably Efficient Interconnection

CEPT   Conference of European Postal and Telecommunications Administrations

CERN   European Council for Nuclear Research

CERT   Computer Emergency Response Team

CES   Circuit Emulation Service

CEV   Controlled Environmental Vault

CGI   Common Gateway Interface (Internet)

CHAP   Challenge Handshake Authentication Protocol

CHL   Chain Home Low RADAR

CICS   Customer Information Control System

CICS/VS   Customer Information Control System/Virtual Storage

CID   Card Identifier (RFID)

CIDR Classless Interdomain Routing (IETF)

CIF Cells in Frames

CIR Committed Information Rate

CISC Complex Instruction Set Computer

CIX Commercial Internet Exchange

CLASS Custom Local Area Signaling Services (Bellcore)

CLEC Competitive Local Exchange Carrier

CLLM Consolidated Link Layer Management

CLNP Connectionless Network Protocol

CLNS Connectionless Network Service

CLP Cell Loss Priority

CM Communications Module (Lucent 5ESS)

CMIP Common Management Information Protocol

CMISE Common Management Information Service Element

CMOL CMIP over LLC

CMOS Complementary Metal Oxide Semiconductor

CMOT CMIP over TCP/IP

CMP Communications Module Processor

CNE Certified NetWare Engineer

CNM Customer Network Management

CNR Carrier-to-Noise Ratio

CO   Central Office

CoCOM   Coordinating Committee on Export Controls

CODEC   Coder-Decoder

COMC   Communications Controller

CONS   Connection-Oriented Network Service

CORBA   Common Object Request Brokered Architecture

COS   Class of Service (APPN)

COS   Corporation for Open Systems

CPE   Customer Premises Equipment

CPU   Central Processing Unit

CR   Change Request

CRC   Cyclic Redundancy Check

CRM   Customer Relationship Management

CRT   Cathode Ray Tube

CRS   Cell Relay Service

CRV   Call Reference Value

CS   Convergence Sublayer

CSA   Carrier Serving Area

CSCF   Call Session Control Function

CSMA   Carrier Sense Multiple Access

CSMA/CA   Carrier Sense Multiple Access with Collision Avoidance

CSMA/CD   Carrier Sense Multiple Access with Collision Detection

CSU   Channel Service Unit

CTI   Computer Telephony Integration

CTIA   Cellular Telecommunications Industry Association

CTS   Clear to Send

CU   Control Unit

CVSD   Continuously Variable Slope Delta Modulation

CWDM   Coarse Wavelength Division Multiplexing

D/A   Digital to Analog

DA   Destination Address

DAC   Dual Attachment Concentrator (FDDI)

DACS   Digital Access and Cross-Connect System

DARPA   Defense Advanced Research Projects Agency

DAS   Direct Attached Storage

DAS   Dual Attachment Station (FDDI)

DASD   Direct Access Storage Device

DB   Decibel

DBS   Direct Broadcast Satellite

DC   Direct Current

DCC   Data Communications Channel (SONET)

DCE   Data Circuit-Terminating Equipment

DCN   Data Communications Network

DCS   Digital Cross-Connect System

DCT   Discrete Cosine Transform

DDCMP   Digital Data Communications Management Protocol (DNA)

DDD   Direct Distance Dialing

DDP   Datagram Delivery Protocol

DDS   Dataphone Digital Service (sometimes Digital Data Service)

DDS   Digital Data Service

DE   Discard Eligibility (LAPF)

DECT   Digital European Cordless Telephone

DES   Data Encryption Standard (NIST)

DID   Direct Inward Dialing

DIP   Dual Inline Package

DLC   Digital Loop Carrier

DLCI   Data Link Connection Identifier

DLE   Data Link Escape

DLSw   Data Link Switching

DM   Data Mining

DM   Delta Modulation

DM   Disconnected Mode

DMA   Direct Memory Access (computers)

DMAC   Direct Memory Access Control

DME   Distributed Management Environment

DMS   Digital Multiplex Switch

DMT   Discrete Multitone

DNA   Digital Network Architecture

DNIC   Data Network Identification Code (X.121)

DNIS   Dialed Number Identification Service

DNS   Domain Name Service

DNS   Domain Name System (IETF)

DOD   Department of Defense

DOD   Direct Outward Dialing

DOJ   Department of Justice

DOV   Data Over Voice

DPSK   Differential Phase Shift Keying

DQDB   Distributed Queue Dual Bus

DR   Data Rate Send (RFID)

DRAM   Dynamic Random-Access Memory

DS   Data Rate Send (RFID)

DSAP   Destination Service Access Point

DSF   Dispersion-Shifted Fiber

DSI   Digital Speech Interpolation

DSL   Digital Subscriber Line

DSLAM   Digital Subscriber Line Access Multiplexer

DSP   Digital Signal Processing

DSR   Data Set Ready

DSS   Digital Satellite System

DSS   Digital Subscriber Signaling System

DSSS   Direct Sequence Spread Spectrum

DSU   Data Service Unit

DTE   Data Terminal Equipment

DTMF   Dual Tone Multifrequency

DTR   Data Terminal Ready

DVRN   Dense Virtual Routed Networking (Crescent)

DWDM   Dense Wavelength Division Multiplexing

DXI   Data Exchange Interface

E/O   Electrical to Optical

EAN   European Article Numbering System

EBCDIC   Extended Binary Coded Decimal Interchange Code

EBITDA   Earnings Before Interest, Tax, Depreciation,
and Amortization

ECMA   European Computer Manufacturer Association

ECN   Explicit Congestion Notification

ECSA   Exchange Carriers Standards Association

EDFA   Erbium-Doped Fiber Amplifier

EDI   Electronic Data Interchange

EDIBANX   EDI Bank Alliance Network Exchange

EDIFACT   Electronic Data Interchange for Administration, Commerce, and Trade (ANSI)

EFCI   Explicit Forward Congestion Indicator

EFTA   European Free Trade Association

EGP   Exterior Gateway Protocol (IETF)

EIA   Electronics Industry Association

EIGRP   Enhanced Interior Gateway Routing Protocol

EIR   Excess Information Rate

EMBARC   Electronic Mail Broadcast to a Roaming Computer

EMI   Electromagnetic Interference

EMS   Element Management System

EN   End Node

ENIAC   Electronic Numerical Integrator and Computer

EO   End Office

EOC   Embedded Operations Channel (SONET)

EOT   End of Transmission (BISYNC)

EPC   Electronic Product Code

EPROM   Erasable Programmable Read-Only Memory

EPS   Earnings per Share

ERP   Enterprise Resource Planning

ESCON   Enterprise System Connection (IBM)

ESF   Extended Superframe Format

ESOP   Employee Stock Ownership Plan

ESP   Enhanced Service Provider

ESS   Electronic Switching System

ETSI   European Telecommunications Standards Institute

ETX   End of Text (BISYNC)

EVA   Economic Value Added

EWOS   European Workshop for Open Systems

FACTR   Fujitsu Access and Transport System

FAQs   Frequently Asked Questions

FASB   Financial Accounting Standards Board

FAT   File Allocation Table

FCF   Free Cash Flow

FCS   Frame Check Sequence

FDA   Food and Drug Administration

FDD   Frequency Division Duplex

FDDI   Fiber Distributed Data Interface

FDM   Frequency Division Multiplexing

FDMA   Frequency Division Multiple Access

FDX   Full Duplex

FEBE   Far End Block Error (SONET)

FEC   Forward Equivalence Class

FEC   Forward Error Correction

FECN   Forward Explicit Congestion Notification

FEP   Front-End Processor

FERF   Far End Receive Failure (SONET)

FET   Field Effect Transistor

FHSS   Frequency Hopping Spread Spectrum

FIB   Forward Indicator Bit (SS7)

FIFO   First In First Out

FITL   Fiber in the Loop

FLAG   Fiber Link Across the Globe

FM   Frequency Modulation

FOIRL   Fiber Optic Inter-Repeater Link

FPGA   Field Programmable Gate Array

FR   Frame Relay

FRAD   Frame Relay Access Device

FRBS   Frame Relay Bearer Service

FSDI   Frame Size Device Integer (RFID)

FSK   Frequency Shift Keying

FSN   Forward Sequence Number (SS7)

FTAM   File Transfer, Access, and Management

FTP   File Transfer Protocol (IETF)

FTTC   Fiber to the Curb

FTTH   Fiber to the Home

FUNI   Frame User-to-Network Interface

FWI   Frame Waiting Integer (RFID)

FWM   Four Wave Mixing

GAAP   Generally Accepted Accounting Principles

GATT   General Agreement on Tariffs and Trade

GbE   Gigabit Ethernet

Gbps   Gigabits per Second (billion bits per second)

GDMO   Guidelines for the Development of Managed Objects

GDP   Gross Domestic Product

GEOS   Geosynchronous Earth Orbit Satellite

GFC   Generic Flow Control (ATM)

GFI   General Format Identifier (X.25)

GFP   Generic Framing Procedure

GFP-F   Generic Framing Procedure-Frame-Based

GFP-X   Generic Framing Procedure-Transparent

GGSN   Gateway GPRS Support Node

GMPLS   Generalized MPLS

GOSIP   Government Open Systems Interconnection Profile

GPRS   Generalized Packet Radio System

GPS   Global Positioning System

GRIN   Graded Index (fiber)

GSM   Global System for Mobile Communications

GTIN   Global Trade Item Number

GUI   Graphical User Interface

HDB3   High Density, Bipolar 3 (E-Carrier)

HDLC   High-Level Data Link Control

HDSL   High-Bit-Rate Digital Subscriber Line

HDTV   High-Definition Television

HDX   Half-Duplex

HEC   Header Error Control (ATM)

HFC   Hybrid Fiber/Coax

HFS   Hierarchical File Storage

HIPAA   Health Insurance Portability and Accountability Act

HLR   Home Location Register

HNO   Host Network Operator

HPPI   High-Performance Parallel Interface

HSS   Home Subscriber Server

HSSI   High-Speed Serial Interface (ANSI)

HTML   Hypertext Markup Language

HTTP   Hypertext Transfer Protocol (IETF)

HTU   HDSL Transmission Unit

I   Intrapictures

IAB   Internet Architecture Board (formerly Internet Activities Board)

IACS   Integrated Access and Cross-Connect System

IAD   Integrated Access Device

IAM   Initial Address Message (SS7)

IANA   Internet Address Naming Authority

ICMP   Internet Control Message Protocol (IETF)

I-CSCF   Interrogating Call Session Control Function

IDP   Internet Datagram Protocol

IEC   Interexchange Carrier (also IXC)

IEC   International Electrotechnical Commission

IEEE   Institute of Electrical and Electronics Engineers

IETF   Internet Engineering Task Force

IFRB   International Frequency Registration Board

IGP   Interior Gateway Protocol (IETF)

IGRP   Interior Gateway Routing Protocol

ILEC   Incumbent Local Exchange Carrier

IM   Instant Messenger (AOL)

IML   Initial Microcode Load

IMP   Interface Message Processor (ARPANET)

IMPRES   Instant Messaging and Presence

IMS   IP Multimedia Subsystem

IMS   Information Management System

InARP   Inverse Address Resolution Protocol (IETF)

InATMARP   Inverse ATMARP

INMARSAT   International Maritime Satellite Organization

INP   Internet Nodal Processor

InterNIC   Internet Network Information Center

IP   Intellectual Property

IP   Internet Protocol (IETF)

IPO   Initial Product Offering

IPX   Internetwork Packet Exchange (NetWare)

IRU   Indefeasible Rights of Use

IS   Information Systems

ISDN   Integrated Services Digital Network

ISO   Information Systems Organization

ISO   International Organization for Standardization

ISOC   Internet Society

ISP   Internet Service Provider

ISUP   ISDN User Part (SS7)

IT   Information Technology

ITU   International Telecommunication Union

ITU-R   International Telecommunication Union-Radio Communication Sector

IVD   Inside Vapor Deposition

IVR   Interactive Voice Response

IXC   Interexchange Carrier

JAN   Japanese Article Numbering System

JEPI   Joint Electronic Paynets Initiative

JES   Job Entry System

JIT   Just in Time

JPEG   Joint Photographic Experts Group

JTC   Joint Technical Committee

KB   Kilobytes

Kbps   Kilobits per Second (thousand bits per second)

KLTN   Potassium Lithium Tantalate Niobate

KM   Knowledge Management

LAN Local Area Network

LANE LAN Emulation

LAP Link Access Procedure (X.25)

LAPB Link Access Procedure Balanced (X.25)

LAPD Link Access Procedure for the D-Channel

LAPF Link Access Procedure to Frame Mode Bearer Services

LAPF-Core Core Aspects of the Link Access Procedure to Frame Mode Bearer Services

LAPM Link Access Procedure for Modems

LAPX Link Access Procedure Half-Duplex

LASER Light Amplification by the Stimulated Emission of Radiation

LATA Local Access and Transport Area

LCD Liquid Crystal Display

LCGN Logical Channel Group Number

LCM Line Concentrator Module

LCN Local Communications Network

LD Laser Diode

LDAP Lightweight Directory Access Protocol (X.500)

LEAF® Large Effective Area Fiber (Corning product)

LEC Local Exchange Carrier

LED Light-Emitting Diode

LENS   Lightwave Efficient Network Solution (Centerpoint)

LEOS   Low Earth Orbit Satellite

LER   Label Edge Router

LI   Length Indicator

LIDB   Line Information Database

LIFO   Last In First Out

LIS   Logical IP Subnet

LLC   Logical Link Control

LMDS   Local Multipoint Distribution System

LMI   Local Management Interface

LMOS   Loop Maintenance Operations System

LORAN   Long-Range Radio Navigation

LPC   Linear Predictive Coding

LPP   Lightweight Presentation Protocol

LRC   Longitudinal Redundancy Check (BISYNC)

LS   Link State

LSI   Large-Scale Integration

LSP   Label-Switched Path

LSR   Label-Switched Router

LU   Line Unit

LU   Logical Unit (SNA)

MAC   Media Access Control

MAN   Metropolitan Area Network

MAP   Manufacturing Automation Protocol

MAP   Mobile Application Part

MAU   Medium Attachment Unit (Ethernet)

MAU   Multistation Access Unit (Token Ring)

MB   Megabyte

MBA™   Metro Business Access (Ocular)

Mbps   Megabits per Second (million bits per second)

MD   Message Digest (MD2, MD4, MD5) (IETF)

MDF   Main Distribution Frame

MDU   Multidwelling Unit

MEMS   Micro Electrical Mechanical System

MF   Multifrequency

MFJ   Modified Final Judgment

MHS   Message Handling System (X.400)

MIB   Management Information Base

MIC   Medium Interface Connector (FDDI)

MIME   Multipurpose Internet Mail Extension (IETF)

MIPS   Millions of Instructions per Second

MIS   Management Information System

MITI   Ministry of International Trade and Industry (Japan)

MITS   Micro Instrumentation and Telemetry Systems

ML-PPP   Multilink Point-to-Point Protocol

MMDS   Multichannel, Multipoint Distribution System

MMF   Multimode Fiber

MNP   Microcom Networking Protocol

MON   Metropolitan Optical Network

MoU   Memorandum of Understanding

MP   Multilink PPP

MPEG   Motion Picture Experts Group

MPLS   Multiprotocol Label Switching

MPOA   Multiprotocol over ATM

MPÏS   Multiprotocol Lambda Switching

MRFC   Media Resource Function Controller

MRFP   Media Resource Function Processor

MRI   Magnetic Resonance Imaging

MSB   Most Significant Bit

MSC   Mobile Switching Center

MSO   Mobile Switching Office

MSPP   Multi-Service Provisioning Platform

MSVC   Meta-Signaling Virtual Channel

MTA   Major Trading Area

MTBF   Mean Time Between Failures

MTP   Message Transfer Part (SS7)

MTSO   Mobile Telephone Switching Office

MTTR   Mean Time to Repair

MTU   Maximum Transmission Unit

MTU   Multitenant Unit

MVNE   Mobile Virtual Network Enabler

MVNO   Mobile Virtual Network Operator

MVS   Multiple Virtual Storage

NAD   Node Address (RFID)

NAFTA   North American Free Trade Agreement

NAK   Negative Acknowledgment (BISYNC, DDCMP)

NAP   Network Access Point (Internet)

NARUC   National Association of Regulatory Utility Commissioners

NAS   Network Attached Storage

NASA   National Aeronautics and Space Administration

NASDAQ   National Association of Securities Dealers Automated Quotations

NATA   North American Telecommunications Association

NATO   North Atlantic Treaty Organization

NAU Network Accessible Unit

NCP Network Control Program

NCSA National Center for Supercomputer Applications

NCTA National Cable Television Association

NDIS Network Driver Interface Specifications

NDSF Non-Dispersion-Shifted Fiber

NetBEUI NetBIOS Extended User Interface

NetBIOS Network Basic Input/Output System

NFS Network File System (Sun)

NGN Next-Generation Network

NGOSS Next-Generation Operations Support System

NIC Network Interface Card

NII National Information Infrastructure

NIST National Institute of Standards and Technology (formerly NBS)

NIU Network Interface Unit

NLPID Network Layer Protocol Identifier

NLSP NetWare Link Services Protocol

NM Network Module

Nm Nanometer

NMC Network Management Center

NMS Network Management System

NMT   Nordic Mobile Telephone

NMVT   Network Management Vector Transport Protocol

NNI   Network Node Interface

NNI   Network-to-Network Interface

NOC   Network Operations Center

NOCC   Network Operations Control Center

NOPAT   Net Operating Profit after Tax

NOS   Network Operating System

NPA   Numbering Plan Area

NREN   National Research and Education Network

NRZ   Non-Return to Zero

NRZI   Non-Return to Zero Inverted

NSA   National Security Agency

NSAP   Network Service Access Point

NSAPA   Network Service Access Point Address

NSF   National Science Foundation

NTSC   National Television Systems Committee

NTT   Nippon Telephone and Telegraph

NVB   Number of Valid Bits (RFID)

NVOD   Near Video on Demand

NZDSF   Non-Zero Dispersion-Shifted Fiber

OADM Optical Add-Drop Multiplexer

OAM Operations, Administration, and Maintenance

OAM&P Operations, Administration, Maintenance, and Provisioning

OAN Optical Area Network

OBS Optical Burst Switching

OC Optical Carrier

OEM Original Equipment Manufacturer

O-E-O Optical-Electrical-Optical

OLS Optical Line System (Lucent)

OMAP Operations, Maintenance, and Administration Part (SS7)

ONA Open Network Architecture

ONS Object Name Service

ONU Optical Network Unit

OOF Out of Frame

OPEX Operating Expenses

OS Operating System

OSA Open Systems Architecture

OSF Open Software Foundation

OSI Open Systems Interconnection (ISO, ITU-T)

OSI RM Open Systems Interconnection Reference Model

OSPF Open Shortest Path First (IETF)

OSS   Operation Support System

OTDM   Optical Time Division Multiplexing

OTDR   Optical Time-Domain Reflectometer

OUI   Organizationally Unique Identifier (SNAP)

OVD   Outside Vapor Deposition

OXC   Optical Cross-Connect

P/F   Poll/Final (HDLC)

PAD   Packet Assembler/Disassembler (X.25)

PAL   Phase Alternate Line

PAM   Pulse Amplitude Modulation

PANS   Pretty Amazing New Stuff

PBX   Private Branch Exchange

PCB   Protocol Control Byte (RFID)

PCI   Peripheral Component Interface

PCI   Pulse Code Modulation

PCMCIA   Personal Computer Memory Card International Association

PCN   Personal Communications Network

PCS   Personal Communications Services

P-CSCF   Proxy Call Session Control Function

PDA   Personal Digital Assistant

PDF   Policy Decision Function

PDH   Plesiochronous Digital Hierarchy

PDU   Protocol Data Unit

PIN   Positive-Intrinsic-Negative

PING   Packet Internet Groper (TCP/IP)

PKC   Public Key Cryptography

PLCP   Physical Layer Convergence Protocol

PLP   Packet Layer Protocol (X.25)

PM   Phase Modulation

PMD   Physical Medium Dependent (FDDI)

PML   Physical Markup Language

PNNI   Private Network Node Interface (ATM)

PoC   Push-to-Talk over Cellular

PON   Passive Optical Networking

POP   Point of Presence

POSIT   Profiles for Open Systems Interworking Technologies

POSIX   Portable Operating System Interface for UNIX

POTS   Plain Old Telephone Service

PPM   Pulse Position Modulation

PPP   Point-to-Point Protocol (IETF)

PPS   Protocol Parameter Selection (RFID)

PRC   Primary Reference Clock

PRI   Primary Rate Interface

PROFS   Professional Office System

PROM   Programmable Read-Only Memory

PSDN   Packet Switched Data Network

PSK   Phase Shift Keying (RFID)

PSPDN   Packet Switched Public Data Network

PSTN   Public Switched Telephone Network

PTI   Payload Type Identifier (ATM)

PTT   Post, Telephone, and Telegraph

PU   Physical Unit (SNA)

PUC   Public Utilities Commission

PUPI   Pseudo-Unique PICC Identifier

PVC   Permanent Virtual Circuit

QAM   Quadrature Amplitude Modulation

Q-bit   Qualified Data Bit (X.25)

QLLC   Qualified Logical Link Control (SNA)

QoS   Quality of Service

QPSK   Quadrature Phase Shift Keying

QPSX   Queued Packet Synchronous Exchange

R&D   Research and Development

RADAR   Radio Detection and Ranging

RADSL   Rate Adaptive Digital Subscriber Line

RAID   Redundant Array of Inexpensive Disks

RAM   Random-Access Memory

RAN   Radio Access Network

RARP   Reverse Address Resolution Protocol (IETF)

RAS   Remote Access Server

RATS   Request for Answer to Select (RFID)

RBOC   Regional Bell Operating Company

READ_DATA   Read Data from Transponder (RFID)

REQA   Request A (RFID)

REQB   Request B (RFID)

REQUEST_SNR   Request Serial Number (RFID)

RF   Radio Frequency

RFC   Request for Comments (IETF)

RFH   Remote Frame Handler (ISDN)

RFI   Radio Frequency Interference

RFID   Radio Frequency Identification

RFP   Request for Proposal

RFQ   Request for Quote

RFx   Request for x, where "x" can be Proposal, Quote, Information, Comment, etc.

RHC   Regional Holding Company

RHK   Ryan, Hankin and Kent (Consultancy)

RIP   Routing Information Protocol (IETF)

RISC   Reduced Instruction Set Computer

RJE   Remote Job Entry

RNR   Receive Not Ready (HDLC)

ROA   Return on Assets

ROE   Return on Equity

ROI   Return on Investment

ROM   Read-Only Memory

RO-RO   Roll-On Roll-Off

ROSE   Remote Operation Service Element

RPC   Remote Procedure Call

RPR   Resilient Packet Ring

RR   Receive Ready (HDLC)

RSA   Rivest, Shamir, and Aleman

RTS   Request to Send (EIA-232-E)

RTT   Round-Trip Translation

S/DMS   SONET/Digital Multiplex System

S/N   Signal-to-Noise Ratio

SAA   Systems Application Architecture (IBM)

SAAL   Signaling ATM Adaptation Layer (ATM)

SABM   Set Asynchronous Balanced Mode (HDLC)

SABME   Set Asynchronous Balanced Mode Extended (HDLC)

SAC   Single Attachment Concentrator (FDDI)

SAK   Select Acknowledge (RFID)

SAN   Storage Area Network

SAP   Service Access Point (generic)

SAPI   Service Access Point Identifier (LAPD)

SAR   Segmentation and Reassembly (ATM)

SAS   Single Attachment Station (FDDI)

SASE   Specific Applications Service Element (subset of CASE, Application Layer)

SATAN   System Administrator Tool for Analyzing Networks

SBLP   Service-Based Local Policy

SBS   Stimulated Brillouin Scattering

SCCP   Signaling Connection Control Point (SS7)

SCM   Supply Chain Management

SCP   Service Control Point (SS7)

SCREAM   Scalable Control of a Rearrangeable Extensible Array of Mirrors (Calient)

S-CSCF   Serving Call Session Control Function

SCSI   Small Computer Systems Interface

SCTE Serial Clock Transmit External (EIA-232-E)

SDH Synchronous Digital Hierarchy (ITU-T)

SDLC Synchronous Data Link Control (IBM)

SDS Scientific Data Systems

SEC Securities and Exchange Commission

SECAM Sequential Color with Memory

SELECT Select Transponder (RFID)

SELECT_ACKNOWLEDGE Acknowledge Selection (RFID)

SELECT_SNR Select Serial Number (RFID)

SF Superframe Format (T-1)

SFGI Startup Frame Guard Integer (RFID)

SGML Standard Generalized Markup Language

SGMP Simple Gateway Management Protocol (IETF)

SGSN Serving GPRS Support Node

SHDSL Symmetric HDSL

S-HTTP Secure HTTP (IETF)

SIF Signaling Information Field

SIG Special Interest Group

SIO Service Information Octet

SIP Serial Interface Protocol

SIP Session Initiation Protocol

SIR   Sustained Information Rate (SMDS)

SLA   Service-Level Agreement

SLIP   Serial Line Interface Protocol (IETF)

SM   Switching Module

SMAP   System Management Application Part

SMDS   Switched Multimegabit Data Service

SMF   Single Mode Fiber

SMP   Simple Management Protocol

SMP   Switching Module Processor

SMR   Specialized Mobile Radio

SMS   Standard Management System (SS7)

SMTP   Simple Mail Transfer Protocol (IETF)

SNA   Systems Network Architecture (IBM)

SNAP   Subnetwork Access Protocol

SNI   Subscriber Network Interface (SMDS)

SNMP   Simple Network Management Protocol (IETF)

SNP   Sequence Number Protection

SNR   Serial Number (RFID)

SOAP   Simple Object Access Protocol

SOHO   Small Office, Home Office

SONET   Synchronous Optical Network

SPAG   Standards Promotion and Application Group

SPARC   Scalable Performance Architecture

SPE   Synchronous Payload Envelope (SONET)

SPID   Service Profile Identifier (ISDN)

SPM   Self-Phase Modulation

SPOC   Single Point of Contact

SPX   Sequenced Packet Exchange (NetWare)

SQL   Structured Query Language

SRB   Source Route Bridging

SRLP   Service-Related Local Policy

SRP   Spatial Reuse Protocol

SRS   Stimulated Raman Scattering

SRT   Source Routing Transparent

SS7   Signaling System Seven

SSCC   Serial Shipping Container Code

SSL   Secure Socket Layer (IETF)

SSP   Service Switching Point (SS7)

SSR   Secondary Surveillance RADAR

SST   Spread Spectrum Transmission

STDM   Statistical Time Division Multiplexing

STM   Synchronous Transfer Mode

STM   Synchronous Transport Module (SDH)

STP   Shielded Twisted Pair

STP   Signal Transfer Point (SS7)

STS   Synchronous Transport Signal (SONET)

STX   Start of Text (BISYNC)

SVC   Signaling Virtual Channel (ATM)

SVC   Switched Virtual Circuit

SXS   Step-by-Step Switching

SYN   Synchronization

SYNTRAN   Synchronous Transmission

TA   Terminal Adapter (ISDN)

TAG   Technical Advisory Group

TASI   Time Assigned Speech Interpolation

TAXI   Transparent Asynchronous Transmitter/Receiver Interface (physical layer)

TCAP   Transaction Capabilities Application Part (SS7)

TCM   Time Compression Multiplexing

TCM   Trellis Coding Modulation

TCP   Transmission Control Protocol (IETF)

TDD   Time Division Duplexing

TDM   Time Division Multiplexing

TDMA   Time Division Multiple Access

TDR   Time Domain Reflectometer

TE1   Terminal Equipment Type 1 (ISDN-capable)

TE2   Terminal Equipment Type 2 (non-ISDN-capable)

TEI   Terminal Endpoint Identifier (LAPD)

TELRIC   Total Element Long-Run Incremental Cost

THIG   Topology-Hiding Interface Gateway

TIA   Telecommunications Industry Association

TIRIS   TI RF Identification Systems (Texas Instruments)

TIRKS   Trunk Integrated Record Keeping System

TL1   Transaction Language 1

TLAN   Transparent LAN

TM   Terminal Multiplexer

TMN   Telecommunications Management Network

TMS   Time-Multiplexed Switch

TOH   Transport Overhead (SONET)

TOP   Technical and Office Protocol

TOS   Type of Service (IP)

TP   Twisted Pair

TR   Token Ring

TRA   Traffic Routing Administration

TSI　Time Slot Interchange

TSLRIC　Total Service Long-Run Incremental Cost

TSO　Terminating Screening Office

TSO　Time-Sharing Option (IBM)

TSR　Terminate and Stay Resident

TSS　Telecommunication Standardization Sector (ITU-T)

TST　Time-Space-Time Switching

TSTS　Time-Space-Time-Space Switching

TTL　Time to Live

TU　Tributary Unit (SDH)

TUG　Tributary Unit Group (SDH)

TUP　Telephone User Part (SS7)

UA　Unnumbered Acknowledgment (HDLC)

UART　Universal Asynchronous Receiver Transmitter

UBR　Unspecified Bit Rate (ATM)

UCC　Uniform Code Council

UDI　Unrestricted Digital Information (ISDN)

UDP　User Datagram Protocol (IETF)

UHF　Ultra-High Frequency

UI　Unnumbered Information (HDLC)

UMTS　Universal Mobile Telephony System

UNI   User-to-Network Interface (ATM, FR)

UNIT   Unified Network Interface Technology (Ocular)

UNMA   Unified Network Management Architecture

UNSELECT   Unselect Transponder (RFID)

UPC   Universal Product Code

UPS   Uninterruptible Power Supply

UPSR   Unidirectional Path Switched Ring

UPT   Universal Personal Telecommunications

URL   Uniform Resource Locator

USART   Universal Synchronous Asynchronous Receiver Transmitter

USB   Universal Serial Bus

UTC   Coordinated Universal Time

UTP   Unshielded Twisted Pair (physical layer)

UUCP   UNIX-UNIX Copy

VAN   Value-Added Network

VAX   Virtual Address Extension (DEC)

vBNS   Very High Speed Backbone Network Service

VBR   Variable Bit Rate (ATM)

VBR-NRT   Variable Bit Rate-Non-Real-Time (ATM)

VBR-RT   Variable Bit Rate-Real-Time (ATM)

VC   Venture Capital

VC   Virtual Channel (ATM)

VC   Virtual Circuit (PSN)

VC   Virtual Container (SDH)

VCC   Virtual Channel Connection (ATM)

VCI   Virtual Channel Identifier (ATM)

VCSEL   Vertical Cavity Surface Emitting Laser

VDSL   Very High-Speed Digital Subscriber Line

VDSL   Very High Bit Rate Digital Subscriber Line

VERONICA   Very Easy Rodent-Oriented Netwide Index to Computerized Archives (Internet)

VGA   Variable Graphics Array

VHF   Very High Frequency

VHS   Video Home System

VID   VLAN ID

VIN   Vehicle Identification Number

VINES   Virtual Networking System (Banyan)

VIP   VINES Internet Protocol

VLAN   Virtual LAN

VLF   Very Low Frequency

VLR   Visitor Location Register (Wireless)

VLSI   Very Large Scale Integration

VM   Virtual Machine (IBM)

VM   Virtual Memory

VMS   Virtual Memory System (DEC)

VOD   Video-on-Demand

VoIP   Voice over Internet Protocol

VP   Virtual Path

VPC   Virtual Path Connection

VPI   Virtual Path Identifier

VPN   Virtual Private Network

VR   Virtual Reality

VSAT   Very Small Aperture Terminal

VSB   Vestigial Sideband

VSELP   Vector-Sum Excited Linear Prediction

VT   Virtual Tributary

VTAM   Virtual Telecommunications Access Method (SNA)

VTOA   Voice and Telephony over ATM

VTP   Virtual Terminal Protocol (ISO)

WACK   Wait Acknowledgment (BISYNC)

WACS   Wireless Access Communications System

WAIS   Wide Area Information Server (IETF)

WAN   Wide Area Network

WAP   Wireless Application Protocol (Wrong Approach to Portability)

WARC   World Administrative Radio Conference

WATS   Wide Area Telecommunications Service

WDM   Wavelength Division Multiplexing

WIN   Wireless In-Building Network

WISP   Wireless ISP

WTO   World Trade Organization

WWW   World Wide Web (IETF)

WYSIWYG   What You See Is What You Get

xDSL   x-Type Digital Subscriber Line

XID   Exchange Identification (HDLC)

XML   Extensible Markup Language

XNS   Xerox Network Systems

XPM   Cross Phase Modulation

ZBTSI   Zero Byte Time Slot Interchange

ZCS   Zero Code Suppression

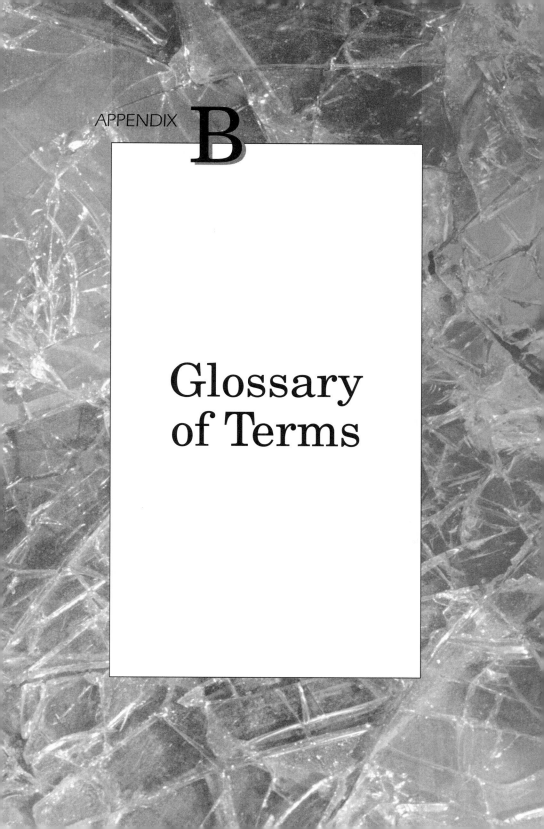

APPENDIX B

Glossary
of Terms

███ Numerical

3G   3G systems will provide access to a wide range of telecommunication services supported by both fixed telecommunication networks and services specific to mobile users. A range of mobile terminal types will be supported and may be designed for mobile or fixed use. Key features of these systems are compatibility of services, small terminals with worldwide roaming capability, Internet and other multimedia applications, high bandwidth, and a wide range of services and terminals.

4G   4G networks extend 3G network capacity by an order of magnitude, rely entirely on a packet infrastructure, use network elements that are 100% digital, and offer extremely high bandwidth.

███ A

Abend   A contraction of the words *abnormal* and *end*; used to describe a computer crash in the mainframe world.

Absorption   A form of optical attenuation in which optical energy is converted to an alternative form, often heat. Often caused by impurities in the fiber; hydroxyl absorption is the best-known form.

Acceptance angle   The critical angle within which incident light is totally internally reflected inside the core of an optical fiber.

Access   The set of technologies employed by a user to reach the network.

Accounts payable   Amounts owed to suppliers and vendors for products and/or services that have been delivered on credit. Most accounts payable agreements call for the credit to be reconciled within 30 to 60 days.

Accounts receivable   Money that is owed to a corporation.

Add/Drop Multiplexer (ADM)   A device used in SONET and SDH systems that has the ability to add and remove signal components without having to demultiplex the entire transmitted transmission stream; this is a significant advantage over legacy multiplexing systems such as DS3.

Aerial plant   Transmission equipment (media, amplifiers, splice cases, etc.) that is suspended in the air between poles.

ALOHA   The name given to the first local area network, which was designed and implemented in Hawaii and used to interconnect the various campuses of that state's university system.

Alternate Mark Inversion   The encoding scheme used in T-1. Every other "1" is inverted in polarity from the "1" that preceded or followed it.

ALU (Arithmetic Logic Unit)   The "brain" of a CPU chip.

Amplifier   A device that increases the transmitted power of a signal. Amplifiers typically are spaced at carefully selected intervals along a transmission span.

Amplitude modulation   (1) A signal-encoding technique in which the amplitude of the carrier is modified according to the behavior of the signal it is transporting. (2) The process of causing an electromagnetic wave to carry information by changing or modulating the amplitude or loudness of the wave.

AMPS (Advanced Mobile Phone System)   The modern analog cellular network.

Analog   A signal that continuously varies in time. Functionally, the opposite of digital.

Analog   A word that means "constantly varying in time."

Angular misalignment   The reason for loss at the fiber ingress point. If the light source is improperly aligned with the fiber's core, some of the incident light will be lost, leading to reduced signal strength.

Armor   The rigid protective coating on some fiber cables that protects them from being crushed and being chewed by rodents.

ASCII (American Standard Code for Information Interchange)
A 7-bit data-encoding scheme.

ASIC (Application-Specific Integrated Circuit)   A specially designed
Integrated Circuit (IC) created for a specific application.

Asset   What a company owns.

Asynchronous   Data that is transmitted between two devices that do
not have a common clock source.

Asynchronous Transfer Mode (ATM)   (1) A standard for switching
and multiplexing that relies on the transport of fixed-size data entities
called cells that are 53 octets in length. ATM has gotten a great deal of
attention lately because its internal workings allow it to provide quality of service (QoS), a much-demanded option in modern data networks. (2) One of the family of so-called fast packet technologies
characterized by low error rates, high speed, and low cost. ATM is
designed to connect seamlessly with SONET and SDH.

ATM Adaptation Layer (AAL)   In ATM, the layer responsible for
matching the payload being transported to a requested quality of service
level by assigning an ALL Type to which the network responds.

Attenuation   The reduction in signal strength in optical fiber that
results from absorption and scattering effects.

Avalanche photodiode (APD)   An optical semiconductor receiver
that has the ability to amplify weak received optical signals by "multiplying" the number of received photons to intensify the strength of the
received signal. APDs are used in transmission systems in which
receiver sensitivity is a critical issue.

Average revenue per user (ARPU)   The average amount of revenue
generated by each customer; calculated by dividing total revenue by the
total number of subscribers.

Axis   The center line of an optical fiber.

B

Back scattering The problem that occurs when light is scattered backward into the transmitter of an optical system. This impairment is analogous to the echo that occurs in copper-based systems.

Balance sheet Provides a view of what a company owns (its assets) and what it owes to creditors (its liabilities). The assets always equal the sum of the liabilities and shareholder equity. Liabilities represent obligations the firm has against its own assets. Accounts payable, for example, represent funds that are owed to someone or to another company that is outside the corporation but that are balanced by a service or physical asset that has been provided to the company.

Bandwidth (1) A measure of the number of bits per second that can be transmitted down a channel. (2) The range of frequencies within which a transmission system operates.

Bar code A machine-scannable product identification label that consists of a pattern of alternating thick and thin lines that uniquely identify the product to which they are affixed.

Baseband In signaling, any technique that uses digital signal representation.

Baud The signaling rate of a transmission system. One of the most misunderstood terms in telecommunications. Often used synonymously with bits per second, baud usually has a very different meaning. Through the use of multibit encoding techniques, a single signal can simultaneously represent multiple bits. Thus, the bit rate can be many times the signaling rate.

Beam splitter An optical device used to direct a single signal in multiple directions through the use of a partially reflective mirror or another optical filter.

BECN (Backward Explicit Congestion Notification) A bit used in frame relay to notify a device that it is transmitting too much information into the network and is therefore in violation of its service agreement with the switch.

Bell System Reference Frequency (BSRF)   In the early days of the Bell System, a single timing source in the Midwest provided a timing signal for all central office equipment in the country. This signal, which was delivered from a very expensive cesium clock source, was known as the BSRF. Today GPS is used as the main reference clock source.

Bend radius   The maximum degree to which a fiber can be bent before serious signal loss or fiber breakage occurs. One of the functional characteristics of most fiber products.

Bending loss   Loss that occurs when a fiber is bent far enough that its maximum allowable bend radius is exceeded. In this case, some of the light escapes from the waveguide, resulting in signal degradation.

Bidirectional   Refers to a system that is capable of transmitting simultaneously in both directions.

Binary   A counting scheme that uses base 2.

Bit rate   Bits per second.

Bluetooth   An open wireless standard designed to operate at a gross transmission level of 1 Mbps. It is being positioned as a connectivity standard for personal area networks.

Bragg grating   A device that relies on the formation of interference patterns to filter specific wavelengths of light from a transmitted signal. In optical systems, these gratings usually are created by wrapping a grating of the correct size around a piece of fiber that has been made photosensitive. The fiber then is exposed to strong ultraviolet light that passes through the grating, forming areas of high and low refractive indexes. Bragg gratings (or filters, as they often are called) are used for selecting certain wavelengths of a transmitted signal and often are used in optical switches, DWDM systems, and tunable lasers.

Broadband   (1) Historically, any signal that is faster than the ISDN Primary Rate (T1 or E1). Today, it means "big pipe"; in other words, a very high transmission speed. (2) In signaling this term means analog; in data transmission it means "big pipe" (high bandwidth).

Buffer   A coating that surrounds optical fiber in a cable and offers protection from water, abrasion, and so on.

Building Integrated Timing Supply (BITS)   The central office device that receives the clock signal from GPS or another source and feeds it to the devices in the office it controls.

Bull's-eye code   The earliest form of bar code, consisting of a series of concentric circles so that the code could be read from any angle.

Bundling   A product sales strategy in which multiple services (voice, video, entertainment, Internet, wireless, etc.) are sold as a converged package and invoiced with a single easy-to-understand bill.

Bus   The parallel cable that interconnects the components of a computer.

Butt splice   A technique in which two fibers are joined end to end by fusing them with heat or optical cement.

 C

Cable   An assembly made up of multiple optical or electrical conductors as well as other inclusions, such as strength members, waterproofing materials, and armor.

Cable assembly   A complete optical cable that includes the fiber itself and terminators on each end to make it capable of attaching to a transmission or receiving device.

Cable plant   The entire collection of transmission equipment in a system, including the signal emitters, the transport media, the switching and multiplexing equipment, and the receive devices.

Cable vault   The subterranean room in a central office where cables enter and leave the building.

Call center   A room in which operators receive calls from customers.

Capacitance   An electrical phenomenon by which an electric charge is stored in a circuit.

Capacitive coupling   The transfer of electromagnetic energy from one circuit to another through mutual capacitance, which is the ability of a surface to store an electric charge. Capacitance is simply a measure of the electrical storage capacity between the circuits. Similar to inductive coupling, capacitive coupling can be both intentional and unplanned.

Capital expenditures (CAPEX)   Wealth in the form of money or property, typically accumulated in a business by a person, partnership, or corporation. In most cases capital expenditures can be amortized over a period of several years, most commonly five years.

Capital intensity   A measure that has begun to appear as a valid measure of financial performance for large telecom operators. It is calculated by dividing capital spending (CAPEX) by revenue.

Cash burn   A term that became a part of the common lexicon during the dot-com years. Refers to the rate at which companies consume their available cash.

Cash flow   One of the most common measures of valuation for public and private companies. True cash flow is exactly that: a measure of the cash that flows through a company during a defined period after factoring out all fixed expenses. In many cases cash flow is equated to earnings before interest, tax, depreciation, and amortization (EBITDA). Usually, it is defined as income after taxes minus preferred dividends plus depreciation and amortization.

CCITT (Consultative Committee on International Telegraphy and Telephony)   Defunct; has been replaced by the ITU-TSS.

CDMA (Code Division Multiple Access)   One of several digital cellular access schemes. Relies on frequency hopping and noise modulation to encode conversations.

Cell   The standard protocol data unit in ATM networks. It consists of a 5-byte header and a 48-octet payload field.

Cell Loss Priority (CLP)   In ATM, a rudimentary single-bit field used to assign priority to transported payloads.

Cell Relay Service (CRS)   In ATM, the most primitive service offered by service providers, consisting of only raw bit transport with no assigned AAL types.

Cellular telephony   The wireless telephony system characterized by low-power cells, frequency reuse, handoff, and central administration.

Center wavelength   The central operating wavelength of a laser used for data transmission.

Central office   A building that houses shared telephony equipment such as switches, multiplexers, and cable distribution hardware.

Central office terminal (COT)   In loop carrier systems, the device in the central office that provides multiplexing and demultiplexing services. It is connected to the remote terminal.

Chained layers   The lower three layers of the OSI model that provide for connectivity.

Chirp   A problem that occurs in laser diodes when the center wavelength shifts momentarily during the transmission of a single pulse. Caused by instability of the laser itself.

Chromatic dispersion   Because the wavelength of transmitted light determines its propagation speed in an optical fiber, different wavelengths of light travel at different speeds during transmission. As a result, the multiwavelength pulse tends to "spread out" during transmission, causing difficulties for the receive device. Material dispersion, waveguide dispersion, and profile dispersion all contribute to the problem.

CIR (Committed Information Rate)   The volume of data a frame relay provider absolutely guarantees it will transport for a customer.

Circuit Emulation Service (CES)   In ATM, a service that emulates private line service by modifying (1) the number of cells transmitted per second and (2) the number of bytes of data contained in the payload of each cell.

Cladding   The fused silica "coating" that surrounds the core of an optical fiber. It typically has a different index of refraction than does the core, causing light that escapes from the core into the cladding to be refracted back into the core.

CLEC (Competitive Local Exchange Carrier)   A small telephone company that competes with the incumbent player in its own marketplace.

Close-coupling smart card   A card that is defined by extremely short read ranges; is similar to contact-based smart cards. These devices are designed to be used with an insertion reader, similar to what often is seen in modern hotel room doors.

CMOS (Complementary Metal Oxide Semiconductor)   A form of integrated circuit technology that typically is used in low-speed and low-power applications.

Coating   The plastic substance that covers the cladding of an optical fiber. Used to prevent damage to the fiber through abrasion.

Coherent   Refers to a form of emitted light in which all the rays of the transmitted light align themselves along the same transmission axis, resulting in a narrow, tightly focused beam. Lasers emit coherent light.

Compression   The process of reducing the size of a transmitted file without losing the integrity of the content by eliminating redundant information before transmitting or storing.

Concatenation   A technique used in SONET and SDH in which multiple payloads are "ganged" together to form a superrate frame capable of transporting payloads greater in size than the basic transmission speed of the system. Thus, an OC-12c provides 622.08 Mbps of total bandwidth, as opposed to an OC-12, which also offers 622.08 Mbps, but in increments of OC-1 (51.84 Mbps).

Conditioning   The process of "doctoring" a dedicated circuit to eliminate the known and predictable results of distortion.

Congestion The condition that results when traffic arrives faster than it can be processed by a server.

Connectivity The process of providing electrical transport of data.

Connector A device, usually mechanical, used to connect a fiber to a transmit or receive device or to bond two fibers.

Core (1) The central portion of an optical fiber that provides the primary transmission path for an optical signal. It usually has a higher index of refraction than does the cladding. (2) The central high-speed transport region of the network.

Counter-rotating ring A form of transmission system that includes two rings operating in opposite directions. Typically, one ring serves as the active path and the other serves as the protect or backup path.

CPU (Central Processing Unit) The chipset in a computer that provides the intelligence.

CRC (Cyclic Redundancy Check) A mathematical technique for checking the integrity of the bits in a transmitted file.

Critical angle The angle at which total internal reflection occurs.

Cross-phase modulation (XPM) A problem that occurs in optical fiber that results from the nonlinear index of refraction of the silica in the fiber. Because the index of refraction varies with the strength of the transmitted signal, some signals interact with each other in destructive ways. Considered to be a fiber nonlinearity.

CSMA/CD (Carrier Sense Multiple Access with Collision Detection) The medium access scheme used in Ethernet LANs; characterized by an "if it feels good, do it" approach.

Current assets The assets on the balance sheet that typically are expected to be converted to cash within a year of the publication date of the balance sheet. Typically include line items such as accounts receivable, cash, inventories and supplies, any marketable securities held by the corporation, prepaid expenses, and a variety of other less critical items that typically fall into the other line items.

Current liabilities   Obligations that must be repaid within a year.

Current ratio   Calculated by dividing the current assets for a financial period by the current liabilities for that period. A climbing current ratio might be a good indicator of improving financial performance but also could indicate that warehoused product volumes are climbing.

Customer relationship management (CRM)   A technique for managing the relationship between a service provider and a customer through the discrete management of knowledge about the customer.

Cutoff wavelength   The wavelength below which a single mode fiber ceases to be single mode.

Cylinder   A stack of tracks to which data can be written logically on a hard drive.

 D

Dark fiber   Optical fiber that sometimes is leased to a client that is not connected to a transmitter or receiver. In a dark fiber installation, it is the customer's responsibility to terminate the fiber.

Data   Raw, unprocessed 0s and 1s.

Data communications   The science of moving data between two or more communicating devices.

Data mining   A technique in which enterprises extract information about customers' behavior by analyzing data contained in their stored transaction records.

Datagram   The service provided by a connectionless network. Often said to be unreliable, this service makes no guarantees with regard to latency or sequentiality.

DCE (Data Circuit Terminating Equipment)   A modem or other device that delineates the end of the service provider's circuit.

DE (Discard Eligibility Bit) A primitive single-bit technique for prioritizing traffic that is to be transmitted.

Debt to equity ratio Calculated by dividing the total debt for a particular fiscal year by the total shareholder equity for the same financial period.

Decibel (dB) A logarithmic measure of the strength of a transmitted signal. Because it is a logarithmic measure, a 20-dB loss indicates that the received signal is one one-hundredth its original strength.

Dense Wavelength Division Multiplexing (DWDM) A form of frequency division multiplexing in which multiple wavelengths of light are transmitted across the same optical fiber. These systems typically operate in the so-called L-Band (1625 nm) and have channels that are spaced 50 to 100 GHz apart. Newly announced products may reduce this spacing dramatically.

Detector An optical receive device that converts an optical signal to an electrical signal so that it can be handed off to a switch, router, multiplexer, or other electrical transmission device. These devices are usually either Negative-Positive-Negative (NPN) or Avalanche Photodiodes (APDs).

Diameter mismatch loss Loss that occurs when the diameter of a light emitter and the diameter of the ingress fiber's core are dramatically different.

Dichroic filter A filter that transmits light in a wavelength-specific fashion, reflecting nonselected wavelengths.

Dielectric Refers to a substance that is nonconducting.

Diffraction grating A grid of closely spaced lines that are used to direct specific wavelengths of light selectively as required.

Digital (1) Refers to a signal characterized by discrete states. The opposite of analog. (2) Literally, "discrete."

Digital Hierarchy   In North America, the multiplexing hierarchy that allows 64-Kbps DS-0 signals to be combined to form DS-3 signals for high bit rate transport.

Digital Subscriber Line Access Multiplexer (DSLAM)   The multiplexer in the central office that receives voice and data signals on separate channels, relaying voice to the local switch and data to a router elsewhere in the office.

Diode   A semiconductor device that allows current to flow only in a single direction.

Direct attached storage (DAS)   A storage option in which the storage media (hard drives, CDs, etc.) are either integral to the server (internally mounted) or directly connected to one of the servers.

Dispersion   The spreading of a light signal over time that results from modal or chromatic inefficiencies in the fiber.

Dispersion compensating fiber (DCF)   A segment of fiber that exhibits the dispersion effect opposite to that of the fiber to which it is coupled. Used to counteract the dispersion of the other fiber.

Dispersion-shifted fiber (DSF)   A form of optical fiber that is designed to exhibit zero dispersion within the C-Band (1550 nm). Does not work well for DWDM because of Four Wave Mixing problems; Non-Zero Dispersion Shifted Fiber is used instead.

Distortion   A known and measurable (and therefore correctable) impairment on transmission facilities.

Dopant   A substance used to lower the refractive index of the silica used in optical fiber.

DS-0 (digital signal level 0)   A 64-Kbps signal.

DS-1 (digital signal level 1)   A 1.544-Mbps signal.

DS-2 (digital signal level 2)   A 6.312-Mbps signal.

DS-3   A 44.736-Mbps signal format found in the North American Digital Hierarchy.

DSL (Digital Subscriber Line)   A technique for transporting high-speed digital data across the analog local loop while in some cases transporting voice simultaneously.

DTE (Data Terminal Equipment)   User equipment that is connected to a DCE.

DTMF (Dual-Tone, Multi-Frequency)   The set of tones used in modern phones to signal dialed digits to the switch. Each button triggers a pair of tones.

Duopoly   The current regulatory model for cellular systems. Two providers are assigned to each market. One is the wireline provider (typically the local ILEC), and the other is an independent provider.

DWDM (Dense Wavelength Division Multiplexing)   A form of frequency division multiplexing that allows multiple optical signals to be transported simultaneously across a single fiber.

 E

E1   The 2.048-Mbps transmission standard used in Europe and some other parts of the world. It is analogous to the North American T1.

Earnings before interest, tax, depreciation, and amortization (EBITDA)   Sometimes called operating cash flow; used to evaluate a firm's operating profitability before subtracting nonoperating expenses such as interest and other core "nonbusiness" expenses and noncash charges. Long ago, cable companies and other highly capital-intensive industries substituted EBITDA for traditional cash flow as a *temporary* measure of financial performance without adding in the cost of building new infrastructure. Because it excluded all interest due on borrowed capital as well as the inevitable depreciation of assets, EBITDA was seen as a temporary better gauge of potential future performance.

Earnings per share (EPS) Calculated by dividing annual earnings by the total number of outstanding shares.

EBCDIC (Extended Binary Coded Decimal Interchange Code) An 8-bit data-encoding scheme.

Edge The periphery of the network where aggregation, QoS, and IP implementation take place. Also where most of the intelligence in the network resides.

EDGE (Enhanced Data for Global Evolution) A 384-Kbps enhancement to GSM.

Edge-emitting diode A diode that emits light from the edge of the device rather than the surface, resulting in a more coherent and directed beam of light.

Effective area The cross section of a single-mode fiber that carries the optical signal.

EIR (Excess Information Rate) The amount of data that is being transmitted by a user above the CIR in frame relay.

Encryption The process of modifying a text or image file to prevent unauthorized users from viewing the content.

End-to-end layers The upper four layers of the OSI model that provide interoperability.

Enterprise resource planning (ERP) A technique for managing customer interactions through data mining, knowledge management, and customer relationship management (CRM).

Erbium-Doped Fiber Amplifier (EDFA) A form of optical amplifier that uses the element erbium to bring about the amplification process. Erbium has the quality that when struck by light operating at 980 nm, it emits photons in the 1550-nm range, providing agnostic amplification for signals operating in the same transmission window.

ESF (Extended Superframe) The framing technique used in modern T-carrier systems that provides a dedicated data channel for nonintrusive testing of customer facilities.

Ethernet A LAN product developed by Xerox that relies on a CSMA/CD medium access scheme.

Evanescent wave Light that travels down the inner layer of the cladding instead of down the fiber core.

Extrinsic loss Loss that occurs at splice points in an optical fiber.

Eye pattern A measure of the degree to which bit errors are occurring in optical transmission systems. The width of the "eyes" (eye patterns look like figure eights lying on their sides) indicates the relative bit error rate.

F

Facilities-based A regulatory term that refers to the requirement that CLECs own their own physical facilities instead of relying on those of the ILEC for service delivery.

Facility A circuit.

Faraday effect Sometimes called the magneto-optical effect; describes the degree to which some materials can cause the polarization angle of incident light to change when placed within a magnetic field that is parallel to the propagation direction.

Fast Ethernet A version of Ethernet that operates at 100 Mbps.

Fast packet Refers to technologies characterized by low error rates, high speed, and low cost.

FDMA (Frequency Division Multiple Access) The access technique used in analog AMPS cellular systems.

FEC (Forward Error Correction) An error correction technique that sends enough additional overhead information along with the transmitted data so that a receiver not only can detect an error but actually can fix it without requesting a resend.

FECN (Forward Explicit Congestion Notification) A bit in the header of a frame relay frame that can be used to notify a distant switch that the frame experienced severe congestion on its way to the destination.

Ferrule A rigid or semirigid tube that surrounds optical fibers and protects them.

Fiber grating A segment of photosensitive optical fiber that has been treated with ultraviolet light to create a refractive index within the fiber that varies periodically along its length. It operates analogously to a fiber grating and is used to select specific wavelengths of light for transmission.

Fiber to the Curb (FTTC) A transmission architecture for service delivery in which a fiber is installed in a neighborhood and terminated at a junction box. From there, coaxial cable or twisted-pair cable can be cross-connected from the O-E converter to the customer premises. If coaxial is used, the system is called Hybrid Fiber Coax (HFC); twisted-pair-based systems are called Switched Digital Video (SDV).

Fiber to the Home (FTTH) Similar to FTTC except FTTH extends the optical fiber all the way to the customer's premises.

Fibre Channel A set of standards for a serial I/O bus that supports a range of port speeds, including 133 Mbps, 266 Mbps, 530 Mbps, 1 Gbps, and, soon, 4 Gbps. The standard supports point-to-point connections, switched topologies, and arbitrated loop architecture.

Financial Accounting Standards Board (FASB) The officially recognized entity that establishes standards for accounting organizations to ensure commonality among countries and international accounting organizations.

Four Wave Mixing (FWM) The nastiest of the so-called fiber nonlinearities. Commonly seen in DWDM systems; occurs when the closely spaced channels mix and generate the equivalent of optical sidebands. The number of these sidebands can be expressed by the equation $\frac{1}{2}(n^3 - n^2)$, where n is the number of original channels in the system. Thus, a 16-channel DWDM system potentially will generate 1920 interfering sidebands.

Frame   A variable-size data transport entity.

Frame relay   One of the family of so-called fast packet technologies characterized by low error rates, high speed, and low cost.

Frame Relay Bearer Service (FRBS)   In ATM, a service that allows relay frame to be transported across an ATM network.

Freespace optics   A metro transport technique that uses a narrow unlicensed optical beam to transport high-speed data.

Frequency-agile   Refers to the ability of a receiving or transmitting device to change its frequency to take advantage of alternative channels.

Frequency-division multiplexing   The process of assigning specific frequencies to specific users.

Frequency modulation   The process of causing an electromagnetic wave to carry information by changing or modulating the frequency of the wave.

Fresnel loss   The loss that occurs at the interface between the head of the fiber and the light source to which it is attached. At air-glass interfaces the loss usually equates to about 4%.

Full-duplex   Two-way simultaneous transmission.

Fused fiber   A group of fibers that are fused together so that they remain in alignment. Often used in one-to-many distribution systems for the propagation of a single signal to multiple destinations. Fused fiber devices play a key role in passive optical networking (PON).

Fusion splice   A splice made by melting the ends of the fibers together.

G

Generally Accepted Accounting Principles (GAAP)   The commonly recognized accounting practices that ensure financial accounting standardization across multiple global entities.

Generic Flow Control (GFC)   In ATM, the first field in the cell header. It is largely unused except when it is overwritten in NNI cells, in which case it becomes additional space for virtual path addressing.

GEOS (Geosynchronous Earth Orbit Satellite)   A family of satellites that orbit above the equator at an altitude of 22,300 miles and provide data and voice transport services.

Gigabit Ethernet   A version of Ethernet that operates at 1000 Mbps.

Global Positioning System (GPS)   The array of satellites used for radiolocation around the world. In the telephony world, GPS satellites provide an accurate timing signal for synchronizing office equipment.

Go-Back-N   A technique for error correction that causes all frames of data to be transmitted again, starting with the errored frame.

Gozinta   "Goes into."

Gozouta   "Goes out of."

GPRS (General Packet Radio System)   An add-on for GSM networks that is not having a great deal of success in the market yet.

Graded index fiber (GRIN)   A type of fiber in which the refractive index changes gradually between the central axis of the fiber and the outer layer instead of abruptly at the core-cladding interface.

Groom and fill   Similar to add-drop; refers to the ability to add (fill) and drop (groom) payload components at intermediate locations along a network path.

Gross domestic product (GDP)   The total market value of all the goods and services produced by a nation during a specific period.

GSM (Global System for Mobile Communications)   The wireless access standard used in many parts of the world; offers two-way paging, short messaging, and two-way radio in addition to cellular telephony.

GUI (Graphical User Interface)   The computer interface characterized by the "click, move, drop" method of file management.

H

Half-duplex   Two-way transmission, but in only one direction at a time.

Haptics   The science of providing tactile feedback to a user electronically. Often used in high-end virtual reality systems.

Headend   The signal origination point in a cable system.

Header   In ATM, the first five bytes of the cell. Contains information used by the network to route the cell to its ultimate destination. Fields in the cell header include Generic Flow Control, Virtual Path Identifier, Virtual Channel Identifier, Payload Type Identifier, Cell Loss Priority, and Header Error Correction.

Header Error Correction (HEC)   In ATM, the header field used to recover from bit errors in the header data.

Hertz (Hz)   A measure of cycles per second in transmission systems.

Hop count   A measure of the number of machines a message or packet has to pass through between the source and the destination. Often used as a diagnostic tool.

Hybrid fiber coax   A transmission system architecture in which a fiber feeder penetrates a service area and then is cross-connected to coaxial cable feeders into the customer's premises.

Hybrid loop   An access facility that uses more than one medium; for example, Hybrid-Fiber Coax (HFC) or hybrids of fiber and copper twisted pair.

I

ILEC (Incumbent Local Exchange Carrier)   An RBOC.

Income statement   Used to report a corporation's revenues, expenses, and net income (profit) for a particular defined time period. Sometimes called a profit and loss (P&L) statement or statement of operations. Charts a company's performance over a period of time. The results most often are reported as earnings per share and diluted earnings per share. Earnings per share is defined as the proportion of the firm's net income that can be accounted for on a per-share basis of outstanding common stock. It is calculated by subtracting preferred dividends from net income and dividing the result by the number of common shares that are outstanding. Diluted earnings per share takes into account earned or fully vested stock options that have not been exercised by their owner and shares that would be created from the conversion of convertible securities into stock.

Indefeasible Rights of Use (IRU)   A long-term capacity lease of a cable. IRUs are identified by channels and available bandwidth and typically are granted for long periods.

Index of refraction   A measure of the ratio between the velocity of light in a vacuum and the velocity of the same light in an optical fiber. The refractive index is always greater than 1 and is denoted n.

Inductance   The property of an electric circuit by which an electromotive force is induced in it by a variation of current flowing through the circuit.

Inductive coupling   The transfer of electromagnetic energy from one circuit to another as a result of the mutual *inductance* between the circuits. May be intentional, as in an impedance matcher that matches the impedance of a transmitter or a receiver to an antenna to guarantee maximum power transfer, or may be unplanned, as in the power line inductive coupling that occasionally takes place in telephone lines, often referred to as crosstalk or hum.

Information   Data that has been converted to a manipulable form.

Infrared (IR)   The region of the spectrum within which most optical transmission systems operate; between 700 nm and 0.1 mm.

Injection laser   A semiconductor laser.

Inside plant   Telephony equipment that is inside the central office.

Intermodulation   A fiber nonlinearity that is similar to four-wave mixing, in which the power-dependent refractive index of the transmission medium allows signals to mix and create destructive sidebands.

Interoperability   (1) Characterized by the ability to share information logically between two communicating devices and be able to read and understand the data of the other. (2) In SONET and SDH, the ability of devices from different manufacturers to send and receive information to and from each other successfully.

Intrinsic loss   Loss that occurs as the result of physical differences in two fibers being spliced.

ISDN (Integrated Services Digital Network)   A digital local loop technology that offers moderately high bit rates to customers.

Isochronous   A term used in timing systems to indicate that there is constant delay across a network.

ISP (Internet Service Provider)   A company that offers Internet access.

ITU (International Telecommunication Union)   A division of the United Nations that is responsible for managing the telecom standards development and maintenance processes.

ITU-TSS (ITU Telecommunication Standardization Sector)   The ITU organization responsible for telecommunications standards development.

J

Jacket   The protective outer coating of an optical fiber cable. The jacket may be polyethylene, Kevlar, or metal.

JPEG (Joint Photographic Experts Group) A standards body tasked with developing standards for the compression of still images.

Jumper An optical cable assembly, usually fairly short, that terminates on both ends with connectors.

K

Knowledge Information that has been acted on and modified through some form of intuitive human thought process.

Knowledge management The process of managing all that a company knows about its customers in an intelligent way so that some benefit is attained for both the customer and the service provider.

L

Lambda A single wavelength on a multichannel DWDM system.

LAN (Local Area Network) A small network that has the following characteristics: privately owned, high speed, low error rate, physically small.

LAN emulation (LANE) In ATM, a service that defines the ability to provide bridging services between LANs across an ATM network.

Large core fiber Fiber that characteristically has a core diameter of 200 microns or more.

Laser An acronym for light amplification by the stimulated emission of radiation. Used in optical transmission systems because lasers produce coherent light that is almost purely monochromatic.

Laser diode (LD) A diode that produces coherent light when a forward biasing current is applied to it.

LATA (Local Access and Transport Area) The geographic area within which an ILEC is allowed to transport traffic. Beyond LATA boundaries the ILEC must hand traffic off to a long-distance carrier.

LEOS (Low Earth Orbit Satellite) A satellite that orbits pole to pole instead of above the equator and offers nearly instantaneous response time.

Liability Obligations a firm has against its own assets. Accounts payable, for example, represent funds that are owed to someone or to another company that is outside the corporation but that are balanced by some service or physical asset that has been provided to the company.

Light emitting diode (LED) A diode that emits incoherent light when a forward bias current is applied to it. Typically used in shorter-distance, lower-speed systems.

Lightguide A term used synonymously with optical fiber.

Line Overhead (LOH) In SONET, the overhead that is used to manage the network regions between multiplexers.

Line sharing A business relationship between an ILEC and a CLEC in which the CLEC provides logical DSL service over the ILEC's physical facilities.

Linewidth The spectrum of wavelengths that make up an optical signal.

Load coil A device that tunes the local loop to the voiceband.

Local loop The pair of wires (or digital channel) that runs between the customer's phone (or computer) and the switch in the local central office.

Long-term debt Debt that is typically due beyond the one-year maturity period of short-term debt.

Loose tube optical cable An optical cable assembly in which the fibers within the cable are loosely contained within tubes inside the sheath of the cable. The fibers are able to move within the tube, allowing them to adapt and move without damage as the cable is flexed and stretched.

Loss   The reduction in signal strength that occurs over distance; usually expressed in decibels.

M

M13   A multiplexer that interfaces between DS-1 and DS-3 systems.

Mainframe   A large computer that offers support for very large databases and large numbers of simultaneous sessions.

MAN (Metropolitan Area Network)   A network, larger than a LAN, that provides high-speed services within a metropolitan area.

Manchester coding   A data transmission code in which data and clock signals are combined to form a self-synchronizing data stream in which each represented bit contains a transition at the midpoint of the bit period. The direction of transition determines whether the bit is a 0 or a 1.

Market cap(italization)   The current market value of all outstanding shares a company has. It is calculated by multiplying the total number of outstanding shares by the current share price.

Material dispersion   A dispersion effect caused by the fact that different wavelengths of light travel at different speeds through a medium.

MDF (Main Distribution Frame)   The large iron structure that provides physical support for cable pairs in a central office between the switch and the incoming and outgoing cables.

Message switching   An older technique that sends entire messages from point to point instead of breaking a message into packets.

Metasignaling virtual channel (MSVC)   In ATM, a signaling channel that is always on. Used for the establishment of temporary signaling channels as well as channels for voice and data transport.

Metropolitan Optical Network (MON)   An all-optical network deployed in a metro region.

Microbend   Changes in the physical structure of an optical fiber, caused by bending, which can result in light leakage from the fiber.

Midspan Meet   In SONET and SDH, the term used to describe interoperability. See also *interoperability.*

Modal dispersion   See *multimode dispersion.*

Mode   A single wave that propagates down a fiber. Multimode fiber allows multiple modes to travel, whereas single mode fiber allows only a single mode to be transmitted.

Modem   A term derived from the words *modulate* and *demodulate.* Its job is to make a computer appear to the network like a telephone.

Modulation   The process of changing or *modulating* a carrier wave to cause it to carry information.

MPEG (Moving Picture Experts Group)   A standards body tasked with crafting standards for motion pictures.

MPLS (Multiprotocol Label Switching)   A level 3 protocol designed to provide quality of service across IP networks without the need for ATM by assigning QoS "labels" to packets as they enter the network.

MTSO (Mobile Telephone Switching Office)   A central office with special responsibilities for handling cellular services and the interface between cellular users and the wireline network.

Multidwelling unit (MDU)   A building that houses multiple residence customers, such as an apartment building.

Multimode dispersion   Sometimes referred to as modal dispersion; caused by the fact that different modes take different amounts of time to move from the ingress point to the egress point of a fiber, resulting in modal spreading.

Multimode fiber Fiber that has a core diameter of 62.5 microns or greater, wide enough to allow multiple modes of light to be transmitted simultaneously down the fiber.

Multiplexer A device that has the ability to combine multiple inputs into a single output as a way to reduce the requirement for additional transmission facilities.

Multiprotocol over ATM (MPOA) In ATM, a service that allows IP packets to be routed across an ATM network.

Multitenant unit (MTU) A building that houses multiple enterprise customers, such as a high-rise office building.

Mutual inductance The tendency of a change in the current of one coil to affect the current and voltage in a second coil. When voltage is produced because of a change in current in a coupled coil, the effect is mutual inductance. The voltage always opposes the change in the magnetic field produced by the coupled coil.

N

Near-end crosstalk (NEXT) The problem that occurs when an optical signal is reflected back toward the input port from one or more output ports. This problem sometimes is referred to as isolation directivity.

Net income A term for bottom-line profit.

Network Attached Storage (NAS) An architecture in which a server accesses storage media via a LAN connection. The storage media are connected to another server.

Noise An unpredictable impairment in networks. It cannot be anticipated; it can only be corrected after the fact.

Non-Dispersion-Shifted Fiber (NDSF) Fiber that is designed to operate at the low-dispersion second operational window (1310 nm).

Non-Zero Dispersion-Shifted Fiber (NZDSF) A form of single mode fiber that is designed to operate just outside the 1550-nm window so that fiber nonlinearities, particularly FWM, are minimized.

Numerical aperture (NA) A measure of the ability of a fiber to gather light; also a measure of the maximum angle at which a light source can be from the center axis of a fiber in order to collect light.

 O

OAM&P (Operations, Administration, Maintenance, and Provisioning) The four key areas in modern network management systems. The term was coined by the Bell System and is still in widespread use.

Operating expenses (OPEX) Expenses that must be accounted for in the year in which they are incurred.

Optical amplifier A device that amplifies an optical signal without first converting it to an electrical signal.

Optical burst switching (OBS) A technique that uses a "one-way reservation" technique so that a burst of user data, such as a cluster of IP packets, can be sent without the need to establish a dedicated path before transmission. A control packet is sent first to reserve the wavelength, followed by the traffic burst. As a result, OBS avoids the protracted end-to-end setup delay and also improves the utilization of optical channels for variable-bit-rate services.

Optical Carrier Level n (OC-n) (1) In SONET, the transmission level at which an optical system is operating. (2) A measure of bandwidth used in SONET systems. OC-1 is 51.84 Mbps; OC-n is n times 51.84 Mbps.

Optical isolator A device used to block specific wavelengths of light selectively.

Optical time-domain reflectometer (OTDR) A device used to detect failures in an optical span by measuring the amount of light reflected back from the air-glass interface at the failure point.

OSS (Operations Support System) Another term for OAM&P.

Outside plant Telephone equipment that is outside the central office.

Overhead The part of a transmission stream that the network uses to manage and direct the payload to its destination.

 P

Packet A variable-size entity normally carried inside a frame or cell.

Packet switching The technique for transmitting packets across a wide area network.

Path overhead In SONET and SDH, that part of the overhead that is specific to the payload being transported.

Payload In SONET and SDH, the user data that is being transported.

Payload type identifier (PTI) In ATM, a cell header field that is used to identify network congestion and cell type. The first bit indicates whether the cell was generated by the user or by the network, and the second indicates the presence or absence of congestion in user-generated cells or flow-related operations, administration, and maintenance information in cells generated by the network. The third bit is used for service-specific, higher-layer functions in the user-to-network direction, such as to indicate that a cell is the last in a series of cells. From the network to the user, the third bit is used with the second bit to indicate whether the OA&M information refers to segment or end-to-end-related information flow.

PBX (Private Branch Exchange) A small telephone switch on a customer premise. The PBX connects back to the service provider's central office via a collection of high-speed trunks.

PCM (Pulse Code Modulation)   The encoding scheme used in North America for digitizing voice.

Phase modulation   The process of causing an electromagnetic wave to carry information by changing or modulating the phase of the wave.

Photodetector   A device used to detect an incoming optical signal and convert it to an electrical output.

Photodiode   A semiconductor that converts light to electricity.

Photon   The fundamental unit of light; sometimes referred to as a quantum of electromagnetic energy.

Photonic   The optical equivalent of the term electronic.

Pipelining   The process of having multiple unacknowledged outstanding messages in a circuit between two communicating devices.

Pixel   A combination of the words picture and element. The tiny color elements that make up the screen on a computer monitor.

Planar waveguide   A waveguide fabricated from a flat material such as a sheet of glass into which are etched fine lines used to conduct optical signals.

Plenum   The air-handling space in buildings found inside walls, under floors, and above ceilings. The plenum spaces often are used as conduits for optical cables.

Plenum cable   Cable that passes fire-retardant tests so that it can be used legally in plenum installations.

Plesiochronous   In timing systems, a term that means "almost synchronized." It refers to the fact that in SONET and SDH systems, payload components frequently derive from different sources and therefore may have slightly different phase characteristics.

Pointer   In SONET and SDH, a field that is used to indicate the beginning of the transported payload.

Polarization   The process of modifying the direction of the magnetic field within a light wave.

Polarization mode dispersion (PMD)   The problem that occurs when light waves with different polarization planes in the same fiber travel at different velocities down the fiber.

Preform   The cylindrical mass of highly pure fused silica from which optical fiber is drawn during the manufacturing process. In the industry, the preform sometimes is referred to as a gob.

Private line   A dedicated point-to-point circuit.

Protocol   A set of rules that facilitates communications.

Proximity-coupling smart card   A card that is designed to be readable at a distance of approximately 4 to 10 inches from the reader. These devices often are used for sporting events and other large public gatherings that require access control across a large population of attendees.

Pulse spreading   The widening or spreading out of an optical signal that occurs over distance in a fiber.

Pump laser   The laser that provides the energy used to excite the dopant in an optical amplifier.

PVC (Permanent Virtual Circuit)   A circuit provisioned in frame relay or ATM that does not change without service order activity by the service provider.

 Q

Q.931   The set of standards that define signaling packets in ISDN networks.

Quantize   The process of assigning numeric values to the digitized samples created as part of the voice digitization process.

Quick ratio   Calculated by dividing the sum of cash, short-term investments, and accounts receivable for a specific period by the current liabilities for that period. Measures the degree of a firm's liquidity.

Quiet zone   The area on either side of the Universal Product Code (UPC) that has no printing.

R

RAM (Random-Access Memory)   The volatile memory used in computers for short-term storage.

Rayleigh scattering   A scattering effect that occurs in optical fiber as a result of fluctuations in silica density or chemical composition. Metal ions in the fiber often cause Rayleigh scattering.

RBOC   Regional Bell Operating Company; today called an ILEC.

Refraction   The change in direction that occurs in a light wave as it passes from one medium into another. The most common example is the "bending" that often is seen when a stick is inserted into water.

Refractive index   A measure of the speed at which light travels through a medium; usually expressed as a ratio to the speed of the same light in a vacuum.

Regenerative repeater   A device that reconstructs and regenerates a transmitted signal that has been weakened over distance.

Regenerator   A device that recreates a degraded digital signal before transmitting it on to its final destination.

Remote terminal (RT)   In loop carrier systems, the multiplexer located in the field. It communicates with the central office terminal (COT).

Repeater   See *regenerator*.

Resilient packet ring (RPR)   A ring architecture that includes multiple nodes that share access to a bidirectional ring. Nodes send data across the ring by using a specific MAC protocol created for RPR. The goal of the RPR topology is to interconnect multiple nodes ring architecture that is media-independent for efficiency purposes.

Retained earnings   Represents the money a company has earned minus any dividends it has paid out. Does not necessarily equate to cash; more often than not it reflects the amount of money the corporation has reinvested in itself rather than paid out to shareholders as stock dividends.

Return on investment (ROI)   The ratio of a company's profits to the amount of capital that has been invested in it. Measures the financial benefit of a particular business activity relative to the costs of engaging in that activity. The profits used in the calculation of ROI can be calculated before or after taxes and depreciation and can be defined either as the first year's profit or as the weighted average profit during the lifetime of the entire project. Invested capital, in contrast, typically is defined as the capital expenditure required for the project's first year of existence. Some companies may include maintenance or recurring costs as part of the invested capital figure, such as software updates. Because there are no hard and fast rules about the absolute meanings of profits and invested capital, using ROI as a comparison of companies can be risky because of the danger of comparing apples to tractors, as it were. Be sure that comparative ROI calculations use the same bases for comparison.

ROM (Read-Only Memory)   Memory that cannot be erased; often used to store critical files or boot instructions.

 S

Scattering   The "backsplash" or reflection of an optical signal that occurs when it is reflected by small inclusions or particles in the fiber.

SDH (Synchronous Digital Hierarchy)   The European equivalent of SONET.

Section Overhead (SOH) In SONET systems, the overhead that is used to manage the network regions that occur between repeaters.

Sector A quadrant on a disk drive to which data can be written. Used for locating information on the drive.

Securities and Exchange Commission (SEC) The government agency responsible for regulation of the securities industry.

Selective retransmit An error correction technique in which only the errored frames are retransmitted.

Self-phase modulation (SPM) The refractive index of glass is directly related to the power of the transmitted signal. As the power fluctuates, so too does the index of refraction, causing waveform distortion.

Shareholder equity Claims that shareholders have against a corporation's assets.

Sheath One of the layers of protective coating in an optical fiber cable.

Signaling The techniques used to set up, maintain, and tear down a call.

Signaling Virtual Channel (SVC) In ATM, a temporary signaling channel used to establish paths for the transport of user traffic.

Simplex One-way transmission only.

Single mode fiber (SMF) The most popular form of fiber today; characterized by the fact that it allows only a single mode of light to propagate down the fiber.

Slotted ALOHA A variation on ALOHA in which stations transmit at predetermined times to ensure maximum throughput and minimal numbers of collisions.

Soliton A unique waveform that takes advantage of nonlinearities in the fiber medium; as a result, a signal suffers essentially no dispersion effects over long distances. Soliton transmission is an area of significant study at the moment because of the promise it holds for long-haul transmission systems.

SONET (Synchronous Optical Network)　A multiplexing standard that begins at DS3 and provides standards-based multiplexing up to gigabit speeds. It is widely used in telephone company long-haul transmission systems.

Source　The emitter of light in an optical transmission system.

Spatial Reuse Protocol (SRP)　A Layer 2 protocol developed by Cisco for use in Resilient Packet Ring (RPR) architectures.

SS7 (Signaling System Seven)　The current standard for telephony signaling worldwide.

Standards　The published rules that govern an industry's activities.

Statement of cash flows　Illustrates the manner in which a firm generated cash flows (the sources of funds) and the manner in which it employed them to support ongoing business operations.

Steganography　A cryptographic technique in which encrypted information is embedded in the pixel patterns of graphical images. The technique is being examined as a way to enforce digital watermarking and digital signature capabilities.

Step index fiber　Fiber that exhibits a continuous refractive index in the core that then "steps" at the core-cladding interface.

Stimulated Brillouin Scattering (SBS)　A fiber nonlinearity that occurs when a light signal traveling down a fiber interacts with acoustic vibrations in the glass matrix (sometimes called photon-phonon interaction), causing light to be scattered or reflected back toward the source.

Stimulated Raman Scattering (SRS)　A fiber nonlinearity that occurs when power from short-wavelength, high-power channels is bled into longer-wavelength, lower-power channels.

Storage area network (SAN)   A dedicated storage network that provides access to stored content. In an SAN, multiple servers may have access to the same servers.

Store and forward   The transmission technique in which data is transmitted to a switch, stored there, examined for errors, examined for address information, and forwarded to the final destination.

Strength member   The strand within an optical cable that is used to provide tensile strength to the overall assembly. The member usually is composed of steel, fiberglass, or Aramid yarn.

Supply chain   The process by which products move intelligently from the manufacturer to the end user, assigned through a variety of functional entities along the way.

Supply chain management   The management methodologies involved in the supply chain management process.

Surface emitting diode   A semiconductor that emits light from its surface, resulting in a low-power, broad-spectrum emission.

SVC (Switched Virtual Circuit)   A frame relay or ATM technique in which a customer can establish on-demand circuits as required.

Synchronous   A term that means that both communicating devices derive their synchronization signal from the same source.

Synchronous Transmission Signal Level 1 (STS-1)   In SONET systems, the lowest transmission level in the hierarchy; the electrical equivalent of OC.

T

T-1   The 1.544-Mbps transmission standard in North America.

T-3   In the North American Digital Hierarchy, a 44.736-Mbps signal.

Tandem   A switch that serves as an interface between other switches and typically does not host customers directly.

TDMA (Time Division Multiple Access)   A digital technique for cellular access in which customers share access to a frequency on a round-robin, time division basis.

Telecommunications   The science of transmitting sound over distance.

Terminal multiplexer   In SONET and SDH systems, a device used to distribute payload to or receive payload from user devices at the end of an optical span.

Tight buffer cable   An optical cable in which the fibers are tightly bound by the surrounding material.

Time-division multiplexing   The process of assigning time slots to specific users.

Token ring   A LAN technique, originally developed by IBM, that uses token passing to control access to the shared infrastructure.

Total internal reflection   The phenomenon that occurs when light strikes a surface at such an angle that all the light is reflected back into the transporting medium. In optical fiber, it is achieved by keeping the light source and the fiber core oriented along the same axis so that the light that enters the core is reflected back into the core at the core-cladding interface.

Transceiver   A device that incorporates a transmitter and a receiver in the same housing, reducing the need for rack space.

Transponder   A device that incorporates a transmitter, a receiver, and a multiplexer on a single chassis. A device that receives and transmits radio signals at a predetermined frequency range. After receiving a signal, the transponder rebroadcasts it at a different frequency. Transponders are used in satellite communications and in location (RFID), identification, and navigation systems. In the case of RFID, the transponder is the tag that is affixed to the product.

Treasury stock Stock that was sold to the public and later repurchased by the company on the open market. It is shown on the balance sheet as a negative number that reflects the cost of the repurchase of the shares rather than the actual market value of the shares. Treasury stock can be retired or resold later to improve earnings-per-share numbers if desired.

Twisted pair The wire used to interconnect customers to the telephone network.

 U

UPS (Uninterruptible Power Supply) Part of the central office power plant that prevents power outages.

V

Venture capital (VC) Money used to finance new companies or projects, especially those with high earning potential. Those companies often are characterized as being high-risk ventures.

Vertical cavity surface emitting laser (VCSEL) A small, highly efficient laser that emits light vertically from the surface of the wafer on which it is made.

Vicinity-coupling smart card A card designed to operate at a read range of up to three or four feet.

Virtual Channel (VC) In ATM, a unidirectional channel between two communicating devices.

Virtual Channel Identifier (VCI) In ATM, the field that identifies a virtual channel.

Virtual Container   In SDH, the technique used to transport subrate payloads.

Virtual Path (VP)   In ATM, a combination of unidirectional virtual channels that make up a bidirectional channel.

Virtual Path Identifier (VPI)   In ATM, the field that identifies a virtual path.

Virtual private network   A network connection that provides privatelike services over a public network.

Virtual Tributary (VT)   In SONET, the technique used to transport subrate payloads.

Voiceband   The 300- to 3300-Hz band used for the transmission of voice traffic.

Voice/Telephony over ATM (VTOA)   In ATM, a service used to transport telephony signals across an ATM network.

 # W

WAN (Wide Area Network)   A network that provides connectivity over a large geographic area.

Waveguide   A medium that is designed to conduct light within itself over a significant distance, such as optical fiber.

Waveguide dispersion   A form of chromatic dispersion that occurs when some of the light traveling in the core escapes into the cladding, traveling there at a speed different from that of the light in the core.

Wavelength   The distance between the same points on two consecutive waves in a chain; for example, from the peak of wave 1 to the peak of wave 2. Wavelength is related to frequency by the equation $\lambda = c/f$ where lambda (λ) is the wavelength, c is the speed of light, and f is the frequency of the transmitted signal.

Wavelength division multiplexing (WDM) The process of transmitting multiple wavelengths of light down a fiber.

Window A region within which optical signals are transmitted at specific wavelengths to take advantage of propagation characteristics that occur there, such as minimum loss and dispersion.

Window size A measure of the number of messages that can be outstanding at any time between two communicating entities.

 X, Y, Z

Zero dispersion wavelength The wavelength at which material and waveguide dispersion cancel each other.

INDEX

Note: Boldface numbers indicate illustrations; italic *t* indicates a table.